P9-BHR-450

11-23-53

THE ORGANIZATION
OF THE
METHODIST CHURCH

THE ORGANIZATION
OF THE
METHODIST CHURCH

*Historic Development and
Present Working Structure*

By
NOLAN B. HARMON
BOOK EDITOR OF THE METHODIST CHURCH

Revised Edition

THE METHODIST PUBLISHING HOUSE

NASHVILLE	CINCINNATI	CHICAGO	NEW YORK
DALLAS	RICHMOND	BALTIMORE	KANSAS CITY
DETROIT	PITTSBURGH	PORTLAND	SAN FRANCISCO

Library of Congress Catalog Card Number: 53-5396

B

SET UP, PRINTED, AND BOUND BY THE
PARTHENON PRESS, AT NASHVILLE,
TENNESSEE, UNITED STATES OF AMERICA

To

MY COMRADES OF THE

OLD BALTIMORE CONFERENCE

OF THE METHODIST EPISCOPAL CHURCH, SOUTH

Who, after one hundred and fifty-five years of un-broken Conference life, inspired by the vision of a United Methodism, voted for a Plan of Union which they knew would destroy their Conference;

Who served together during the last year of their Conference's life as calmly and steadily as though they had another one hundred and fifty-five years ahead of them;

824918

Who in October, 1939, met in their last Conference, set their affairs in order, made disposition of their precious documents, provided for the care of their Conference claimants, told each other good-by and went immediately into four different Conferences, where they continue to serve to this day loyally and efficiently—and all without missing a single step in the forward march of Methodism.

PREFACE

IN 1939 THE METHODIST EPISCOPAL CHURCH, THE METHODIST EPIS-
copal Church, South, and the Methodist Protestant Church united to
become The Methodist Church. Since that union there has been need
for a comprehensive study of the constitution and working structure of
the reorganized church. The great works of Neely, Stevens, Drinkhouse,
Tigert, Buckley, and other constitutional authorities on Methodist organization and polity, were sufficient for their day, although each one of
these was somewhat restricted in scope, being written primarily for one
special branch of the church. But the last of these writings appeared
many years ago, and since the beginning of the twentieth century a
steady and perceptible modification in fundamental Methodist attitudes
and procedure has been taking place. This development has perhaps
been no more than Methodism's way of making adjustment to the
vastly quickened tempo of the modern age, in which new occasions are
continually teaching new duties. The world has moved with astonish-
ing swiftness in the lifetime of this present generation, and even before
union each of the three churches was conscious of increasing change.

Thus when Methodist union came about in 1939, the plan and structure of the reorganized church partook not only of Methodism's own
historic attitudes and constitutional forms, but embodied also other
features for which the newer age seemed to call. Some of these features
were not new in ecclesiastical life; some were. And although the reorganized church has scarcely passed through its second quadrennium,
it is not too soon to make a careful study of its constitutional features
and practical operative structure.

In making this study it is necessary first to understand the historic
transmission and development of the various institutions and procedures
which are found in the present complex organization of The Methodist
Church. The roots of all present features—with one or two important
exceptions—reach far back in the past, and to understand the present
church one must understand the long process of past development.

But the present is more important than the past, and the prime pur-
pose of this book is to examine the structure and organization of The
Methodist Church as that was determined, or came into being, in 1939.
Description and explanation are accompanied where possible with de-

tails regarding its practical working. Where suggestions for modification or amendment seem to be coming from responsible quarters, such moves and suggestions are called to attention as belonging to the life of the church. This book, however, purposes to explain and describe rather than to plead for some special feature or viewpoint.

One profound reason for this study is that each present-day Methodist has an unconscious tendency to think of the church as the perpetuation and prolongation of that branch of the Methodist Church with which he was familiar before union. Legally The Methodist Church is exactly that—the continued life and operation of the Methodist Episcopal Church, the Methodist Episcopal Church, South, and the Methodist Protestant Church. These three are now legally and organically one. But in their coming together the resultant church has modified vastly former processes known or followed in one or the other of the uniting bodies. In some cases there have been adopted new patterns of structure which no Methodist Church had before 1939, and new institutions or novel processes are always puzzling to those who have not known them before. To explain the processes and ideals of one of the uniting Methodisms in terms of the others—or to the others—is a prime task of this writing.

Since the two churches representing Episcopal Methodism—the Methodist Episcopal Church, and the Methodist Episcopal Church, South—were very much larger bodies than was the Methodist Protestant Church, it was natural and inevitable that their institutions and processes should have more greatly influenced the Plan of Union and the structure of the present church than did Methodist Protestantism. If, therefore, the following pages fail to indicate in certain instances the Methodist Protestant tradition or polity, this is because of the overwhelming dominance of the larger bodies in shaping final forms. In those vastly important areas where Methodist Protestantism did make its distinctive contribution, I have been at pains to point this out in proper perspective.

The substance of this book was delivered as The Southwestern University Lectures of 1946, and it is with grateful appreciation that I remember the courtesy and consideration of President J. N. R. Score and that of the members of the faculty of Southwestern University while I was with them during the week of the lectureship. Special thanks are due to Dr. James R. Joy, librarian of the New York Methodist Historical Society, who helped me greatly as I expanded the lectures for the present book and did research for the volume. Dr. Joy not only placed at my disposal the wealth of material in the society's historical library at 150 Fifth Avenue, New York, but assisted by many helpful criticisms and suggestions in the actual compilation of the manuscript. A complete file of General Conference *Journals* and *Daily Advocates* of the Methodist Episcopal Church, the Methodist Episcopal Church, South, and the Methodist Protestant Church, respectively, kept in this library, were within convenient reach where I might check the historic record at almost any point.

Others are also to be thanked: The bishops wrote letters giving their judgment and comment upon the Methodist episcopacy as they from personal experience have been able to evaluate the many duties and present status of the office of bishop in The Methodist Church. Bishops John M. Moore, G. Bromley Oxnam, and James H. Straughn read the section of this book treating of episcopacy and made many helpful suggestions. Dr. James E. Skillington, the well-known authority on Methodist parliamentary law and practice, read the section of the manuscript dealing with the conference system of the church, and his able criticism and well-stated comment was of great help toward a final revision. For similar help in the way of suggestion and criticism on specific sections the following are gratefully mentioned: Dr. Francis R. Bayley, chairman of the Judicial Council, and the Honorable Walter McElreath, of Atlanta, Georgia, on the judicial processes of the church; Dr. Ralph E. Diffendorfer, Dr. Earl R. Brown and Miss Henrietta Gibson, on the Board of Missions and Church Extension; Dr. John Q. Schisler and Dr. H. W. McPherson, on the Board of Education; Dr. Fred D. Stone, on the Board of Publication; Dr. Thomas A. Stafford, on the Board of Pensions; Dr. Harry F. Denman and George II. Jones, on the General Board of Evangelism; Dr. George L. Morelock, on the General Board of Lay Activities; Dr. Thomas B. Lugg, on the General Commission on World Service and Finance; Dr. Karl P. Meister, on the Board of Hospitals and Homes; Dr. Deets Pickett, on the Board of Temperance; Dr. Charles F. Boss, on the Commission on World Peace; Dr. John L. Seaton, on the University Senate; and Dr. Ralph Stoody, on the Commission on Methodist Information.

In dealing with as broad a subject as the history and working structure of The Methodist Church, and in tracing the evolution of that structure through three separate church organizations, it will be strange indeed if I shall not be thought to have overemphasized some things, underemphasized or overlooked others, or even at certain points misinterpreted the intent or meaning of past history or even present law. Where there is guiding law or disciplinary enactment, I have endeavored to rely upon that, and where there is none, I have been guided by the informed judgment and opinions of other Methodist authorities. The Judicial Council itself, the final interpreter of Methodist law, has not passed upon many matters which may conceivably be referred to it in future, and any General Conference may see fit to modify at any time the present statutory law herein cited. The reader should keep in mind what I have reminded myself throughout this study, that the book of *Discipline* of The Methodist Church is the final authoritative code of Methodist law today as it has been in the past; all findings and all pronouncements, even those of the Judicial Council, are referred to and guided by its provisions. This volume is put forth in the endeavor to make the disciplinary language— both constitutional and statutory—more plain and understandable.

The structure and working organization of the largest and most widely distributed Protestant church of what is admittedly the most powerful nation in the world cannot but be of some moment. Out of a profound love and admiration for the church of my fathers, and for my own church, I have written these pages.

Nolan B. Harmon

PREFACE TO THE REVISED EDITION

Since this book first appeared certain important changes in the organizational structure of the church were called for by the General Conference of 1952. These changes affected primarily the organization of the local church, and recast and rearranged certain general boards and agencies of the church. The present revision of this book takes account of these changes and indicates the importance and scope of each one. Future changes may of course be called for as succeeding General Conferences feel the necessity of modifying from time to time our church organization.

N.B.H.

CONTENTS

PART ONE

EPISCOPACY

PART TWO

THE CONFERENCE SYSTEM

PART THREE

THE JURISDICTIONAL DIVISION

PART FOUR

METHODIST LAW AND THE JUDICIAL COUNCIL

THE ORGANIZATION OF THE METHODIST CHURCH
PART FIVE
The Executive Agencies

I

OF ORIGINS

We agreed to form a Methodist Episcopal Church.
—Journal of the Rev. Thomas Ware

JOHN WESLEY, WHO WAS UNDER GOD THE FOUNDER OF METHODISM, was by that same fact its controlling head and directing power. Methodist superintendency and the fundamentals of Methodist organization, whatever subsequent development these have experienced, stem directly and historically from John Wesley. He spoke of himself once, when his right to set apart men for America was questioned, as being "as Scriptural an *episcopos* as there is in Europe." He had lived long enough by that time to see somewhat objectively the results of his own work, and to recognize what Methodism was going to mean in the record of universal history. He knew that to a great degree he had put his own stamp upon its subsequent life. Certainly while Wesley lived his leadership was never questioned and his will in Britain scarcely ever challenged.

The calling of the first conference by Wesley in 1744 marked the beginning of the conference system. But the Conference of 1744 was not at all similar to a present-day conference. To be sure, the question-and-answer pattern of doing business was there inaugurated—a procedure we are familiar with—but it was John Wesley who asked the questions and Wesley who answered them or directed the answering. Later Wesley recalled with considerable vigor that he did not call this or any subsequent conference together that he might be *controlled* by it. He called it to be *advised* by the brethren present. He made it clear that he felt it his duty to lead, and while he declared several times that he would have turned over to others his leadership if he could have found a way to do it, the fact remains that he never did. He explained:

I did not seek any part of this power; it came upon me unawares; but when it was come, not daring to bury that talent, I used it to the best of my judgment. Yet I never was fond of it; I always did, and do now, bear it as my burden, the burden which God lays upon me, and therefore I dare not lay it down. But if you can tell me any one, or any five men, to whom I may transfer this burden, who can and will do just what I do now, I will heartily

13

thank both them and you. . . . Preaching twice or thrice a day is no burden to me at all; but the care of all the preachers and of all the people is a burden indeed.[1]

As part of this duty of governing, Wesley directed his "helpers" or "assistants" where they were to preach, and fixed for congregations what preachers they were to have. This tremendous power over the lives and habits of other men provoked great discussion. "This is shackling free-born Englishmen," said some. "Who gave this man authority to reign over us?" To this Wesley replied in his tart, laconic way, that he had no authority over anyone save what that person had given to him; that he did not compel anyone to join his organization nor to be his "assistant"; and that if men did not like this relationship, they were at liberty to terminate it. But he made it quite clear that if anyone was to "assist" him, that person must not attempt to *amend* his rules but *keep* them.

Wesley continued "stationing the preachers," and holding conferences as long as he lived. Such conferences met, argued, and advised, but went no further. They recorded those who were admitted, who were to remain on trial, and called the regular questions, but they never authorized anyone to be ordained, nor did they make laws in the sense in which we legislate today. The conferences kept their minutes carefully, the members supported each other loyally, and the preachers went home —or wherever they were told to go.

The Wesleyan system was transported in the late seventeen-sixties to America. Preachers here were also "assistants" to Wesley. They followed his leadership on this side of the Atlantic, and continued the pattern of his government, obeying the one whom he appointed to be chief assistant. Into this position eventually came Francis Asbury, who set his stamp upon Methodism in America just as definitely as Wesley had laid his mind upon English Methodism.

Francis Asbury was much the same type as John Wesley. Both were ascetic and indefatigable. Both were in the prophetic succession. Asbury lacked Wesley's incisive mind, merciless logic, classical scholarship, and the catholicity of viewpoint which came from a thorough grounding in the fundamentals of the classics and history of the Christian ages. The pioneer bishop in America was no Oxonian. He could never have answered the Quaker, Robert Barclay, on the one hand, nor the English prelates on the other, as did Wesley. Nor could he have guided the Methodist movement in England as did its founder, keeping it prac-

[1] *Minutes,* 1776. In Wesley's *Works,* American ed., V, 220-22.

tically a church within a church through the long decades. Wesley managed to avoid the shallows of mysticism and enthusiasm on the one hand, and on the other kept out of the uncharted deeps which a break with the Establishment would then have meant.

But Francis Asbury had qualities which John Wesley lacked—a more sure evaluation of men and their motives, an uncanny intuition regarding the value and import of proposed moves, a complete appreciation of locale, especially of the American scene, and an unerring sense of "timing," that is, when, as well as what, action should be taken. Put Asbury at the head of the Methodists in England and he would have made a poor apologist for the people and cause he led. Put Wesley in America and he would have found himself terribly miscast, as the Savannah experience showed. He would never have felt at home or at ease, either with people or preachers on these shores. But put Wesley in Britain, and Asbury in America, and slow down communication between them to the leisurely tempo of an eighteenth-century sailing ship, and the world can yet marvel at the result in ecclesiastical structure.

Wesley, who exercised a complete sovereignty over all Methodism, no doubt expected to transmit a great part of this to Asbury when in due time it was necessary for him to "set off" American Methodism. But at the very time of this transmittal, when a new church was to be begun in America, an unforeseen factor suddenly appeared. On this side of the ocean something new was met which had not been within the calculation of Wesley. That new thing was the emergence of a sovereign conference, not advisory but autonomous in its own right. It was destined to assume the sovereignty hitherto exercised by the founder alone, and to order and direct all future Methodist life and organization on these shores. The steps that brought this about may be briefly narrated.

When Wesley sent over Thomas Coke to ordain Asbury as superintendent in 1784, Asbury refused the ordination unless, and until, the Methodist preachers who were his assistants should agree to elect him to such an office. This was unexpected. Wesley had directed Coke to kneel before him and be ordained as a superintendent; and that Coke, in turn, should go to America and have Asbury kneel before *him* and be ordained a superintendent. Coke obediently knelt before Wesley—in fact a great many think Coke's consuming ambition was to get such an ordination. But in America Asbury refused to kneel before Coke until the preachers could be heard from. The preachers therefore were summoned and met, "three score or more of them," and organized the

15

Methodist Episcopal Church in Baltimore in 1784. They did elect Asbury superintendent, as well as electing, or rather accepting the superintendency of Coke. But the principle which Asbury unexpectedly relied upon marked the emergence of sovereign conference power in America. In rapid time it brought about that great difference between the polity of Methodism on these shores and that which was followed through for a long time by our British brethren.

In England Wesley's death left British Methodism organized as a conference, indeed, but a truncated one, divided against itself, with some persons anxious to remain within the Establishment and some calling for complete separation. Not until many years after Wesley's death did British Methodism finally find itself and become the powerful, united organization it has since become. In America, from the first, the power of the conference was determinative. In England it was not.

A close study of the Methodist organization in 1784 ought not to stop with a bare statement that Methodist sovereignty at once began to rest upon a distinctive conference basis. The bare framework of sovereignty was not the only thing which determined the form, shape, and life of the Methodist Episcopal Church in America, though certain writers seem to assume that this is so. Proper attention has never yet been fully paid to certain unwritten but powerful directive forces which also came to American Methodism in 1784. The part the Prayer Book, or the Wesleyan edition of the English Book of Common Prayer, played in the organization of early American Methodism has never been fully appreciated. It must be remembered that there was at that time no overhead organization holding the ministers together, only a loose "connection" which they then proposed to organize into a church. As the English Prayer Book, with which they were all familiar, has been in a sense the constitution of the English Church, so these Methodist ministers, at their organization, formally adopted an abridgment of the English Prayer Book (the "Sunday Service") prepared for them by Wesley, as their connectional bond and guiding symbol. The question and answer here are historic:

Question 3: As the ecclesiastical, as well as civil, forces of these United States have passed through a very considerable change by the Revolution, what plan of church government shall we pursue?

Answer: We will form ourselves into an episcopal church under the direction of superintendents, elders, deacons, and helpers, according to the

Forms of Ordination annexed to our liturgy and the form of Discipline set forth in these Minutes.[2]

This, of course, is the final answer to the question as to the "plan of church government." The "forms of ordination," which were in the liturgy sent over by Wesley, embodied principles and procedures which had been in the very lifestream of the English Church. Wesley intended them to be used and perpetuated among the American ministers. "Else these provisions," said Bishop Tigert, arguing for the importance of the forms for ordination, "had been irrelevant and unnecessary."

It is strange that in the many writings which Methodist scholars have given to their church regarding its constitution, no one has paid great heed to the incontrovertible fact that there came to American Methodism at its origin an actual order of procedure by which its ministry itself was constituted, by which it was to continue to be constituted in future. It was not altogether a new church which in 1784 came into being. It was a church which in its method of ordaining its ministry and consecrating its superintendents was careful to stay within the Christian tradition and to conform to the English Rite. Whatever of constitutional procedure came to Methodism in 1784 was certainly not the product of any previous General Conference action, for there was no previous General Conference. Conference action approved, adopted, and used the forms and methods of a historic ministry, both in its ordination and in its official functioning, but it did not originate them. Methodism too has its "succession."

Furthermore not enough attention has ever been paid to the almost unseen but ever-present strength of the English Use in shaping Methodist worship and polity. The first American Methodists desired, for themselves and their children, the usages and forms of the Church of England when it came to administering the sacraments and carrying on the work of the church. Wesley's ordination parchment for the first Methodist bishop begins:

WHEREAS—
Many of the people in the southern provinces of North America, who desire to continue in my care and still adhere to the doctrines and discipline of the Church of England, are greatly distressed for want of ministers to administer the sacraments . . . according to the usage of the said Church . . . ;

[2] *Minutes of Several Conversations Between the Reverend Thomas Coke, LL.D.; the Reverend Francis Asbury and Others*, Philadelphia, 1784, p. 3. Bound with the Sunday Service of 1784.

know all men that I, John Wesley, think myself to be providentially *called at this time to set apart some persons for the work of the ministry in America*.[3]

The italics are mine and call attention to the fact that Wesley found the majority of his people in the colonies to be not Presbyterians, Baptists, or Dissenters but evangelical persons whose roots were fastened deep in the habits and ways of the English Church. The "Sunday Service," as Wesley's abridgment of the Prayer Book was called, was brought over to America in loose sheets, but on these same loose sheets were transferred to this country some of the strongest features in our connectionalism. These embodied, as has been seen, a plan for the perpetuation of the ministry under which plan Methodist ministers in America to this very day continue to perpetuate that ministry itself. They transmitted into the life of the church the ethos and influence of an age-old church, and these same loose-leaf pages acted as a connectional bond in holding together what had else been scattered societies. Thus with an episcopacy or superintendency established, a ministry ordained and functioning, a liturgy adopted, and the Methodist practice of holding conferences firmly fixed in the plan of the new church, Methodism in America began. It was destined to grow rapidly and, like any other living organism, at once began to discard those features which it found no longer usable or serviceable. In turn it adopted, and to this day continues to adopt, such other forms and practices as it might need for the better expression of its own life.

[3] John J. Tigert, *Constitutional History of American Episcopal Methodism* (rev. ed., 1904), p. 174.

PART ONE

Episcopacy

II

METHODIST EPISCOPACY

There shall be an episcopacy.
—Constitution, Div. III, Art. I

METHODIST EPISCOPACY HAS BEEN THE TRADITIONAL STORM CENTER of the whole Methodist organization. It has, at the same time, been one of the pillars upon which the entire constitutional structure of the church rests. The tension which has always been present regarding the episcopacy came about partly by reason of an ambiguity involving its origin and powers, but more because of the exercise of these powers themselves.

When the Methodist Episcopal Church in America took its origin, it was not certain just what powers John Wesley intended Methodist episcopacy to have—indeed, whether he intended that there should be an episcopacy at all. He called for a "superintendent," not a bishop. It was not certain for some time after 1784 what powers Methodist bishops themselves thought they might justly claim. The history of the early years is most informative on this point. Every General Conference that met from 1784 until 1808 debated this matter and any one of them could have altered or done away Methodist episcopacy by a majority vote at any time. Indeed several General Conferences came near doing exactly that, with Francis Asbury himself once sitting outside one of these early conference assemblies, waiting to hear what the verdict of the conference might be in a matter that touched to the quick all the powers he exercised.

The peculiar power of the Methodist bishop, and that which is the cornerstone of the superintendency, has been his power to appoint men to their particular places of work. This appointive power carries with it, naturally, the ability to control the pulpit as far as each local church is concerned. The bishop, and the bishop alone, has the right to say where each preacher shall preach. He, and he alone, has the power to tell every church, and every lay member in every church, what preacher shall be theirs to follow as pastor, what man they are to hear Sunday after Sunday, and to what man they shall give their financial support. This vast

21

power has been modified through the years but still exists, and it is this tremendous fact which is the nub of the whole "episcopal controversy," as it has sometimes been called. Grant to any man the right to sit in a chair before several hundred of his brother ministers and allow him the unquestioned right to tell each and every one of them where they shall live, what pulpit they must preach in, what sort of house their families shall have, what their salaries shall be, and what schooling their children may get (for all these things hang on the individual appointment), and you have lodged in that one man an almost incalculable power. Nor does this control cease with the ministry. It puts the bishop in complete charge of the local churches and lay people also, for these must wait upon the bishop to send them a man who will be to them pastor, preacher, counselor, and spiritual leader. Thus it is that the guidance and leadership of countless churches, as well as of hundreds of individual ministers, are in the hands of the bishop. No wonder a man in such a position finds himself sought after, entertained, flattered, and praised with sometimes an adulation and servility which bishops themselves have often deplored. No wonder that men of small caliber elected to this powerful office have come to think more highly of themselves than they—or the church—ought to have thought. No wonder that the bludgeoning of circumstance and the increasing pressure through the long years have gradually forced a modification of Methodism's pristine episcopacy, so that while in theory it has been, and is, absolute, in practice it is a long way from being so. No wonder that episcopacy itself has been glad to relinquish, at first little by little and then in later years by much more definite moves, some of the weight of responsibility inherent in its absolute appointive power.

The history of the exercise of this appointive power by the Methodist bishop is so closely bound up with the entire history of the episcopacy in our economy, that it is no very great exaggeration to say that the appointive power is Methodist episcopacy. Although bishops have many things to do besides the making of the appointments—to ordain men, to preside over conference sessions, to carry through the church's program and the like—Methodist episcopacy yet stands or falls in relation to its own power to station the preachers. "If a bishop can make good appointments," said Bishop Warren A. Candler, "he is a good bishop." Episcopacy has been strongest when it exercised the appointive powers most strongly. It has grown weaker during successive years as it has in measure relinquished some of its power to district superintendents, conference recommendations, and to congregational committees. It has always been termed a "modified episcopacy," and perhaps that is the best name for it. But to understand our present church structure one must understand the part episcopacy has played and is playing in the present church.

So closely has its official superintendency been woven into the life of the church that to outline in a broad way the successive steps by which Methodist episcopacy has come down to the present will be in effect to review the history of the church itself. These steps have been, roughly speaking, four in number, though episcopacy itself has been one continuous power from the beginning until now. There was first a formative period when Methodism took its origin and fixed its character, dating from 1784 to 1808. Then came growth and tension, from 1808 to 1844, with the organization of the Methodist Protestant Church, a nonepiscopal body, and with two differing attitudes manifesting themselves in Episcopal Methodism itself. From 1844—when the division of the church occurred—to 1939 there came a further development of these two somewhat different concepts regarding episcopal power; and since 1939 and the recently consummated union of Methodism the church lives under a much more moderate episcopacy inherent in the organization of the new church. To review in a brief manner these successive periods will be the next task.

THE FIRST PERIOD—1784 TO 1808

At the organization of the Methodist Episcopal Church in America in 1784, Francis Asbury, after his election and ordination as superintendent, assumed the right to continue stationing the preachers. He had been doing this all along by virtue of Wesley's personal appointment of himself as his "assistant" in America. For a time Wesley withdrew this power from Asbury and vested it in Thomas Rankin, but the power itself was always in effect, as Rankin, during his tenure, also stationed the preachers. But Rankin, who never was at home in America, fled before the Revolution had progressed far, and Asbury, at Wesley's appointment, became "assistant" again. As assistant he unhesitatingly directed the preachers where they were to travel, after the pattern of itineracy, which had become as customary among Methodists in this country as it was in England. Therefore in 1784, after Asbury's election and ordination as superintendent, it was nothing new for him to continue assigning the preachers to their field of labor. But it was a new church, with a new name, in a vigorous, new democratic nation, and the fact that in the formal organization of this new church there should be one man who would and could direct the lives of all the others brought at once objection and recoil.

We misread the bitterness of the whole "episcopal controversy" unless we get clearly in mind the background of life at the early period and understand something of the thought processes of the newly freed American people. The Revolution had been fought to a victorious conclusion by a people who had risked their all and suffered bitterly in their struggle to be free. Liberty was no mere political shibboleth or catchword stamped on a coin to the robust people of 1784. It was a priceless thing, and the frontiersman, the pioneer, the farmer, the townsman, who had faced British bullets and lost their property to obtain it, knew it for what it was. The new nation, as the very songs of the age show, was full to the bursting with the idea of man's right to be free. Under the dynamic spirit of the times the American people had already caught that sense of destiny, that mission to explore wildernesses and conquer lands which marked the throwing forward of the whole frontier. Nor was this an American ideal only. Across the ocean the French Revolution was shaking the earth, and the troops of France were soon to take their banners marked "Liberty, Equality, and Fraternity" into almost every capital in Europe. It was an age of boundless freedom in every department of life. He who thinks of our own age as "the century of the common man" may get his history in reverse if he is not careful. With all that we have attained as a great and powerful nation, it is doubtful that we have yet come to (and certainly we have not kept) that exultant idealism and untrammeled individual freedom which the early nineteenth century knew.

It is with a clear realization of all this that we can better appreciate what happened when the Methodist Episcopal Church, with a powerful centralized control, found itself organized among such newly freed people. In six short years after 1784 the Methodist superintendent frankly dropped that long name and adopted for himself the title of "bishop," after the nomenclature of the English Church—and bishops, as everyone knew, were ecclesiastical peers who lived in palaces, and some of them sat in the House of Lords. They also, as it was immediately remembered by the American Methodists, lorded it over their brethren, and considered themselves to have a higher churchly grade than mere priests or deacons. "Is this," asked the simple Methodist brethren on the Eastern seaboard, "the liberty in which we have been made free?" Furthermore, with all the power an English bishop had, he never could control the movements of men as could Francis Asbury and "Dr. Coke," as the

Americans persisted in calling the other superintendent. "Is it for this we have fought to be free?" men asked. One can see at once the tension that could arise.

The situation was complicated and bitterness increased over a difference of opinion and interpretation as to what John Wesley intended Coke and Asbury to be. Wesley was known to reject the idea of the bishop as representing a third ecclesiastical order. Indeed he could not have ordained Coke if he had believed in the third order, for he himself was not a bishop. Nor did he give Coke or Asbury the title, "bishop," but "superintendent." He did not pretend to ordain at all by the authority of any episcopal grace but said frankly of the ordinations: "We formed a presbytery"—that is, a group of priests ("elders," as Wesley called them). Furthermore, though no historian that I have ever read has ever mentioned this before, Wesley omitted from the prayer book which he sent to American Methodism, the Order of Confirmation, that order by which persons are admitted to membership in the Church of England and which requires the imposition of the hands of a bishop to be valid. Wesley left out the whole office and made no mention whatever of any such rite among American Methodists. He may have done so because he did not believe that the gate to the church was confirmation, but baptism only; or he may not have believed in giving to any one man the power to admit others to membership in the church; or he may have had no idea of and no desire to give his Methodist superintendent any semblance of a power that might make him appear to be very like an English bishop.

Wesley wrote a bitter letter to Asbury when he heard in 1788 that he had allowed himself to be called "bishop." "Men may call me a knave or a fool, a rascal, a scoundrel and I am content. But they shall never by my consent call me Bishop," was Wesley's acid message to his American superintendent.[1]

But what did Wesley mean by giving a third ordination to Thomas Coke and thus "setting him apart" for American superintendency? Why did he instruct Coke to give that same type of ordination to Asbury, and why did he send over with him a printed office embodying that third ordination, one which is almost a replica of "The Form for the Ordaining and Consecrating of a Bishop or Archbishop" in the Church of England? Further, that Wesley did not object to the organization of a Methodist Episcopal Church in America seems to be quite obvious, though exactly what Wesley expected his American superintendent to do or to be when he got to America is not at all clear.

[1] George Eayrs, *Letters of John Wesley* (London: Hodder & Stoughton, 1915), p. 280.

No one has yet been able fully to interpret Wesley's mind upon these questions which were deeply involved in the organization of American Methodism. But over the main point and the real issue in the subsequent episcopal controversy, which was not the *name* but the *power* of the American bishop, Wesley left no one in uncertainty. Certainly he never registered any objection to the powers which Coke and Asbury exercised, whatever may have been his objection to the name by which they called themselves. In fact, if his own attitudes and appointments are considered, Wesley must have approved the way things were managed upon the American shores. He stationed preachers himself, with none gainsaying, as long as he lived; and while he "never expected to create an American General Conference," as Tigert aptly says, he did expect Asbury to perpetuate the Methodist appointive system in America itself. And it was this appointive system, not the name by which it was known, that was the crux of the whole matter.

Soon after the new church had taken its origin, Bishops Coke and Asbury themselves put on record their own mind toward the type of episcopacy they were carrying on. In their notes appended to the *Discipline* of 1798 the pioneer bishops took frank cognizance of the objection to their own supreme power. In a document that remains as their own personal as well as official apology, they frankly claimed the power of stationing the preachers, not because of prelatical custom or the desire for churchly supremacy, but for the very practical reason that the bishop *must have this power in order to establish and maintain the itinerant system*. The bishops made it clear that they considered themselves perfectly subject to the General Conference in all points. But they also made it clear that they believed it was necessary for them to station the preachers if the not yet fully proved system of itineracy should become integrated into the church they were endeavoring to lead. To establish itineracy, not episcopacy, was Asbury's prime policy.

But although these notes of 1798 breathe an air of lofty apology, they were unable to hush the storm of objection. Move after move in General Conference after General Conference in these early years makes that unmistakably clear. At one conference the debate was on the right of a minister to appeal his appointment to the conference, if and when he thought himself wronged by the bishop's decision. At another it was over the election of the presiding elders, when able men maintained that the election of presiding elders should be in the hands of the conference, so that the elders themselves should not become creatures of the bishop. This move too was defeated. As early as 1792 James O'Kelly,

26

losing his motion that the minister should have the right to appeal to his conference if he did not like his appointment, walked out with a few followers and so left the church. At every General Conference from 1784 to 1808 the power of the episcopacy provided the subject for debate, and at any one of these conferences that power might have been radically changed or modified by a majority vote. Had it been modified, the bishop would have been compelled to yield, and Methodist episcopacy would then have had a different rating on the parchment of universal church history. But in every case the effort to denature the Asburian episcopacy failed. Then in 1808 the delegated General Conference was created and this took over the entire power and direction of the church, except in certain vastly important particulars. One of these had to do with the episcopacy. The third Restrictive Rule, written and adopted by the church in 1808, held that, as an exception to the sweeping powers given to the General Conference, it should not possess the right "to do away episcopacy or destroy the plan of our itinerant general superintendency." Thus episcopacy—as it then was—was established, and the plan of itinerant general superintendency, with whatever features the brethren of 1808 thought that comprehended, was put beyond the reach of General Conference action. Methodist episcopacy was frankly recognized for what it had always been—a co-ordinate part of the church's government.

But before 1808 crystallized and set the pattern of Methodist episcopacy in that form which the fathers of that date thought should be forever beyond the reach of General Conference action, there had taken place one important modification in the power of episcopacy itself. That had to do with what the later church learned to call the "time limit"; that is, the length of time a pastor might be allowed to stay on any one charge. Like other changes and modifications which the years were to bring, this arose out of practical necessity. It came about in this way.

There was in Albany in 1800 a pastor by the name of Stebbins, who was very popular with the people but whose reappointment for that special place, Asbury felt, would be a mistake. But to move the man, it was evident, would cause dissension and division in the local church, and, against his better judgment, the venerable bishop did as other bishops have often done in subsequent years—he yielded to the local pressure and reappointed Stebbins again and again.

This situation was much discussed among the connection and Aaron Hunt was bold enough to suggest to Asbury that, in order to take care of it, the General Conference should pass a measure forbidding the reappointment of any minister for a term longer than two years. Asbury, with the keen discernment which marked him, saw at once what effect this would have on the superintendency.

"So then you would restrict the appointive power?" he asked pleasantly enough, but alert to what the suggestion meant.

"Nay, sir," was Hunt's reply, "we would aid its execution for in the present instance it seems deficient."

"So, so," musingly replied Asbury, as though he were thinking. But his failure to object encouraged Hunt, and at the ensuing General Conference, he, with Totten of the Philadelphia Conference, presented the resolution asking for a three-year time limit—and saw it passed.[2] Subsequent General Conferences through the years acted to modify the time limit, lengthening it a year or so at a time as the decades passed, until it was finally removed altogether. But this action in 1804 was an exercise of the sovereignty of the General Conference, restricting the power of the bishop. So in 1808, when the delegated General Conference was created, the episcopacy, as it then was, was put beyond reach of that conference. As the bishop in 1808 already found the appointive power "restricted," as Asbury put it, with reference to the outside limit of a man's term of appointment, there was not then, nor has there ever been since, any question as to the constitutional right of a General Conference to limit the bishops as to the number of years they may reappoint any man to any place. All appointments, of course, are made for a year at a time—the "time limit" had to do with the number of years beyond which a man could not be reappointed to the same charge.

Long after this, indeed within recent years—in 1924—in the Methodist Episcopal Church, there was pending a measure designed to limit the term of the district superintendents. Opponents of the measure contended that it would curtail the powers of the episcopacy and was therefore unconstitutional. The Judiciary Committee of the General Conference was appealed to for a ruling on this matter. The committee affirmed that "the Bishop has always exercised the power of appointment but was directed as to where and how long he should apply it, as the pastor's time limit was always considered not a limitation of the Bishop's power, but of when he should exercise it." [3] Asbury evidently saw the effect of the time limit much more clearly than did the 1924 committee.

[2] James M. Buckley, A History of Methodism in the United States (1897), I, 367.

[3] Journal, 1924, pp. 470-77.

The Second Period—1808 to 1844

But the constitutional enactment of 1808 and the Restrictive Rule with reference to episcopacy in no way quieted the anti-episcopal storm. It merely punctuated it. That the bishop could now claim the protection of constitutional law for his power did not make that power less objectionable. It was the thing itself and not its legal establishment which was at the heart of the difficulty.

Furthermore the language of the Third Restrictive Rule was open, as the years proved, to a variety of interpretations. It was perfectly evident that episcopacy itself could not be "done away," but could it not be greatly modified? And as to the plan of itinerant general superintendency, could that not be altered without being destroyed? The bishops were, of course, personally amenable for their proper conduct to the General Conference, as they had been from the first. Thus was opened a very curious situation which to an extent persists yet—the bishop able at any time to fix the appointment of any man in the church, and of any man in the General Conference, but these men themselves when in the General Conference (now the Jurisdictional Conference) controlling the bishop in the sense of sitting as judges upon him in the personal and official performance of his duty, including that of stationing *them*.

Adding force and strength to the elements in the church which continued after 1808 to oppose the power of the episcopacy was the movement which increasingly registered itself under the cry for "lay rights." Methodism, it was swiftly pointed out, though composed of loyal laymen everywhere, was in effect a preacher's church. Preachers, and preachers only, composed the General and Annual Conferences. Certain writers hold that during these years no layman was admitted even as an "unofficial observer" to Annual Conference sessions, and that a "gallery" of visitors was scarcely known even at General Conferences. Preachers, and preachers only, made all the laws for the whole connection; preachers made all the appointments—indeed, one preacher, the bishop, made them all by himself. The only right which the lay people had was to raise money and be obedient to Methodist discipline. They could, of course, petition for a certain preacher to be sent them or for a preacher's removal, but even petitions were frowned upon as un-Methodistic in these early years. The whole system was clearly of the preachers, by the preachers, and—so said the objectors—for the preachers. Why could not the local congregation, which paid all the bills, have the right to appeal to the conference when it was evident that the preacher to be sent them was one whom they did not want; or why did they not have some recourse when their own beloved minister was to be "moved," perhaps against his consent?

This cry for lay rights tied in with and reinforced the anti-episcopal elements in the church, and became more and more formidable as the General Conferences of 1816, 1820, and 1824 were held. And why not? Given the American background of boundless freedom, even those who came up in the episcopal branches of Methodism can see today the validity of the demand made by the Snethens and Stocktons of that early era. What if today there were ministers only in the Annual Conference, ministers only in the General Conference, ministers only on the Judicial Council or on the great boards of the church? All our laymen left out of the lawmaking body, and given no voice whatever in the control of the church they love and support? To mention such a situation is to show us how far we have come from 1828 and how much the Methodist Protestant tradition has become a part of the present life of Methodism.

But today is not 1816 or 1820, and the church then was succeeding in a marvelous manner. Those who were opposed to laity rights or to decentralizing the power of the bishop had the pragmatic argument of success on their side. Members were being added, and the "old Methodist system," as the fathers of 1816 were even then reverently terming it, was functioning effectively—if multiplied numbers and influence mean anything (as they do). The constitutional historian is sometimes so enamored of vast structural changes and epochal developments that he may overlook the fact that in the marvelous growth of Methodism it was not the actions of General Conferences or debates over great issues which determined the progress of the church. Rather it was the preaching of the countless circuit riders, the testimony and work of the innumerable class leaders, the vital ministry of a growing church filled with evangelistic fervor, and the irresistible testimony of men and women that they had been redeemed from sin and found life sweet and purposeful. It was in church on Sunday, or in the class meeting at early candlelight, or in the fervor of camp meeting throngs, in the work of a happy exultant people, singing—sometimes shouting—that Methodism found its best expression. Its organization has played indeed a great part in its success, but perhaps not as much as the constitutional historian sometimes thinks.

In 1820 the fight to decentralize the power of the bishop came to a head with the presentation of a resolution in the General Conference granting power to the Annual Conferences to elect their own presiding elders. This was a proposal which had been up before from time to time. It was certainly democratic in intent and was agreeable to a great

30

number. Others, however, rightly saw in it a drastic curtailment of the bishop's power—which it was.

"The office of Presiding Elder is coeval with the Methodist Episcopal Church," explained Bishop Osmon C. Baker,[4] while Bishops Coke and Asbury declared that this office was

so necessary that they [Asbury and the District Conferences] agreed to enlarge the number and give them the name by which they are at present called. . . . In 1792 the General Conference, equally conscious of having such an office among us, not only confirmed everything that Bishop Asbury and the district conferences had done, but also drew up, or agreed to, the present section for the explanation of the nature and duties of the office.[5]

But it remained for William McKendree to recognize the real function and status of this office, and in 1812 he summoned the presiding elders to meet with him when he was preparing to make the appointments for the preachers. Thus originated "the cabinet"—the bishop with his presiding elders sitting in council on the stationing of the preachers, a procedure which has become fixed in Methodism since that day.

Bishop Holland N. McTyeire, himself a protagonist, not to say exemplar, of the strong episcopacy, once declared:

The presiding elder, ever since the office was created in 1792, is the agent or assistant of the Bishop; is part of the executive government; and in his district is authorized to discharge all the duties of the absent Bishop except ordination. The authority by which the Bishop is enabled to "oversee the business of the church" consists largely therefore in the power of appointing the presiding elders.[6]

It may be said here, in order to avoid confusion in the later pages of this study, that the name "presiding elder" was changed to "district superintendent" in the Methodist Episcopal Church in 1908, and so remains in The Methodist Church. The Methodist Episcopal Church, South, retained the old name "presiding elder" until union in 1939. An effort to adopt the name "district elder" in The Methodist Church failed at the Uniting Conference.

Those who have endeavored to make it appear that the district superintendency is something entirely apart from the administration of the church—"a fifth wheel"—have never been able to make out their case.

[4] A Guide Book in the Administration of the Discipline (1873), p. 63.
[5] Discipline, 1798. Coke and Asbury's notes.
[6] History of Methodism (1884), p. 570.

31

At the Methodist Episcopal General Conference of 1908 a delegate, R. A. Chase, aptly described the district superintendency as the "applied end of the episcopacy." [7]

The district superintendency, were there no bishops, would mean proconsular anarchy; a bishop with no district superintendents under his control would stand bereft of his executive assistants, if he could stand at all. It was this latter fact which made the fight for the elective superintendency in 1820 such a crucial one.

However, the resolution calling for the election of presiding elders passed, and it would undoubtedly have gone into effect but for the unexpected and dramatic stand taken against it by one man, Joshua Soule. For Soule, who was elected bishop by this same General Conference, refused to allow himself to be ordained to the office, affirming that he believed the office to which he had just been elected was being radically changed by the measure the conference had just adopted. "I cannot with my conviction of propriety and obligation enter upon the work of an itinerant general superintendent." So ran his message to the General Conference. "I was elected under the constitution and government of the Methodist Episcopal Church unimpaired, and under no other consideration than that of their continuance would I have consented to be considered as a candidate for a relation in which were incorporated such arduous labors and awful responsibilities." [8]

The stand of Soule, it was soon evident, had the full support of Bishop William McKendree, who was, after Asbury, the most influential figure in early Methodism. In fact, while the whole matter was pending and at the time Soule's refusal was made known, a communication from McKendree was read to the conference in which the senior bishop flatly pronounced the resolution "unconstitutional and therefore destitute of the proper authority of the Church." McKendree, however, evidently did not feel that his pronouncement would have the effect of actually blocking the resolution, for later on in his paper he declared, "Under the influence of this sentiment . . . I enter this protest." [9]

The other two bishops, George and Roberts, were undecided in the matter, the one through "amiable impartiality," and the other through "judicial weakness," as McTyeire later put it. But McKendree, supporting Soule, and both carrying on the Asburian tradition, felt that the elective

[7] *Daily Christian Advocate*, May 18, 1908.
[8] Robert Paine, *Life and Times of Bishop McKendree* (1874), I, 420-21.
[9] *Ibid.*, I, 418-19.

eldership would be a direct blow at the heart of the whole episcopal system. So Episcopal Methodists subsequently and almost invariably held.

This view came to prevail, but in the formative years it was not so evident. Even the two junior bishops, as well as a great number of brethren, felt that to allow the conferences the right to elect their own presiding elders would not greatly interfere with episcopal supervision. Soule and McKendree felt otherwise.

Soule himself was a man of deep conviction. He had been the author of a large part of the plan for the delegated General Conference adopted in 1808. The Restrictive Rules, including that protecting the episcopacy, were written by his pen, and that a man of his stature and understanding in church government should feel so deeply on this question made a profound impression. The result was that a state of compromise was reached by the passage at this same conference of a resolution, by a 45 to 35 vote, which declared that the "rule passed by this conference respecting the nomination and election of presiding elders be suspended until the next general conference." This much of a compromise having been achieved, it was thought that Soule would yield and accept the episcopacy. But as the matter had not been decided but only held in suspense, he again refused and the session ended with the same bishops continuing to oversee the business of the church.

McKendree, who was a hard fighter, appealed to the Annual Conferences on the matter, and presented the question of the elective eldership in conference after conference. The protagonists of the measure were not idle and a deeper cleavage began to manifest itself. It soon became evident that the conferences were going to support the senior bishop. The prestige of his name and the stand of Soule combined to lend great strength to the "movement against reform," as their antagonists termed it. Curiously enough a sectional cleavage began to appear also, with the Northern conferences generally supporting the suspended resolution, the Southern against. In 1824, however, as the General Conference convened, it was evident that the elective presiding eldership had lost. So the event proved. Soule was then again elected bishop, accepted, and was ordained, and the conference ended with the whole movement for lay rights and decentralization effectually blocked—or so it appeared.

Great bitterness resulted. The movement for reform found a powerful advocate in a well-edited journal *Wesleyan Repository*, which in a short while became *Mutual Rights*, edited by a committee whose chairman, S. K. Jennings was a physician. The *Methodist Magazine*, edited by such stalwarts as Nathan Bangs and John Emory, stoutly defended the *status quo.* These last followed the time-hallowed editorial plan of refusing to publish writing of a controversial character "which would go to disturb the peace and harmony of the Church." [10] Thus the minority had little chance for official rejoinder. The protagonists of lay rights turned elsewhere, and "Union Societies" began to be organized in which the reformers could express themselves and demand redress. *Mutual Rights* became very polemic. Controversy filled the air. Men were expelled from the Methodist Episcopal Church simply for subscribing to *Mutual Rights*—and without trial.

Agitation continued, but after 1824 it became increasingly evident that all efforts within the church to obtain "reform"—by which was meant lay representation, the appeal of the minister concerning an appointment, and the elective presiding leadership—all this was futile. A break with the whole system was all that was left for those who had championed the reform measures. This definite break came with, and after, the General Conference of 1828.

It will not be possible to go into all the details connected with the organization of the Methodist Protestant Church. The importance of that organization, however, and the part it has played in all subsequent Methodist history, and which it now plays in the Methodist Church, warrants at least a brief outline of its formation and early years.

After the 1824 General Conference a meeting was held composed of distinguished members of the conference and other persons from different parts of the country. These, imbued with the seriousness of the situation, decided to call on those who wished reform to organize "Union Societies" of all persons who were "favorable to a change in the government of the Methodist Episcopal Church." In November, 1827, the representatives of the Union Societies and those desirous of reform, met in a convention in Baltimore. There were one hundred delegates present, representing seven states. This convention drew up and arranged for presentation to the General Conference of the next year (1828) a well-wrought memorial praying for the admission of laymen into the legislative councils of the church.

But the reformers got nowhere in the General Conference itself. Late in the year, on November 12, 1828, they met again in Baltimore and created a provisional organization which they termed The Associated Methodist Churches. They decided to call a full and representative conference two years later in 1830.

[10] Edward J. Drinkhouse, *History of Methodist Reform and of the Methodist Protestant Church* (1899), II, 34.

Pursuant to this, in St. John's Church, Baltimore, on November 3, 1830, the Methodist Protestant Church was organized. The organizing conference drew up a constitution which "recognized Christ as head of the church and all the elders of the Church as equal." It secured to every adult layman the right to vote and to be represented in every church meeting; and to every itinerant the right to appeal from what he regarded as an oppressive appointment, and gave him a veto upon his removal from a charge, while in the regular discharge of his duty, until the expiration of his term. The Methodist Protestant Church made trials for matters of opinion impossible, and did away with what the reformers called "the modern Episcopacy" and presiding eldership, terming both "unnecessary." The Methodist Protestant *Discipline* of 1936 states with all the vigor of the Methodist Protestant fathers of that earlier day that "as they were Americans and not Englishmen, they believed in a Church without a bishop and a state without a king."   824918

The Methodist Protestant Church, thus organized in 1828-30, embodied within itself the reform measures which the organizing members felt should have belonged to all Methodism. It did away with episcopacy entirely, as has been said, allowing each Annual Conference to choose a "president," who should serve for a definite term only, and who should "travel the district." The appointments were made by a "stationing committee" elected by each Annual Conference. On this, laymen usually served, though each conference made its own rules and established the type of its own committee. Pastoral appointments were read openly in the Annual Conference, and where there was objection to an appointment by a minister, he could appeal. If his appeal was allowed, the stationing committee had to give him another appointment.

Lay rights were fully taken care of by the inclusion of laymen to share in the Annual Conferences and in the lawmaking body of the church— the General Conference. Thus for Methodist Protestantism the episcopal controversy and tensions over variant interpretations of a bishop's power were forever ended. Full democracy had been achieved—and there were no bishops.

The Methodist Protestants, of course, remained Methodist in doctrine and discipline, and while they lacked episcopal supervision and the close and vigorous shepherding of presiding elders, they did retain itineracy, which was the pulse beat of the whole system. They also kept practically every other essential form of administration and organization known then in Methodist polity. But in their swing away from centralized authority the "reformers" went further—certainly their church did—than they had originally intended. "Authority was diffused among Annual Conferences and local churches to such an extent that denominational adhesiveness and unity were definitely subordinated. It took nearly a hundred years for the church to realize and act on this discovery," states Bishop James H. Straughn. Fortunately for all Methodism, just as the Methodist Protestants of the twentieth century awoke to the need for more centralized control, Episcopal Methodists awoke to the value of Methodist Protestantism in the larger stream of Methodism itself.

In the unrolling of the years and in the overwhelming growth of the two Episcopal Methodisms the historian is tempted sometimes to see an adverse judgment against Methodist Protestantism as such. To take such a view, however, would be—I write as an Episcopal Methodist—quite *ex parte*. Granted that there was more authority to place men in needed positions and to keep them there in Episcopal Methodism, and more authority on the part of the general church to put into effect the strategy of its leaders, even that would scarcely tell the whole story. Methodist Protestants were Methodists, and in that fact lay the glory and weakness of their organization. When Methodist Protestants moved into new communities they were at once absorbed into the Methodist bodies already residing there. It was not in 1939 that Methodist Protestantism went down "without a trace in the troubled jurisdictional seas," as Bishop Edwin Holt Hughes expressed it. It had been doing something like that through its long and noble career.

DIVIDING EPISCOPAL SUPERVISION

It was during the eighteen-twenties that there came to the fore the problem of maintaining a united general superintendency in a rapidly growing Church. Asbury's idea, and the theory of episcopacy, which until 1939 was in effect in Methodism, held that a bishop in one place is a bishop in every place. Superintendency must be "general," that is, not diocesan or effective only in one special area but everywhere. As long as the church was small and there were at most but three bishops, all under the tutelage of Asbury, it was customary for the bishops to travel together. Any appointment made by one was understood to be made by all. But as American Methodism grew enormously with the fast-growing nation, and as conference after conference was added to the connection, with vast distances separating the various fields of labor, it was seen that no one bishop could possibly oversee the whole work. And since there were by this time several bishops, it was quite natural that these bishops themselves should agree on a division of their labor. One bishop would oversee certain conferences for a year or two, another would supervise others.

Asbury, and McKendree after him, did not look kindly upon this plan. It had always been "Coke-and-Asbury," then "Asbury-and-Whatcoat," then "Asbury-and-McKendree," attending together all the conferences where practicable. But in 1816, when Enoch George and Robert R. Roberts were added to the episcopal group, a new turn was taken. McKendree explained that the three bishops mutually agreed among themselves to "attend the Conferences alternately, thus changing their work every year; and for the Bishop, whose turn it might be to attend a Conference, to be the responsible president of it; and the other Bishops, if present, to be his counselors." [11]

Thus began the practice of dividing the work and superintending the conferences. But it was a practice put into effect by the bishops themselves. Although the General Conference of 1824 passed a resolution stating that it was "highly expedient for the Bishops to meet both at the General Conference and in the intervals between to form their plan of travelling through their charge," [12] it was the bishops who were expected and requested—but not ordered—to do this. Indeed in the General Conference of 1824, when the resolution above cited was pending, there was a proposal that the conference should divide up the church for the quadrennium into episcopal districts so that the bishops might be able better to oversee the work. To this proposal William Winans, of Mississippi, made a ringing rejoinder, citing the impossibility, under the Third Restrictive Rule, of any General Conference undertaking to so break in upon the plan of itinerant general superintendency.

Even in the later Methodist Episcopal Church, where the episcopacy was admittedly "completely subject to the General Conference in all things," there was no strong support for the right of the General Conference to district the bishops, or fix for the Council of Bishops the outlines of special areas, until late in the century. This will be discussed later.

Nevertheless, although the bishops retained the right to divide out the work, and did divide it out, and although a bishop anywhere was a bishop everywhere, in actual practice in both the Methodist Episcopal Church and the Methodist Episcopal Church, South—when this was organized—and in the present church for that matter, the superintendency was bound to be much more local than general in its effective function-

[11] John J. Tigert, *Constitutional History of American Episcopal Methodism* (rev. ed., 1904), p. 335.

[12] *Journals*, I, 301-2.

ing. Each bishop was superintendent in his own area; in that of the next bishop he was on an equal rank in a titular way, was received in visitation with the honor due his office, and welcomed as a brother beloved by the resident bishop. But he knew, and the preachers knew, and the other bishop knew that he was not the presiding bishop of that area. Theoretically the bishop in the Boston Area could transfer a man from Denver to Seattle if he pleased; and in the South the bishop in Atlanta could put a man from Vicksburg, Mississippi, into First Church, Dallas, but practically such moves were and are impossible. "Comity agreements" Tigert called the inhibiting power here, but it was something that went deeper than that. Anarchy and confusion would have resulted had bishops irrupted into each other' area. Also a bishop must always be a gentleman, and Christian consideration compelled and compels him ever to think first of his brethren. These principles combined to make an unwritten law which no general superintendent ever felt he could break. So general superintendency became of necessity a "majestic constitutional abstraction" as the church grew beyond its swaddling years. In the process of growth either the "general" or the "superintendency" had to be denatured, one or the other, and it will not be hard to understand which survived in the life of a tremendously vital organization. Nevertheless the pristine, august idea was safely enshrined in the constitutional structure of the church, and there it remains today, though since the adoption of the constitution of 1939 there has been put in effect—as will be described later—a regionalizing of the episcopacy due to the jurisdictional division of the church, which is providing a much more decisive division than comity agreements ever did.

But any division of the superintendency, no matter how necessary from a practical standpoint, can have evil consequences if not done by the superintendents so as to avoid parochialization. Indeed Tigert held that part of the responsibility for the split between the South and North in 1844 came about by reason of the fact that in dividing the work of the superintendency in the eighteen-twenties, the superintendents who knew the North never came to the South, and vice versa. Bishop Hedding, from 1824 to 1844, made but a single tour to the Southern conferences, and that in 1831, seven years after he became a bishop. In the same year Bishop Soule made his first episcopal visitation to the North. The bishops, perhaps unconsciously, became sectionalized. Again and again Roberts and Soule advanced as far north as the Baltimore Conference and returned again on their southern track; again and again George and Hedding came as far south as the Philadelphia Conference, and retreated again into New York, New England, or Canada. Said Tigert: "Bishop McKendree's plan of such an episcopal itinerancy as would make the superintendency truly general failed and great hurt came to the Church thereby." [13]

The Church Divides

In 1844 occurred the epochal division of the Methodist Episcopal Church. The adoption by the General Conference of that year of the Plan of Separation, and the subsequent organization of the Methodist Episcopal Church, South, are matters of record. But involved in the separation, and bitterly debated by the General Conference itself, was the now well-worn question of the meaning of Methodist episcopacy. The issue was joined over a proposal properly before the conference that a certain Southern bishop, James O. Andrew, of Georgia, who was a slaveowner (albeit an unwilling one), should cease to exercise his episcopal functions so long as he did own slaves.

At the risk of rehashing an old controversy which were better left to gather its own dust, the actual moves of this historic occasion may be delineated here with some detail so that the part which episcopacy played in the ensuing separation may be made more clear. The Finley resolution calling for the setting aside of Bishop Andrew read as follows:

WHEREAS, The law of our Church forbids the doing of anything calculated to destroy our itinerant general superintendency, and whereas Bishop Andrew has become connected with slavery by marriage and otherwise, and this act having drawn after it circumstances which, in the estimation of the General Conference, will greatly embarrass the exercise of his office as itinerant general superintendent, if not, in some places, entirely prevent it;

Therefore, Resolved, That it is the sense of this General Conference that he desist from the exercise of this office so long as this impediment remains.[14]

Backing the resolution was the full power of the Northern conferences in which, by that time, antislavery feeling had grown to tidal proportions. Against the resolution was the roused-up South, the Southern delegates seeing in the effort to unseat one of their bishops an attack upon episcopacy, as well as upon their own social institutions. Neither side quite realized the might of the ideas and forces which separated them. Neither realized how fatefully this division in a national Christian church foreshadowed the soon-to-be-divided nation. In the debates over Methodist episcopacy in 1844 the historian can hear the drums of Gettysburg.

[13] Op. cit., p. 393.
[14] Journal, 1844, pp. 65-66.

In the effort to rid the Methodist Episcopal Church of the onus of carrying as one of its bishops a man who was a slaveowner, the Northern delegates were forced to maintain—or did maintain—their own ably documented contention that the bishop in Methodism was simply an officer of the General Conference with no extraordinary powers inherent in himself. "A constitutional right to be a Bishop!" exclaimed Jesse T. Peck, of the Troy Conference, later a bishop himself. "You might as well talk of the constitutional right to be an editor or book agent or any other General Conference officer." [15] In the effort to defend Bishop Andrew and the social institution with which the life of their people was so closely involved, the Southern delegates took a position for which they likewise adduced powerful support. They affirmed that bishops were not creatures of the General Conference to be made or unmade at the will of that body. "To say that we can deprive a Bishop of his office and yet not censure him," said Benjamin F. Drake, of the Mississippi Conference, "to say that we can depose and yet leave his episcopal robe unstained, is to my mind absurd in the extreme." [16] "I am astonished," exclaimed George F. Pierce, of Georgia, later a bishop, in answering Peck, "to hear that a Bishop has no constitutional right to be a Bishop." [17]

In the protest which the Southern group prepared and entered on the record after the Finley resolution was passed, this position was stated at great length and with force and cogency. It held in brief that Methodist episcopacy had functioned from the beginning as a constitutional part of the church, just as had the General Conference; that the Third Restrictive Rule specifically put episcopal rights and prerogatives beyond the reach of General Conference action; that while the General Conference might elect a bishop, it had no right to remove him unless after due process and trial it should be proved that he were guilty of personal or official dereliction; and as episcopacy was a co-ordinate part of the church's government, just as was the General Conference, one could not destroy or denature the other. "Once a bishop, always a bishop," became a Southern slogan.

In response to this protest the Northern group set forth in an able paper their opposing conception. The reply to the protest, as it was termed, quoted the 1798 notes of Coke and Asbury in which these two first bishops had declared that they [bishops] were "perfectly subject to the General Conference." Leonidas Hamline, who was on the com-

[15] Journal, 1844, p. 116.
[16] Ibid., p. 106.
[17] L. G. Smith, Life and Times of George F. Pierce (1888), p. 131.

mittee appointed to write the reply to the protest, had already affirmed in a great speech that as episcopacy was an office and not an order, men could be put into it or taken out of it at the will of any General Conference:

Our church constitution recognizes the episcopacy as an abstraction and leaves the body to work it into a concrete form in any hundred or more ways we may be able to invent. We may make one, five or twenty bishops; and, if we please, one for each conference. We may refuse to elect another until all die or resign; and then to maintain the episcopacy, which we are bound to do, we must elect one at least. As to his term, we may limit it at pleasure or leave it undetermined. But in this case is it undeterminable? Certainly not. The power which elected may then displace.[18]

Both the protest and its answer spun out at great length the diverse arguments and opposing views. Both papers were duly made a part of the record. But meanwhile the Finley resolution setting aside Andrew had been passed, almost by a straight sectional vote, and the separation was on.

Underneath the whole conflict, as has been suggested, were greater forces than were playing upon the surface. It has sometimes been affirmed that the tension and eventual war between the sections was brought on by a few hotheads and that far-seeing and clear-thinking men might have effected a compromise without the bitter bloodshed of internecine strife. Perhaps. But as one views the situation in the light of the historic perspective, it is impossible not to see that there was a social, political, and economic cleavage so deep and fundamental that either complete separation or conclusive combat appear to have been the only alternatives. In the Methodist Church this meant separation; in the nation it meant war.

Had there been no division and no debate on episcopal prerogatives in 1844, the signs are not lacking that even so there would have been something of a difference between the Northern and Southern sections in the development of the Methodist episcopacy. The bishop through the years had come to occupy a proportionately stronger position in the South than in the North. This may have been due somewhat to the influence of the episcopal tradition, for the very name "bishop," from Colonial times on, meant more in Virginia, for instance, than it did in Massachusetts. The social organization of the South also would be more friendly to the bishop as belonging to the traditional ruling class than

[18] Walter C. Palmer, *Life and Letters of Leonidas L. Hamline* (1866), p. 156.

could be expected in the more democratic North. We have already noted the fact, stressed with regret by Tigert, that there was a sectional division in episcopal supervision which would tend to perpetuate in either section the personal differences or peculiarities of the bishops in whom these inhered. Roberts and Soule never went North; George and Hedding never went South. If there was a differing emphasis in the two sections this would help to perpetuate it.

As it was, the Plan of Separation was adopted, the Methodist Episcopal Church, South, was organized, and thereafter there were two episcopal Methodisms carrying on two diverse connectional lines. These two had, however, a common tradition in doctrine, worship, hymnody, and polity. The further development of episcopacy in that polity will soon be followed.

METHODIST PROTESTANT DIVISION

It has not been generally known among episcopal Methodists that the Methodist Protestant Church suffered a serious division for many years also because of a difference within that connection over slavery. As early as 1838 the Methodist Protestant Annual Conferences in what were then called the Free States, expressed dissatisfaction with the policy of the Baltimore *Methodist Protestant*, the official organ of the church, which refused to admit any discussion of slavery. A rival weekly *The Western Recorder* was started in 1839 to reflect the views of those who opposed slavery. This publication continued as a private enterprise until 1855, when it was taken over by the Northern and Western Conferences and removed from Zanesville, Ohio, to Springfield, Ohio, and renamed the *Western Methodist Protestant*. This followed an action by the Methodist Protestant General Conference of 1854, which authorized two "conventions" to adjust publishing and other matters of difference between the two different conference groups.

Accordingly the conventions met in Zanesville in 1854, and in Baltimore in 1855, and agreed that there should be two publishing houses— at Springfield and Baltimore—with two papers.

In 1858 the nineteen conferences in the Free States met at a convention and issued what was practically an ultimatum to the Methodist Protestant Church, declaring that they would have nothing more to do with it unless it purged itself of any connection with slavery. This ultimatum the Methodist Protestant General Conference rejected.

In 1866 the disaffected "western" conferences voted to join a similar group who had withdrawn from the Methodist Episcopal Church on the

42

same grounds, and had organized the Wesleyan Methodist Church. The merged body adopted the name of The Methodist Church, and issued a book of *Discipline* under that name. But the plan of union failed to materialize, and the former Methodist Protestant group continued on by themselves. In 1871 their publishing house removed from Springfield, Ohio, to Pittsburgh, Pennsylvania.

It was not long after the end of the Civil War that the two divided Methodist Protestant groups began to draw together, never having had any differences which the war had not removed. After several years of negotiations a basis of union was reached and in May, 1877, the first General Conference of the reunited Methodist Protestant Church met in Baltimore.

The occasion was not without drama. The delegates from the two "sections" paired off and walked arm in arm to the old Starr Church, where the ceremonies connected with their reunion were held.

However, it was considered wise to keep the two publishing houses, one in Pittsburgh and one in Baltimore, in order to better serve the whole connection. These centers of Methodist Protestant publication continued to exist as such until Methodist Union in 1939. The two papers, *The Recorder*, and the *Methodist Protestant*, were merged in 1930 to become the *Methodist Protestant Recorder*, published in Baltimore.

III

THE TWO EPISCOPACIES—1844-1939

The Bishops ought not to enter into small details. It is not their calling. To select the proper men who are to act as their agents—to preserve in order and in motion the wheels of the vast machine—to keep a constant and watchful eye upon the whole—and to think deeply for the general good—form their peculiar and important avocation.

—Notes by Coke and Asbury, Discipline, 1798

A THIRD PERIOD OF METHODIST EPISCOPACY BEGAN IN 1844 AT WHAT some historians have been wont to call the bisection of the church. It came to an end at Kansas City in 1939 when the Plan of Union was adopted as the constitution of reunited Methodism. This sweep of ninety-five years was by all odds the most momentous epoch in the history of the church, covering, as it did, first the continental expansion of Methodism, and then its world-wide growth and power.

In spite of the somewhat different attitudes toward episcopacy taken officially by the Methodist Episcopal Church and the Methodist Episcopal Church, South, during these years, the development of the office in both communions shows an amazing parallel. The Methodist Episcopal Church, South, in its first *Discipline*, 1846, kept the exact language of the 1844 *Discipline* of the Methodist Episcopal Church, that treated of the powers of the General Conference. Except for two important differences, which will be pointed out, the two churches met the special problems which the years pressed upon their episcopal establishments in almost the same way. Both inherited from the unbroken church the plan of having a Committee on Episcopacy in every General Conference. Both relaxed the time limit on the pastorate little by little, and finally removed it entirely. Both faced the problem of missionary bishops or of a special superintendency for the foreign field at about the same time, though each met it in a different way; the limitation of term for the presiding elder or district superintendent was in due time adopted by both churches, as was the age limit for the retirement of the bishops themselves. The question of term episcopacy, or of electing a bishop for a definite number of years, arose to agitate both connections late in this period; and both churches were subjected to increasing and eventually overwhelming pressure on the part of the local churches, to the end that these local churches might have a direct control in the making or unmaking of their own pastoral appointments. Because of this parallel development it will be simpler to trace as one record Methodist episcopacy through both the episcopal branches during these crucial years.

Naturally enough, just after the division of the church each branch of Methodism swung at once to the extreme limit of its own proclaimed position. There had been vague differences over episcopal power and prerogative before 1844, but after that date the fathers in both camps saw to it that differences should be absolutely unmistakable. Certainly they both made plain after 1844 what they had argued about in 1844. Both sections had gone on record in a fierce debate and had parted in a bitter separation. Both had issued forceful documents and these very documents were to guide and direct future attitudes in the separate communions. For from that day and for many years afterward all the ecclesiastical historians and apologists in either camp simply reiterated and reinforced the contention of their own particular fathers and brethren. What the Pecks and Hamlines had declared, the Neelys, Stevens', and Buckleys of the Methodist Episcopal Church later echoed with power and ability; and what the Winans and Pierces of the South had affirmed, the McTyeires, the Tigerts, and the Dennys were to restate with increasing fervor. Years and experience were to modify something of the sharp line early drawn by the recoil after division, but it is a noteworthy fact that the two distinctive features which differentiated between the episcopacy in the Methodist Episcopal Church and that in the Methodist Episcopal Church, South, both came into effect a few years after the separation. These features were: the tremendous power given the bishops in the Church, South, to act as the final judges of Methodist law and to block any legislative action on the part of the General Conference which they believed to be unconstitutional; and in the Methodist Episcopal Church a distinctive modification of the Third Restrictive Rule, in order that "missionary bishops," who were not to be general superintendents, might be created. Both these features will be studied in turn.

JUDICIAL POWER OF THE BISHOPS

In early conferences, bishops, as presiding officers, were compelled to rule from time to time upon matters of Methodist law. In 1840 this power was frankly recognized and established by a disciplinary direction empowering the bishops to: "decide all questions of law in an annual conference, subject to an appeal to the General Conference; but in all cases the application of law shall be with the conference." [1]

This regulation remained in every *Discipline* of the Methodist Episcopal Church in substantially these words, and was carried over into The Methodist Church where it remains today in the constitution as ruling law. The practical import of this regulation will be discussed later in the section devoted to judicial processes.

In the Methodist Episcopal Church, South, the above regulation was left out of its first two *Disciplines*, but re-inserted in 1854 with a sweeping addition, emphasized below in italics:

He [the bishop] shall decide all questions of law coming before him in the regular business of an annual conference, and may require such questions to be presented in writing, and, on the order of the conference, such questions and the decisions of the bishop shall be recorded on the journal of the conference. When the bishop shall have decided a question of law, the conference shall have the right to determine how far the law thus decided or interpreted is applicable to the case then pending. An annual conference shall have the right to appeal from such decision *to the college of bishops, whose decision in such cases shall be final. And no episcopal decision shall be authoritative except in the case pending, nor shall any be published, until it shall have been approved by the college of bishops. And each bishop shall report in writing to the episcopal college . . . such decisions as he has made, . . . and all such decisions, when approved by the college of bishops, shall be either recorded in a permanent form, or published in such manner as the bishops shall agree to adopt; and when so approved, and recorded or published, they shall be authoritative interpretations or constructions of the law.*[2]

Thus it is seen that very early in this period there was lodged in the bishops of the Methodist Episcopal Church, South, a power that was reserved to the General Conference in the Methodist Episcopal Church —to act as the final interpreter of Methodist law. As the years rolled by the "episcopal decisions" of the Southern Church became a body of law binding upon all the members of that communion; just as the "Reports of the Committee on Judiciary," when these had been adopted by the General Conference of the Methodist Episcopal Church, became a part of the *corpus legis* of that body. In the South the recoil against an all-powerful General Conference served to take away from that body its judicial power and to lodge it in the bishops; in the North the all-powerful General Conference continued to be all-powerful, acting as the

[1] *Discipline*, 1840, p. 27.
[2] *Discipline*, 1854, pp. 49-50.

judge and interpreter of its own law. The Board of Bishops of the Methodist Episcopal Church was wont, in formal communications, to ask the General Conference to "decide questions of law or interpret the *Discipline*." In the South the reverse was the case. The General Conference asked the College of Bishops to make the interpretations.

But the Church, South, went even further. In 1854 it invested its College of Bishops with the right to block or check any General Conference action which in its judgment contravened the constitution of the church. The fact that in 1844 there had been no third party to which an appeal might have been taken, but the majority of the General Conference was then able to act as judge, jury and—according to Southern ideas—as executioner, showed the need of some sort of check or balance here. The "all-powerful General Conference" had already become a Southern *bête noire*, as all commissions on church union were later to discover. To guard against that the following regulation was proposed and adopted in 1854:

Provided, that when any rule or regulation is adopted by the General Conference which, in the opinions of the bishops is unconstitutional, the bishops may present to the General Conference their objections to such rule or regulation, with reasons thereof, and if, after hearing the objections and reasons of the bishops, two-thirds of the members of the Conference present shall vote in favor of the rule or regulation so objected to, it shall have the force of law, otherwise it shall be null and void.[3]

This important measure was passed by the General Conference of the Methodist Episcopal Church, South, by majority vote and as simple legislation. But that it was a structural constitutional change, and not a mere statutory one, was clearly evident. The situation was much discussed in the Methodist Episcopal Church, South, and finally in 1870 an able paper treating of the entire matter was presented to the General Conference by Dr. Leroy Lee, of the Missouri Conference, the chairman of the Committee on Episcopacy. Dr. Lee's well-wrought and ably reasoned report made clear the constitutionality, or unconstitutionality, of the measure passed in 1854 and pointed the way out.[4] The General Conference thereupon passed the same measure again—with slight verbal changes—by the requisite constitutional majority and sent it down to the Annual Conferences for their vote. This was given during the quadrennium and at the next General Conference the bishops reported that the

[3] *Ibid.*, p. 39.
[4] *Journal*, 1870, pp. 281-87.

measure had now become part of the constitution of the Methodist Episcopal Church, South.

The adoption of this measure did not give the bishops a "veto power" as was often erroneously stated, but it did give them the power to block or check what they considered unconstitutional legislation, until such legislation should be adopted by constitutional processes. A veto in American political parlance means the power to kill or suppress a measure not favored by the executive. The 1870 measure simply enabled the Southern bishops to "lay down an episcopal check," as Bishop Collins Denny once expressed it. Its effect, paradoxically, was to make constitutional whatever the bishops declared to be unconstitutional.

Parenthetically it may be said that this exact power then given to the Southern bishops is now entrusted to the Judicial Council of The Methodist Church. But that power, whether wielded by the Southern bishops in the heyday of their glory or by the present Judicial Council, has never been expected to be legislative, that is, to oppose or advance any particular measure which the General Conference is considering. The Judicial Council is expected, as were the Southern bishops, to pronounce on the constitutionality of actions of the General Conference when these actions, supposedly simple—that is, nonconstitutional— legislation, are in the view of the council in reality constitutional. In practice, unless the Judicial Council calls in question or pronounces an action of the General Conference unconstitutional, the actions of that body are legal and binding and become authoritative Methodist law.

The action of 1854 and 1870 gave the episcopacy in the Southern church a very great power. Equitably enough, however, in spite of the power given, there were only two instances—so Bishop Collins Denny told the Commission on Unification in 1918—when the Southern bishops used their power to check the General Conference.[5] It is somewhat heartening, therefore, to record that the General Conference of the Methodist Episcopal Church, which had the right to determine all matters of constitutionality arising before it, never abused its privilege, all powerful though it was; and that the bishops of the Methodist Episcopal Church, South, having the right to sit in judgment on the acts of their General Conference, even those affecting their own interests, never abused their privilege.

The adoption of the 1870 constitutional enactment bestowing supreme judicial power upon the bishops of the Church, South, marked the high tide of Methodist episcopacy in any branch of Methodism. It was, of

[5] See H. M. Du Bose, *History of Methodism* (1916), p. 115.

course, the era of strong superintendents who made the appointments by personal fiat, and who assumed the power to do so as part of their office. It is not strange, therefore, to find that there has perhaps been in the South, and in the conferences of the present church which formerly adhered to the Southern church, a more exalted idea of Methodist episcopacy than was, or is, the case in the North. Even at the time of church union in 1939 it was quite usual for bishops in the Methodist Episcopal Church, South, to make many important appointments by their own direct will, sometimes even to the disregard of both cabinet and local pulpit committees.

In 1934, however, the power of the Southern bishops to pass upon the constitutionality of General Conference legislation was taken away. This was done by a constitutional move which created a Judicial Council and gave to that council all appellate power, including the power to appeal from any act of the General Conference. The story of this Judicial Council will be told later, but suffice it to say here that the creation of the Judicial Council in the Southern church in 1934 ended for Southern episcopacy its unique power to check for constitutional reasons General Conference action, as well as its right to act as an appellate court interpreting Methodist law.

This move was, of course, to the distaste of certain elements in the Methodist Episcopal Church, South, who felt that the Judicial Council was an innovation and therefore dangerous. I remember hearing Bishop Collins Denny address an Annual Conference and argue against the adoption of the measure setting up the Judicial Council. But the Southern conferences agreed to the change and the council was duly set up.[6] Thereafter questions of law were no longer to be interpreted by "bishops' decisions" but by the new "Supreme Court," as the brethren liked to call it. But as the Southern church itself was on the verge of union with the Methodist Episcopal and Methodist Protestant churches just at the time its council commenced to function, and as the new church—The Methodist Church—was to have a Judicial Council also, as part of the Plan of Union, the judicial power of the Southern bishops was practically co-extensive with the life of the Southern church. Today the bishops' decisions of the Methodist Episcopal Church, South, remain as part of the historic records of the entire church, and will be able to give guidance on many points to those who shall be entrusted with the duty of interpreting Methodist law.

[6] Journal, 1934, p. 30.

MISSIONARY BISHOPS

The question of electing men to be bishops for special missionary areas came to the fore in this period. When the church was small it was easy enough to allow certain bishops to make missionary journeys into pioneer territory, either on the American continent or abroad. Indeed, Dr. Coke was more a missionary bishop and traveler of the high seas than he was an American general superintendent. So was every early bishop a missionary bishop to a degree, some going to the Indians, some to the Western outposts, or perchance to Canada. After a time, as mission churches developed in foreign lands, the need for a superintendency which could acquaint itself with local conditions and reside with the native people was more fully appreciated.

In 1856 this demand came to a head in the Methodist Episcopal Church with the request from Liberia that a bishop be elected especially for that particular field. There the work had been growing, and there was a need felt for a resident superintendency. But to elect a bishop for one special area or land was to alter the plan of general superintendency; for either the bishop so elected could claim his place as a general superintendent of the whole church, in which case he could not be "localized"; or, if he were elected for only one area, the "plan of general superintendency" would be done away. Therefore a proposal that the Third Restrictive Rule be altered to allow for the election of a "missionary bishop" was put before the General Conference of 1856. It read as follows:

They shall not alter or change any part or rule of our government so as to do away episcopacy or destroy the plan of our intinerant general superintendcy, *but may appoint a Missionary Bishop or Superintendent for any of our foreign missions, limiting his episcopal jurisdiction to the same respectively.*

The amendment to the Third Restrictive Rule is indicated above by italics. It was passed by the General Conference of 1856,[7] and sent down to the conferences. These concurred in adopting it during the ensuing quadrennium. However, by a curious oversight on the part of the editor of the *Discipline*, the change in the rule did not appear in the book until the issue of 1868, and not until the second edition of that. So certain, however, were the fathers of 1856 that the amendment would be adopted that they provided for the ordination of a missionary bishop in the interim between General Conferences, "when the restrictive rule should be changed." So as Dr. David Sherman records it, "Liberia was allowed to

[7] *Journal*, 1856, pp. 146-47, 184.

choose a Bishop by a vote of two-thirds, and to have the usual discount on our books." [8]

The missionary bishop thus became a part of the episcopal economy of the Methodist Episcopal Church, and continued so until Methodist union in 1939. Missionary bishops who were such at the time of union were continued as such in The Methodist Church, but it was understood that no new ones were to be authorized. A missionary bishop was always elected by the General Conference of the entire church, but elected for one special field. In that field he exercised full episcopal power, but could not claim such power in the homeland or elsewhere than in his own area. He was not, therefore, considered as a "general" superintendent. In the Methodist Episcopal *Discipline* the names of the missionary bishops were listed separately from those of the regular bishops until the General Conference of 1920. At that time an issue was made of the matter and the whole question as to the status and privileges of missionary bishops was opened up. The General Conference thereupon by special ballot elected the three effective missionary bishops to be general superintendents of the Methodist Episcopal Church and all effective bishops were thereafter listed in one roll in the *Discipline*.[9] The five retired missionary bishops of that date, however, did not profit by this action and continued to have their names published separately under the title "retired missionary bishops." [10] Subsequently, in 1928, Bishop Edwin F. Lee, and in 1936, Bishop John M. Springer were elected missionary bishops, and occupied such status at the time of union in 1939.

As the several mission fields of the Methodist Episcopal Church became more and more autonomous within comparatively recent years, there came a natural demand on the part of mission areas that they be allowed to elect their own bishops. With the formation of Central Conferences, as the respective General Conferences in mission fields were called, this power was granted them, and general superintendents for the respective regions were thereupon duly elected by the Central Conferences. Such superintendents were amenable to their own empowering and ordaining Central Conferences, and in these conferences and areas enjoyed full episcopal power. Likewise the missionary bishop sent out and consecrated by the Methodist Episcopal Church at home had full episcopal power, and this mutual relationship of "native bishops," who might not be natives at all, and missionary bishops, provided something of a

[8] *History of the Revisions of the Discipline* (1874), p. 53.
[9] *Journal*, 1920, pp. 337-38.
[10] *Discipline*, 1920, ¶ 540.

field for speculative discussion. However, good spirit and organizational ability usually overcame the minor difficulties which such intertwined superintendencies might be expected to have. Some of the autonomous churches, however, decided to elect their bishops for a term of years, not for life. Such Central Conference term episcopacy made something of a difference in the way in which such superintendents were regarded by the church in America.

In 1920 it was decided by the General Conference of the Methodist Episcopal Church to elect two bishops from among the Negro constituency of the church, who should be general superintendents in the full sense of the term. The action of the General Conference determining this move came as Report No. 2, of the Committee on Episcopacy:

Your Committee recommends:
1. The election by this General Conference of two Negro General Superintendents.
2. That the Negro General Superintendents be elected on a separate ballot. Adopted, May 11.[11]

Under this mandate two bishops, Matthew W. Clair and Robert E. Jones, were duly elected and took their places in the Board of Bishops. It was tacitly understood that the assignment of these two bishops should usually be to the Negro Conferences of the Methodist Episcopal Church, though, as bishops of the church, they were expected to travel at large and be accorded all the rights and privileges appertaining to their office. Their election, however, may be noticed in connection with that of missionary bishops, though a somewhat reverse situation prevailed. In electing a missionary bishop, the bishop elected was to be for a definite area or region, and not to be a general superintendent. In the case of the Negro bishops, these were by mandate elected from a certain group, but were to be general superintendents of the whole church. The comparison is interesting only from an academic standpoint.

The Methodist Episcopal Church, South, had, of course, bishops appointed to superintend the work in mission areas, but there was no special legislation regarding them, nor were they known as "missionary bishops." They were regular members of the College of Bishops, duly assigned certain mission conferences and areas for their particular oversight. Any bishop might be assigned to any area at home or abroad, and the mission appointments were made so as to provide from the homeland all needed episcopal supervision. Certain bishops, of course, having

[11] *Journal*, 1920, p. 455.

come to be familiar with definite foreign areas, might be reassigned to these from time to time, and some, notably Bishop Walter R. Lambuth, were relieved by the other bishops from home conference superintendency that they might devote their entire time to travel and supervision abroad. Indeed the fact that a bishop was to be given a foreign assignment necessarily meant that he must be relieved somewhat at home. Bishop Arthur J. Moore, in the latter years of the Methodist Episcopal Church, South, was assigned conferences in Europe, the Orient, and Africa, whereupon he observed with great geniality that he had "three continents" to supervise. Naturally such an assignment precluded one's taking, during these years, any home conference. But Southern bishops were all of a piece in the episcopacy and there was no list of special missionary bishops as in the Methodist Episcopal Church, nor was there ever a proposal to amend the restrictive rule to allow for special superintendents.

TERM EPISCOPACY

In the later years of the two Episcopal Methodisms there came the proposal for "term episcopacy." This was a provision that bishops should be elected for a term of years, not for life. As proponents of the measure usually outlined their plan, it provided that the period for which a man was to be elected to serve as bishop should be fixed by the General Conference, and that each bishop should be eligible for re-election at the conclusion of his term. Proponents of the measure took full advantage of the Methodist contention that bishops were not a "third order," but only elders set apart for a special duty. They held, therefore, that neither the episcopal office nor any of its essential prerogatives were impaired by this limitation of tenure; and that if the bishop were truly an elder and no more, it would be entirely proper to return him to his Annual Conference for a traveling preacher's appointment when or if he should not be re-elected to the episcopacy.

Term episcopacy had to commend it also the undeniable fact that the church in both episcopal branches had from time to time made serious mistakes in selecting men for the episcopacy. Persons who managed to impress one General Conference very greatly would absolutely fail with another, and men who in some one particular crisis measured up in an outstanding way would often fall short at other times. Furthermore the duties of a general superintendent are so complex, and of such nature, that until a man was actually invested with the office and began to assume its duties, it was—and still is—impossible to be certain of his fitness for it. Great preachers and pulpit orators do not always make good administrators, nor do executives who are adept at handling administrative details always prove to have the public presence or broad statesmanship of those who should be leaders of a great people. If Methodist episcopacy might be selected as a whole, if the body of bishops were in truth a unitary body functioning always as an organic commission or general board, then upon it the church would do well to put men of varying types and capacities—some great preachers, some great organizers, some ecclesiastical statesmen, some profound scholars, outstanding pastors, and an expert or two in other fields. But the bishops do not function, except at their stated meetings, as an organic body. They act as individual leaders directing the spiritual and temporal affairs of great conferences which are put entirely in their special charge. Therefore they stand as individuals and must be elected as individuals. Sometimes the church has made a palpable mistake which is realized almost immediately. But there is no recourse under Methodism's present and time-honored construction of its constitution. Both bishop and church must suffer the consequences of an electing conference's mistaken judgment until the bishop in question dies or superannuates.

It was to obviate this practical danger that the proposal for term episcopacy was put forward. If bishops should be elected for a term of years, it was urged, those who do not make acceptable bishops would not, as they should not, be re-elected. The mistake of one General Conference would be corrected by another. Proponents of the measure also argued that bishops themselves, knowing that they would be held accountable for their position at every General Conference, would be apt to give the church the very best they had.

But this argument cut two ways. Indeed term episcopacy was eventually defeated, not only by the conservatives and those who objected to change, but by a practical-minded group who felt that it would vastly increase the unrest and excitement in the church if every bishop were compelled to stand for re-election at every quadrennial gathering. "If men do scheme to be elected bishop," so ran this counterargument, "how much more will they be involved if they are to be re-elected at recurring intervals? If there is 'politics' in the election of one new superintendent, how greatly would this be magnified if we are to expect all superintendents to be re-elected at each General Conference!" This reasoning had great weight.

The issue over term episcopacy first came to the fore in the General Conference of the Methodist Episcopal Church in 1888. The measure was after some debate referred to the Judiciary Committee, which was asked to rule upon its constitutionality. The committee did so by affirming that "a lifelong tenure of office is one of the attributes of that episcopacy, originated by our fathers, and which the General Conference 'may not do away or destroy.' "

But to this report a minority of the committee took exception and presented to the General Conference a contrary argument:

We believe that the Third Restrictive Rule carefully guards the office of the episcopacy and its prerogatives, but that it does not touch its tenure.

It is our opinion, therefore, that it is within the power of the General Conference, in its wisdom, to limit the term of office of Bishops to be elected, as it may deem best.[12]

Both these reports were presented and both laid on the table on May 17, 1888. Neither one, for unexplained reasons, was taken up again.

Years after, in 1924, in the Methodist Episcopal Church the fight for term episcopacy was renewed, and the point was made that the 1888 body had never made a decision adverse to its principle. But on this later occasion the measure was defeated after a sharp debate.[13]

In the Methodist Episcopal Church, South, as part of a powerful revolt against its very strong episcopacy, the years preceding church union saw a campaign for term episcopacy almost succeed. In the General Conference of 1930, when a proposed constitution for the Methodist Episcopal Church, South, was being debated point by point, an amendment was offered for insertion, proposing in effect that the General Conference should have the power to limit the term of office for which each bishop might be elected. After a heated debate the amendment was written into the proposed constitution, but when that document had been "perfected," as its opponents sarcastically put it, it overwhelmingly failed of adoption. Many who might have supported the proposed constitution for the other statesmanlike proposals which it incorporated, were against it because it seemed to inaugurate term episcopacy.

The fight was renewed in the Southern church in 1934, when the "termites," as one of their leaders publicly stated they were called, again put forth their proposal. But again the Southern church refused to admit that once a bishop a man might be something else later on. "An ex-bishop, save the mark!" one irate antagonist exclaimed. In the same year the newly elected Judicial Council of the Methodist Episcopal Church, South, came forward with a strong pronouncement upon the real mean-

[12] Arthur Benton Sanford, Reports of the Committee on Judiciary (1924), pp. 257-58.
[13] Journal, 1924, pp. 488-98.

ing and intent of Methodist episcopacy, affirming rather ably the time-honored Southern position.[14] Then the matter rested, waiting for the day which all by that time saw was near at hand—Methodist union.

It is easy to see that had term episcopacy been adopted, a radically different type of supervision would at once have been in effect in the church adopting it. It is true that Methodism emphasizes the office as a special administrative position and not as a churchly order. But she also demands, and from the first has demanded, that men set apart for this office shall be invested as persons with tremendous power and inducted into it through an august ceremony which is an almost exact replica of the Church of England's episcopal ordination and which John Wesley himself was not afraid to call "The Form for the Ordaining of a Superintendent." The vows the bishop-elect takes are exactly those of the time-honored episcopacy of the Church of England, with minor differences. The brethren who have affirmed in recent General Conferences that the substitution in this office of the word "consecrating" for "ordaining" would do much to obviate the implications of a third order, have failed to read the original office which Wesley sent over, or to give full weight to the disciplinary direction that a bishop is to be constituted by the laying on of hands of other bishops, or by Methodist elders. What is this direction for, as John Emory argued long ago, if not to certify that there is to be in the investiture of this man, as he goes into this office, something that is not to be temporary or ephemeral, but for life? To this day The Methodist Church has officially so regarded it.

SUPERANNUATION OF A BISHOP

The superannuation of Methodist bishops has always admittedly been under the complete control of the General Conference. Asbury himself spoke often of asking the conference to allow him the privilege of retiring, though, as it turned out, he never did so ask in such a way as to make it clear he really wished to retire. He died in active service, a feeble old man, still threading endlessly the long trail.

Subsequent bishops were granted superannuation in the due course of time by respective sessions of the General Conference, unless, of course, they died while in active service. A man's health, as well as his age, was always a factor to be considered with a bishop, as with any minister. In time the Committee on Episcopacy at each General Conference, North and South, called the names of the several bishops, heard their reports, and then recommended their individual names and persons to

[14] *Journal*, 1934, pp. 306-12.

the General Conference for continued active service or for superannuation, as the case might be.

Certain bishops have anticipated action by the General Conference and themselves requested superannuation. In practically every case their wish was granted. Some objected to superannuation though they took it well enough when it was voted. But there have been instances where a bishop who was recommended for retirement against his will waxed rather bitter about the whole proceeding, protesting that he was physically active and mentally capable of continuing in the superintendency. In some such cases a bishop whose health or capacity was questioned on account of age, was able to secure friends on the Committee of Episcopacy or before the General Conference, and these friends would publicly urge his continuance in the episcopal office. To vote against them and for the retirement of the bishop, involved personalities and passing public judgment on the bishop's capacity in such a way as to bring on a very embarrassing situation in several instances. To obviate this and to spare the Committee on Episcopacy and the General Conference from such embarrassment, both the Methodist Episcopal Church and Methodist Episcopal Church, South, at length passed legislation automatically retiring bishops at a specified age.

In the case of the Methodist Episcopal Church, bishops in 1912 were granted the right to retire voluntarily at seventy years of age and automatically at the General Conference nearest their seventy-third birthday.[15] But in 1932 the age limits were dropped so that a bishop or a missionary bishop could retire "voluntarily at sixty-seven, and automatically at the General Conference nearest his seventieth birthday." A minority report, ably supported on the floor of the General Conference of 1932, when this measure was pending, attempted to modify it so that it would be possible to prolong the effective life of a bishop after the retirement age, in certain instances where this might be deemed wise. But after much parliamentary jockeying this measure failed.[16]

In the Methodist Episcopal Church, South, the General Conference of 1930 passed a measure automatically retiring bishops at the General Conference nearest their seventy-second birthday. The legislation as then passed also recognized the right of a bishop to be superannuated at his own request.[17]

The passage of the automatic retirement measure was in a sense a con-

[15] Journal, 1912, p. 533.
[16] Journal, 1932, pp. 280-84, 536.
[17] Journal, 1930, pp. 161-63.

fession on the part of the churches involved that their machinery for the appraisal of a bishop's health and effectiveness was not adequate. Everyone admitted that there was a great difference in mental and physical abilities between bishops; that some men were ready for retirement and worn out early, while others could continue long past three-score-and-ten, active and energetic. "The calendar is no proper measure of any man's effectiveness," ran the rather sound argument here. But against this it was urged that Committees on Episcopacy were notoriously lax in facing up to the personal and unpleasant duties which devolved upon them in passing upon a bishop's effectiveness, and that even with the best intent in the world no committee could be sure it was acting wisely. "I'll trust the calendar before I will the committee," one General Conference delegate said, as he voted for the automatic retirement measure. Mistakes are made by either method, but the calendar at least takes away the onus of being responsible for weighty and often mistaken judgments

Bishop Francis J. McConnell, at a banquet honoring him as he was retiring in 1944 from a long and active career as a bishop, expressed himself as in favor of the automatic retirement at a fixed age. He said in substance that in many respects a man's vigor and intellectual powers are not impaired by age, but that in carrying out "important executive work" there is always an unconscious slowing down. A man's "willingness to make hard decisions, to take measures which as a younger man he would not hesitate to take," such abilities and capacities, Bishop McConnell declared, were noticeably weaker in an administrator when he got near the seventy-year line; and since administration is the prime act of a present-day bishop, the move to relieve him of it at or around seventy years of age is wise. So affirmed this bishop who has served the church for many years in almost every capacity in which a Christian minister is called upon to act.

It should be noted here that the constitutionality of the measure to retire bishops was never called in question, not even in the Methodist Episcopal Church, South, where the bishop was always upon something of a pinnacle. At the organization of The Methodist Church, the General Conference, acting under the authority given it by the constitution to "provide a uniform rule for their [Bishops'] superannuation," did this by allowing episcopal retirement under certain specified conditions of age or health, and also inserted a provision allowing retirement "for any reason deemed sufficient by his Jurisdictional Conference." [18] If a bishop's seventieth birthday precedes the first day of a regular session of his Juris-

[18] *Discipline*, 1940, ¶ 336 (2).

dictional Conference, he "shall be released at the close of that Conference from the obligation to travel through the Connection at large, and from residential supervision." [19] This means that the bishop is to be automatically retired at that age.

A retired bishop may, on vote of the Council of Bishops, "be appointed to take charge of an Episcopal Area, or parts of an Area, in case of the death, resignation, or disability of the Resident Bishop or because of judicial procedure." [20] The Council of Bishops, however, cannot so appoint a retired bishop unless a majority of the bishops of the Jurisdiction where the proposed appointment is to be made shall request such an appointment; nor can such a re-employed bishop continue in such position "beyond the next session of his Jurisdictional Conference." A retired bishop, unless so put back into active service, cannot preside over any Annual Conference, provisional Annual Conference or mission, nor at the Jurisdictional or Central Conference sessions, except temporarily when asked so to do by the bishop presiding.[21] He cannot make appointments at all and while he may participate in the meeting of the Council of Bishops the Uniting Conference decided that in doing so he shall have no vote.[22] Otherwise, as the *Discipline* states blandly: "A Bishop who has been released under any of the foregoing provisions [that is, who has been retired] may continue to exercise all the rights and privileges which pertain to the Episcopal office, except as herein otherwise provided." [23] No other rights and privileges of the active episcopal office are left, however, except the title of bishop, and the power to ordain, if and when requested or empowered to do so by a competent authority.

There were three instances in the Methodist Episcopal Church of bishops who resigned from office. In 1882 Bishop L. L. Hamline resigned on account of ill health. A later instance was that of Bishop Fred B. Fisher, who had served for some years as bishop in India. At the General Conference of 1932 the Committee on Episcopacy recommended that the resignation of Bishop Fred B. Fisher from the office of General Superintendent be received and considered to take effect as of May 15, 1930.[24] This was done. At the same conference the committee recommended that Bishop George R. Grose, who had also tendered his resignation from the

[19] *Ibid.*, sec. 1.

[20] *Ibid.*, sec. 4.

[21] *Discipline*, 1944, ¶ 437.

[22] *Discipline*, 1939, ¶ 405 (1). For the Judicial Council's decision on this matter see page 79.

[23] *Ibid.*, sec. 2.

[24] *Journal*, 1932, p. 541.

office of general superintendent, be allowed to resign and that his resignation take effect as of May 18, 1932.[25] This also was adopted.

The Methodist Church allows a bishop to resign from the episcopal office on his own volition "at any session of his Jurisdictional Conference." A bishop so resigning shall surrender to the secretary of the Jurisdictional Conference his consecration papers and in turn shall be furnished with a certificate of resignation. This will entitle him to "membership as a traveling elder in the Annual Conference of which he was last a member or its successor." [26]

As no bishop may hold membership in an Annual Conference unless he resign from the episcopal office as above stated—in which case he is no longer a bishop—retired bishops sustain no relation to one conference which they do not sustain to all. They are a charge upon, and the revered fathers of, that whole church which they have so faithfully served.

A Bishop's Conference Membership

The bishops in Episcopal Methodism were always members of the General Conference and up to the time of union their names were called as part of the conference roll. Their characters were "examined and passed," just as are the characters of the ministers at the Annual Conference, though in the later years this was done almost entirely by the Committee on Episcopacy. In early days bishops participated actively in the affairs of the General Conference. Bishops Asbury and Coke made motions frequently, and evidently debated the same.[27] "On motion from the Chair" is the way one of Asbury's plans is introduced.[28] But as the years went by the bishop became more of a General Conference president than a General Conference member. In 1840 Bishop Soule did offer a series of resolutions which were adopted by a three-to-one vote (97 to 27) [29] but after that date no episcopal member ever seems to have taken the floor. "Later usage, based on a generally accepted view of Episcopal propriety or of ecclesiastical constitution—perhaps both," are the reasons given for this by Bishop Collins Denny. "The Bishops do not formally introduce motions or cast votes; neither do they claim that right. The influence exerted by them, in the chief Synod of the Church, is less positive and direct." [30]

[25] Ibid., p. 542.
[26] Discipline, 1944, ¶ 435 (2).
[27] Journals, I, 73-74, 78-79, 81.
[28] Ibid., p. 79.
[29] Journal, 1840, p. 109.
[30] A Manual of the Discipline (1931), p. 84.

Bishops in The Methodist Church are not listed or referred to as members of the General Conference. They are, however, constitutionally its presiding officers. At the General Conference of 1940, upon motion of James E. Skillington, the conference, in adopting its rules of order, ordered that "the Secretary of the Council of Bishops shall report the number of Bishops who are present, providing the Secretary, for record, a list of their names." [31] The secretary of this The First General Conference of The Methodist Church did indeed call the names of the bishops who had died since the previous (Uniting) conference; and the General Conference later held appropriate exercises in connection with the expected superannuation of certain bishops. But the roll call of the bishops present was furnished to the secretary of the conference by the secretary of the Council of Bishops, and as bishops are amenable to their Jurisdictional Conferences, it is presumed that such membership as they had in the General Conference of the former Methodist Episcopal and Methodist Episcopal Church, South, has been transferred to their respective Jurisdictional Conferences. They therefore are not members of the General Conference in The Methodist Church. The Jurisdictional Conferences of 1944, and not the General Conference of that year, provided the exercises which were had in connection with the superannuation of the bishops then retiring in the respective jurisdictions.

BISHOPS AS ANNUAL CONFERENCE MEMBERS

Whether or not a bishop could be considered as a member of an Annual Conference after he had been elected and consecrated bishop was heatedly discussed in two General Conferences of the former Methodist Episcopal Church. In 1904 Bishop C. C. McCabe, who was much more of a church builder than a parliamentarian, gave the deciding vote in order to break a tie in the Central Illinois Conference, with reference to the admission of a minister who had been expelled. The Judiciary Committee of the ensuing General Conference, to whom this action was subsequently appealed, said flatly: "The Bishop erred in voting in the case, as the Bishops are not members of the Annual Conference, and have no right to vote therein in any circumstances." [32]

The General Conference agreed with the committee. But later, in 1912, when the Committee on Judiciary was asked about the conference membership of Bishop Willam F. Oldham, it held that this bishop, any bishop, did not lose his Annual Conference membership by his

[31] *Journal*, 1940, p. 189.
[32] *Journal*, 1904, pp. 304, 513-14.

election and assumption of the office of bishop. Its decision, however, the committee qualified by asserting that "during his incumbency of his office of Bishop he can exercise only such rights as are compatible with said office." [33]

The report of the Committee on Judiciary was adopted although there was a powerful dissenting opinion, and the view that the bishop was in "suspended relationship with his Annual Conference" was adopted (in 1912) as the judgment of the Methodist Episcopal Church

To clarify this ruling a definite set of questions were referred to the Committee on Judiciary in 1920. The crux of the question lay in the 1912 pronouncement concerning what actions were or were not "compatible" with the episcopal office.

The committee of 1920, the General Conference concurring, issued a rather sweeping report outlining how and in what manner a bishop might keep his Annual Conference membership. He could be counted in making up the list of clerical members for General Conference representation, but could not vote in case of a tie, or on a constitutional question, or for General Conference delegates. [34]

But since the organization of The Methodist Church, Bishop Charles W. Flint, presiding over the Central New York Conference, made a ruling which was destined, after approval by the Judicial Council, to set at rest the whole matter. Bishop Flint, whose own name, together with that of Bishop Frederick T. Keeney, was carried on the roll of Central New York Conference, ruled that "a Bishop effective or retired is not a member of an Annual Conference," and should not be counted in reporting the total membership of the conference for statistical purposes: "No provision should be made by the Annual Conference for him as a Conference claimant; the provision has been made by the General Conference." Bishop Flint's ruling further held that a bishop was not eligible to election as a delegate representing the Annual Conference in the General or Jurisdictional Conferences, and that he was not entitled to vote in electing delegates; that when a man is elected bishop, if he is a member of the electing conference, his membership immediately ceases and his place is to be filled by the proper alternate; that if a bishop shall resign his office "he is returned by definitely prescribed procedure to membership of the Annual Conference, of which he ceased to be a member when elected Bishop."

This ruling was affirmed and adopted as its own by the Judicial Coun-

[33] Journal, 1912, p. 587.
[34] Journal, 1920, pp. 429, 506.

cil of the church, and so sets at rest this long-debated question. Bishops may and do have their names continued upon their former conference roll for sentimental reasons, but they are not, even by courtesy, members of the body.[35]

As it has been decided that bishops cannot be members of an Annual Conference, and as the constitution does not mention bishops as belonging to either the General or the Jurisdictional Conference, the question has been asked: Where then may the bishops' church membership be found? Methodist common law in Episcopal Methodism seems to have held the bishops as members of the General Conference up to the time of union, though they were not allowed to vote or sit with the delegations or take part in debate. The Plan of Union does not make bishops amenable now to their Jurisdictional Conferences, but the General Conference, by statutory enactment, has done so;[36] and has also provided that the bishops assigned to a jurisdiction shall be counted "in all elections in a Jurisdictional Conference which are based on the number of church members within that jurisdiction." [37] It may therefore be argued that since the bishops are amenable to their respective Jurisdictional Conferences, and are to be counted as church members within their respective jurisdictions, their conference and church membership is therefore in their respective Jurisdictional Conferences; and that while the legislation so determining their amenability and membership was not constitutional but statutory, it was passed by a General Conference which has the constitutional right "to define and fix the powers, duties, and privileges of the episcopacy." [38]

AREAS AND RESIDENCES

In the Methodist Episcopal Church, where the bishop was admittedly "subject to the General Conference" in all things, the question continued to come up during the latter half of the nineteenth century regarding the assignment of the bishops to definite conferences and localities. In 1864 the Committee on Episcopacy affirmed: "The Bishops ought and therefore are respectfully requested so to distribute their residences as to be the most accessible to, and in the intervals of the Conference to be able to oversee every part of our extended work as far as possible." [39] In 1868 the General Conference went a bit further and named the cities which it

---

[35] Daily Christian Advocate, May 3, 1944.
[36] Discipline, 1944, ¶ 531.
[37] Ibid., ¶ 534.
[38] Constitution, Div. Two, Sec. I, Art. IV, 5.
[39] Journal, 1864, Committee on Episcopacy, Report 4.

thought the bishops should occupy, but asked the bishops to choose such places in order of their seniority. In 1876 this action was in substance repealed. There was debate but no special action on the matter for some years. Challenged as to its rights to assign bishops, however, in 1884, the General Conference adopted the report of its Judiciary Committee touching the right of the conference to fix episcopal residences, and flatly affirmed: "The General Conference has power to fix the residence of any of its Bishops in any part of the territory occupied by the Methodist Episcopal Church." [40]

But the General Conference appeared loath to avail itself of the privilege which it had declared itself to have, and moved haltingly for some years. The matter, however, would not down, and in 1896 the General Conference decided that the episcopal residences should be designated quadrennially, and that bishops must reside in the cities to which they were assigned.[41]

In 1900, after the Committee on Episcopacy had reported that "the time has come when the General Conference should directly decide where each individual should reside," the General Conference authorized that committee to plan the assignments, subject to General Conference approval.

In 1904 the General Conference went a bit further and fixed the residential cities but left the assignments—that is, manning these residences—to the bishops. In 1908 the General Conference "requested" the bishops to form "groups of Annual Conferences" around their respective residences.[42] In 1912 Report Number One of the Committee on Episcopacy was entitled "Contiguous and Continued Episcopal Supervision." The bishops were to arrange at least four "divisions," and to assign groups of conferences about each episcopal residence to the resident bishop.[43] In 1916 the Committee on Episcopacy assigned the bishops to their residences,[44] and the conferences were grouped by the bishops about their contiguous "residences." There was no mention of "divisions." In 1920 the term "episcopal area" was first applied to such groups of conferences. These area groupings, arranged by the bishops, were formally approved by the General Conference.[45]

Thus came about, step by step, the "area system" and "presidential

[40] Journal, 1844, pp. 160, 369.
[41] Journal, 1896, Committee on Episcopacy, Report 3.
[42] Journal, 1908, p. 436.
[43] Journal, 1912, pp. 428-29, 530.
[44] Journal, 1916, pp. 416, 482.
[45] Journal, 1920, pp. 461-64.

and residential" superintendency in the Methodist Episcopal Church, the latter term or expression being somewhat puzzling to the brethren of the Methodist Episcopal Church, South, when union came about, although in the South episcopal areas, consisting of groups of conferences, had likewise become a feature of the polity of that communion in the years previous to union. But in the South the bishops had complete power to fix areas and establish their own residences in or outside of these areas as they chose. The Committee on Episcopacy of the General Conference of the Methodist Episcopal Church, South, during the later years of that Church, did make suggestions to the bishops as to how the church might best be served by episcopal assignment and strongly urged the bishops to reside in the areas they were to superintend. But to petition and advise was as far as the committee or General Conference itself dared, or could, go. It was understood that the actual division of the church into areas—that is, Annual Conferences grouped as such—was something which would be worked out by the general superintendents themselves. This, of course, was true in the North also, and is true now within the jurisdictions, as far as grouping of conferences is concerned.

The plan of episcopal visitation, for which the constitution makes the bishops of The Methodist Church responsible, is in essence what Annual Conferences the bishops shall preside over, not what residences they shall individually occupy. The bishops always, everywhere, and to this day, have had the right to make their own plan of episcopal supervision with relation to the Annual Conferences which they are to oversee. That was and is now a constitutional right of episcopacy. What the Methodist Episcopal Church did, and what The Methodist Church now does through the Jurisdictional Conferences, is to fix the residences of the bishops. To assign the bishops to residences and the residential sites which the church provides for them was within the power of the General Conference, and is now within the power of the Jurisdictional Conferences. To assign bishops to definite Annual Conferences or Annual Conferences to bishops is not. That prerogative belongs to the bishops themselves. The way The Methodist Church at union came to adopt the present plan will be narrated in the section dealing with the present episcopacy.

THE METHODIST PROTESTANT SUPERINTENDENCY

The Methodist Protestant Church had no episcopacy and no presiding elders. Each of the conferences of that church elected a president at each session. He served both as moderator during the session, and usually as reader of the appointments after these had been duly made. The General Conference of the church elected a president and other officers for its essential work at the quadrennial meetings. Nor were these officials ministers in every case. A distinguished layman Dr. J. W. Hering, of Westminster, Maryland, was twice chosen—in 1892 and 1896—to be the president of the General Conference. But such presidents, while enjoying the highest honor their church could offer, had, until recent years, scarcely more power than does the moderator at any great church gathering. But in 1920 the Methodist Protestant Church, yielding to a demand for more and wider supervision, made the president a full-time officer. The first person to occupy this position was Dr. Thomas Hamilton Lewis.

This action was revolutionary, but, when done, met with almost universal approval. Broadly speaking, the president after 1920 was charged with the duties of Annual Conference visitation, and was a member of each of these conferences with all privileges save suffrage. He was chief connectional officer, chairman of the powerful Executive Committee, and a member of all the boards elected by the General Conference.

This was the acceptance of a church-wide superintendency. It differed from Methodist episcopacy in that the president had no essential relation to the Stationing Committees which made the actual appointments in each of the Annual Conferences.

Methodist Protestants, however, always maintained that their objection to Episcopal Methodism was not because of the bishops, but because of its lack of lay rights and its undemocratic appointment system. To episcopacy as such they had no great antipathy provided their other objections were met. Thus, when union came about, the Methodist Protestant Church did not find it difficult to accept episcopacy, since in the meanwhile both of the other churches had accepted lay representation.

It is important to observe that in every Methodist Protestant conference the "Stationing Committee" was created by the conference itself. Laymen usually served on the committee. Sometimes there were three laymen, three ministers, and the conference president, though each conference had its own method of creating the committee. Sometimes the president alone, as in Maryland, was entrusted with the power of making appointments. The slate of pastoral appointments was made in due time and given a preliminary reading before the conference in order that any minister might have an opportunity to appeal for a change if anyone deemed an appeal to be necessary. The final or last reading came after this opportunity for appeal had been duly given.

Surprisingly enough to episcopally trained Methodists, there is no record of any great number of appeals. "Although our President has always made the plan of appointments quite after the fashion of a bishop," observed Dr. Thomas H. Lewis, "and his plan is never voted on, yet I have never heard of but one church rejecting its pastor in the whole history of the Conference." [46]

Bishop James H. Straughn comments: "The 'Appeal' occasionally was ·resorted to by ministers but usually by some disaffected person whose appeal was not allowed by the Committee on Appeals. This regulation, however, was always considered a salutary provision and it was never changed from 1830."

This lack of appeals may have been due to the fact that as Methodist Protestant conferences were usually small, the pattern of appointments could be worked out fairly well in the minds of the conference members even before conference met—a "kitchen cabinet" procedure in which Methodist ministers of all groups are expert. Furthermore it was recognized among the Methodist Protestants, as among all Methodists, that a connectional church must have its appointments made as a whole, not as isolated instances. To allow one brother to change his appointment would force out another man who was perhaps greatly satisfied, force out perhaps two or three, thus entailing unrest and complaint for a long while. So objections, unless very well founded, were not likely to succeed. In spite of their theory of strong individual rights, the Methodist Protestants, as all other Methodists, realized that the whole was greater than the parts, the church greater than the charges.

[46] John M. Moore, *The Long Road to Methodist Union* (1943), p. 109.

IV

THE PRESENT EPISCOPACY

There shall be an episcopacy in The Methodist Church of like plan, powers, privileges, and duties as now exist in The Methodist Episcopal Church and The Methodist Episcopal Church, South.

—Constitution, Div. III, Art. I

THE DECLARATION OF THE PLAN OF UNION CITED ABOVE ASSUMES THAT the two episcopacies mentioned were identical. The language so implies and the entire church by adopting the Plan of Union with no questions on this point seems to have ratified this conclusion. No attempt can therefore be made to go behind this constitutional affirmation, now the fundamental law of the church. Should there be some subsequent question as to whether any special feature of either one of the merging episcopacies inheres in the present episcopacy, the Judicial Council of the church, and that alone, will have the right and duty to declare what these features are and may mean.

The Methodist Episcopal Church, South, by taking from her bishops in 1934, just previous to union, their power to interpret church law as a court of final resort, and also their power to check, on constitutional matters, any General Conference action during the sessions of that body, removed one distinct feature which for many years differentiated between the two episcopacies. Likewise the "missionary bishops" of the former Methodist Episcopal Church, and the constitutional power of that church to elect bishops who should be bishops only in special areas, was ignored in the Plan of Union, and therefore done away by the new constitution. This was decided by the Judicial Council at the 1944 General Conference.[1] It is therefore not out of place to hold that the Methodist episcopacy, which was recognized and established by the Plan of Union, is all of a piece—a perpetuation and continuation of the historic episcopacy of the past with such common modifications as time had wrought in both branches of Episcopal Methodism.

The Methodist Protestant Church, as has been said, through its accredited representatives and commissions, made it clear rather early in the

[1] *Journal*, 1944, p. 928.

negotiations looking toward union that there would be no objection on the part of that communion to an episcopal form of government. The principle of lay representation having been introduced in both episcopal Methodisms through the years, and, of course, firmly perpetuated and strengthened in the Plan of Union, the Methodist Protestants felt, and with justice, that their contention had been recognized as valid and that they had no occasion to quarrel over a matter of names. It was therefore early seen that Methodist union would come about under an episcopal organization, though with a greatly modified episcopacy, whose modifications would be plainly written into the new constitution. So the event proved.

Under the Plan of Union it was agreed that the delegates representing the Methodist Protestant Church in the Uniting Conference should "have the authority and power to elect to the office of bishop two ministers of their church who, upon ordination or consecration at the Uniting Conference by the bishops of the other two churches, shall become effective bishops of The Methodist Church." [2] Under this warrant or mandate, James H. Straughn and John Calvin Broomfield were elected by the Methodist Protestant delegates and duly consecrated as bishops. Each of these two eminent Methodist Protestant leaders had served as the president of the General Conference of his church. The occasion when they were ordained and consecrated bishops of The Methodist Church proved to be one of the high moments of the Uniting Conference.

The episcopacy, as has been intimated somewhat in the previous pages, has never in Methodist thought been considered a "third order," as is the episcopacy of the Protestant Episcopal Church, the Church of England, or the Roman Catholic Church. It is rather the investiture of an "elder" —who belongs to the highest ministerial order in Methodism—with certain definite executive functions and powers. These powers belong to and constitute the peculiar superintendency of The Methodist Church, today as in the past.

In reinforcing this position within late years there have been actions by successive General Conferences instructing the editors of the *Discipline* and *Ritual* to see that the word "consecrating" and not "ordaining" shall be put at the head of the office whereby a bishop is set apart for his distinctive office. The word "ordain" was felt by many to imply the investiture of a new "order." "This Service is a Consecration, not an Ordination, of an Elder or Presbyter to the duties of General Superintendency in the Church"—so in the Ritual ran the rubric before the office in

[2] Constitution. Div. III, Art. VI.

question. But the great power of the bishop in Methodist polity, coming not from his ecclesiastical rank but from his right to station the preachers, has always made for an anomalous situation in evaluating the exact position of this office. "What avails it to split hairs in affirming that the bishop is only an 'elder equal to his brethren,' but at the same time to give him power over all his brethren?" one Methodist Protestant writer once pointedly asked. Certainly the Methodist bishop has always enjoyed more actual executive power than any bishop in the Anglican or Episcopal Church, although the latter claims the churchly rank of a third order, while the Methodist bishop does not. I once heard an old Methodist minister casually but aptly refer to "this curious kind of episcopacy which we have got."

JURISDICTIONAL EPISCOPACY

When the new constitution was adopted for The Methodist Church, individual episcopacy as a general superintendency for the whole church was finally and officially ended. This came about by the provision of the Plan of Union that bishops were thenceforth to be elected by the Jurisdictional Conferences and by these alone, and that the supervisory powers of any bishop (with carefully prescribed exceptions) were thenceforth to be confined to the particular jurisdiction which elected him or to which the Plan of Union assigned him.[3]

Before the adoption of the Plan of Union a bishop anywhere was a bishop everywhere. So he is now in title, honor, and power to ordain. But formerly he was a general officer of a connectional church, and while the bishops in practice assigned themselves to specific areas and conferences, they still preserved, in theory at least, the idea that each was a "general" superintendent. A bishop in Omaha was a bishop in New York; a bishop in Atlanta might order a change in appointments in Louisville—at least theoretically. But the Plan of Union did away with all that by the jurisdictional division of the church. This took the election of bishops out of the hands of the General Conference and placed such elections in the Jurisdictional Conferences and these alone, and so arranged it that bishops today are to serve each within his own jurisdictional area and in that only. Within these jurisdictional areas, however, the bishops elected for, or assigned to, any respective episcopal area possess all residential and presidential powers. They make their own plan of visitation of intrajurisdictional episcopal "areas" just as did the Board

[3] *Ibid.*, Arts. II, IV, V.

70

of Bishops of the former Methodist Episcopal Church, and after the same pattern.

At the Uniting Conference there was discussion and considerable debate upon the power of the General Conference or Jurisdictional Conferences to "assign" the bishops to their respective appointments. Under the Plan of Union the Uniting Conference was directed to assign the effective bishops "for service to the various Jurisdictional Conferences." [4] At the Uniting Conference there was much parliamentary maneuvering as to whether these assignments were to be made by a special committee or by the regular Committee on Ministry and Judicial Administration. To the latter committee the task was finally entrusted. The committee, following the pattern of the Methodist Episcopal Church, which assigned bishops to residences, brought forward a schedule outlining the jurisdictional affiliation of each active bishop, and naming within each jurisdiction certain residence cities, as well as nominating bishops who were to be assigned to each one of these.[5] When the question arose as to the right of the Uniting Conference or of any conference to assign the bishops to residences, the whole matter was referred to the Committee on Judiciary of the Uniting Conference. That committee brought in a report holding that the Uniting Conference not only had a right but the constitutional duty of assigning the bishops to the respective jurisdictions, and that it also would have the right to assign bishops "to definite areas and residences if such a law or regulation is contained in any one of the Disciplines of the Churches united." [6]

The committee went on to state that it could find no such provision in the Discipline of the Methodist Episcopal Church, South, nor in the body of the Discipline of the Methodist Episcopal Church, but that there was a provision in the appendix of the Discipline of the Methodist Episcopal Church which "by constant usage and judicial decision at least has had all power of law." The Committee on Judiciary doubted whether this provision, occurring in such an appendix, could be used as the basis of firm legislation, and regarded as unwise the "pressing of the question of power" to a decision at the Uniting Conference. The committee, however, did recommend that a schedule of episcopal assignments to jurisdictions and residences be made by the Uniting Conference, and that the bishops be "requested to accept such assignments subject only to such

[4] Ibid., Art. VI.
[5] Journal, 1939, p. 235.
[6] Ibid., p. 819.

adjustments and modifications as to the Council of Bishops may seem wise." [7]

The bishops at the Uniting Conference accepted this report—that is, the schedule of residential assignments—and so did the church. This move was certainly final in its assignment of bishops to jurisdictions. Also, since that time subsequent Jurisdictional Conferences have followed the plan of residential assignment of individual bishops which was then made, and no question has been raised as to constitutionality. It was the Judiciary Committee of the Uniting Conference, and not the Judicial Council, it should be noted, which passed upon this matter for the Uniting Conference in 1939.

By acceding to the custom of assigning bishops to residences, which by 1939 had the force of law in the Methodist Episcopal Church, both the bishops and the united church have strengthened that law greatly since the time of union. In practice, the jurisdictions, through their respective Committees on Episcopacy, fix residence cities and assign bishops by name to such residences. The bishops themselves, under their constitutional mandate to "arrange the plan of episcopal supervision," group together the conferences which are to be superintended by each one of them. There is thus a technical difference between an episcopal area and an episcopal residence. The Jurisdictional Conference, as is said elsewhere, apparently has the right to fix a residence and name the bishop who is to reside in it, but it has no right to tell that bishop what conferences he shall supervise. Of course, the Annual Conferences almost inevitably go with the residences, but this is not necessarily the case, nor has the question whether the Jurisdictional Conference has the power to assign a bishop to a definite residence ever been directly appealed to the Judicial Council. The "question of power has not been pressed," to quote the Uniting Conference *Journal* again. Perhaps it will never be, as all recognize that the utmost co-operation is required between the General Conference, the Jurisdictional Conferences, and the bishops, if there shall be the most effective manning of the work.

To date the Committees on Episcopacy of the respective jurisdictions have continued the residence cities fixed by the Uniting Conference. When episcopal assignments are being made at the Jurisdictional Conference, a subcommittee from the jurisdictional Committee on Episcopacy usually meets with a committee representing the bishops and agrees upon a plan which takes care of the entire matter of residence, area, and

[7] *Ibid.*

episcopal personnel. When this is agreed upon the Committee on Episcopacy reports the entire slate of episcopal assignments to the Jurisdictional Conference which adopts it as its own.[8]

There are two or three exceptions to the rule that a bishop may not serve as a presiding bishop outside his own jurisdiction. If a Jurisdictional Conference shall request that a certain bishop shall be transferred to its jurisdiction, the Council of Bishops may make such a transfer; or if a request is made by a majority of the bishops of a certain jurisdiction that a bishop from another jurisdiction shall be assigned to theirs for presidential purposes, the Council of Bishops may make such a transfer, provided that it shall not be for more than a year. And in an emergency in any jurisdiction, through death or disability of any of its bishops, the Council of Bishops, without waiting for a request from the bishops of the receiving jurisdiction, but dependent upon the consent of a majority of these bishops, may assign one or more bishops from other jurisdictions "to the work of the said jurisdiction." [9]

In the case of Central Conferences, bishops of these areas arrange their plan of visitation as does the College of Bishops in the jurisdictions of the United States. The Council of Bishops, representing the whole church, may assign one of their number to visit such Central Conferences as an envoy of the church, and when requested by the majority of the bishops of the Central Conferences, such an episcopal visitant "may exercise therein the functions of the episcopacy." [10]

A study of the above paragraphs will make it clear that the jurisdictional division of the episcopacy is well-nigh complete as far as any possible action of the Council of Bishops is concerned. The jurisdictions themselves have the right to "elect over," or take over, bishops from other jurisdictions, the Council of Bishops agreeing; and the Council of Bishops can for one year or during an immediate emergency, put bishops across jurisdictional lines with the consent, or at the request, of the receiving jurisdiction. But any permanent departure from the plan of the jurisdictionally divided episcopacy in The Methodist Church is beyond the reach either of the Council of Bishops or the General Conference. The present Methodist episcopacy is jurisdictionally determined. Even the superannuation of a bishop is to be granted and arranged for by his Jurisdictional Conference, though this last is a statutory power vested in the Jurisdictional Conference, not a constitutional one.[11]

[8] *Discipline*, 1944, ¶ 532.
[9] Constitution, Div. III, Art. V.
[10] *Ibid.*, Div. II, Sec. VI, 5.
[11] *Discipline*, 1940, ¶ 336.

THE COUNCIL OF BISHOPS

Offsetting to a degree, however, this division of the episcopacy is the establishment by the constitution of the Council of Bishops as a distinct collective entity. The constitutional provision in question reads:

There shall be a Council of Bishops composed of all the bishops of all the Jurisdictional and Central Conferences. The council shall meet at least once a year and plan for the general oversight and promotion of the temporal and spiritual interests of the entire church.[12]

This recognition and establishment of the Council of Bishops as an integral whole thus gives official status to a true general superintendency which now inheres, not in any one bishop but in the bishops organized as a council. There are no longer any individual "general" superintendents because of the jurisdictional plan, but there is now a general superintendency perpetuated, or it may be, established, by the constitution quoted above.

To a certain extent this collective power of the bishops is, or can be, more powerful than was the joint action of either of the former groups of bishops in either one of the former Methodist Episcopal churches. In these churches the bishops met with each other as individuals to plan their work, and while they formed an organization of their own, their joint action was scarcely more than the sum of their individual might. Neither "College" nor "Board," as the Southern and Northern churches termed their bishops, had constitutional standing, though the individual bishops did. Now, however, in the Plan of Union, the Council of Bishops is recognized constitutionally, and to it is frankly mandated episcopal oversight over the whole church. It must, and does, exercise over the whole connection its joint and complete superintendency. The individual bishop may be jurisdictionalized but the constitutionally established Council of Bishops is not. It "shall meet" and must "plan" for the temporal and spiritual interests of the entire church. It can, in fact, under certain conditions to which it may agree within itself, put its own members into other jurisdictions than the ones which elected them, though only for an annual or emergency visit.

The incorporation within the Plan of Union of these several measures was not done without a full realization of their import. The regionalizing of the episcopacy was in effect part and parcel of the jurisdictional plan, by which alone it was felt that union could be constituted. This plan, in its larger implications, will be discussed in another section, but the dis-

[12] Constitution, Div. III, Art. III.

cussions regarding episcopacy, as the Plan of Union was drawn up, explored every possibility inhering in the whole idea.

In the Commission on Union of 1918 and also in the final discussions of the Joint Commission on Union previous to 1939, there was a determined effort to arrange it so that while bishops might be elected by the Jurisdictional Conferences, they should be confirmed, or at least consecrated, by a subsequent General Conference. But for reasons which will afterward be pointed out, this measure failed of adoption and the present regulations were written into the constitution of The Methodist Church. These regulations call for an election by a Jurisdictional or Central Conference, and ordination and consecration "in the historic manner of episcopal Methodism." The time and place of such ordination or consecration is, however, to be fixed by the General Conference, not the electing one. As it now stands, the General Conference, by statutory enactment, has fixed the time for such ordinations "at the session of the Jurisdictional or Central Conference at which the election or elections take place." [13] The jurisdictions have the right to decide details concerning their method of electing bishops, but the General Conference of 1940 recommended to the jurisdictions that they require a three-fifths majority of votes cast in order to declare a person elected bishop. All the jurisdictions since that date seem to have followed this recommendation.

That the Jurisdictional and Central Conferences alone have the power to elect bishops was made clear by the Judicial Council of the church at the General Conference of 1944. On the motion of Dr. L. O. Hartman, later bishop, who stated that he wished to test the constitutionality of a proposal to elect missionary bishops, there was presented to the General Conference a resolution: "Resolved, That in order to provide adequate supervision for Central Conferences as they so arise, the General Conference shall elect one or more Missionary Bishops for administration in such areas."

The term "missionary bishop," as used in this resolution, was itself a technical one, carrying in the minds of those who had been in the former Methodist Episcopal Church the idea of a bishop who was to be confined in his superintendency to the special area for which he was elected. To those who had been connected with the former Methodist Episcopal Church, South, the term "missionary bishop" meant a bishop who should be a missionary—that is, a traveler to mission lands but nevertheless a bishop with full power of superintending the church at home and

[13] Ibid., ¶ 423.

abroad. The question as to whether in The Methodist Church there were to be missionary bishops in the technical sense in which the former Methodist Episcopal Church had this office was involved in this motion, as well as the right of the General Conference to elect the bishops. Dr. Hartman stated that he wished the conference to pass his resolution in order that the whole issue might be appealed at once to the Judicial Council for determination. In an atmosphere of some uncertainty the Hartman resolution passed and an appeal was immediately taken to the Judicial Council.

The Judicial Council, after taking the matter under close advisement, and after hearing arguments presented by able representatives, announced its unanimous decision:

There is no provision for the election of a Bishop by the General Conference. Since the General Conference cannot go beyond the clear powers granted it in the Constitution, we must declare that it would be unconstitutional for the General Conference to elect Missionary Bishops.[14]

This decision set that particular matter at rest but left in the air the whole problem of providing episcopal supervision for mission fields outside the territory of a Jurisdictional Conference. To meet this situation the General Conference adopted the following provision which was added to the legislation treating of the number of bishops alloted to each jurisdiction:

Provided that the General Conference may authorize any Jurisdictional Conference to elect one or more bishops beyond the quota herein specified in order to provide episcopal supervision for mission fields outside the territory of a Jurisdictional Conference.[15]

Pursuant to this enactment the General Conference empowered various jurisdictions to provide "Presidential, Visitational and Residential Episcopal Supervision of territory embraced in Provisional Central Conferences," and also to take care of "emergency situations in Central Conferences." [16] A distinction was made between the visitational and the residential supervision in the general plan covering the various mission fields and areas. Three of the jurisdictions, the Southeastern, the Central, and the Northeastern, were empowered to provide residential episcopal supervision for Southern Europe, for Liberia, and for Central and South-

[14] *Journal*, 1944, p. 291.
[15] *Discipline*, 1944, ¶ 439.
[16] *Journal*, 1944, p. 770.

ern Africa respectively. Other jurisdictions were empowered to provide "Supervision" but this empowerment did not carry with it the duty of electing any new bishops.

Subsequently, at later dates, these recommendations of the General Conference were carried out, but in a somewhat different manner. The Northeastern Jurisdiction elected for the African Provisional Conference a bishop by a specially ordered separate ballot.[17] The unprecedented step of having nominations from the floor for such episcopal election was put into effect by the Northeastern Jurisdictional Conference. The Central Jurisdiction also elected by a separate ballot a bishop for Liberia. The Southeastern Jurisdiction, in order to provide needed residential episcopal supervision for the area put under its charge, elected by regular ballot one more bishop than would normally have been allotted to its jurisdiction. All these bishops thus elected are bishops of The Methodist Church, though the Northeastern Jurisdiction, and to an extent the Central, made a definite attempt to secure a bishop for the superintendency in Africa who would be thoroughly familiar with and perhaps committed to that particular field.

[17] Journal, Second Northeastern Jurisdictional Conference, p. 53.

V

DUTIES AND RESPONSIBILITIES

*Episcopacy did not make the bishop; the bishop made epis-
copacy. . . . The only men who can seriously damage the episcopacy are the bishops themselves.*

—Bishop Edwin D. Mouzon

THE EPISCOPACY ESTABLISHED OR PERPETUATED WITHIN THE METHODIST
Church by the Plan of Union gives definite written constitutional power
to the bishops to "arrange the plan of episcopal supervision" within the
respective jurisdictions,[1] and to have "residential and presidential supervision in the Jurisdictional Conferences in which they are elected." [2] The
bishops are also given the right to decide questions of law when they are
presiding in a District, Annual, or Jurisdictional Conference.[3] The episcopacy is presumably shielded from the General Conference by the old
third (now the second) Restrictive Rule, which affirms in time-honored
phraseology: "The General Conference shall not change or alter any
part or rule of our government so as to do away episcopacy, or destroy the
plan of our itinerant general superintendency." However, the same
constitution which thus restricts the General Conference with this provision, gives to the General Conference, in a previous paragraph, the
right "to define and fix the powers, duties, and privileges of the episcopacy, to adopt a plan for the support of the bishops, to provide a uniform
rule for their superannuation, and to provide for the discontinuance of a
bishop because of inefficiency or unacceptability." [4]

That this was a sweeping grant of power to the General Conference
was made clear by an issue which arose since union. This had to do with
the right of the General Conference to legislate concerning the voting
of retired bishops in the Council of Bishops. It was provided by the
Uniting Conference that retired bishops should "participate in the
Council of Bishops, but without vote." [5] This was the law respecting retired bishops in the Methodist Episcopal Church at the time of union.

[1] Constitution, Div. III, Art. IV.
[2] *Ibid.*, Art. V.
[3] *Ibid.*, Art. VII.
[4] *Ibid.*, Div. II, Sec. I, Art. IV, 5.
[5] *Journal*, 1940, p. 490.

But this regulation, passed by the Uniting Conference and continued by succeeding General Conferences,[6] was held to infringe the historic right of episcopacy, and more especially that section of the constitution which provides for the Council of Bishops and gives it general supervisory powers. The bishops appealed to the Judicial Council for a ruling on this matter.

The Judicial Council held that

the Constitution has given the General Conference the power "To define and fix the powers, duties, and privileges of the episcopacy." In the exercise of that power it has provided that a retired Bishop may participate in the Council of Bishops, "but without vote." . . . As against the implication of the right to vote implied by membership in the Council of Bishops, is the clear and definite restriction imposed by the General Conference in Paragraph 437.

There is no such conflict of authority in these two portions of the Constitution sufficient to justify our holding the action of the General Conference unconstitutional.[7]

The matter hinged on whether the Council of Bishops, which is a constitutional entity, could have its membership delimited as to voting power by act of the General Conference, which is another constitutional entity. Also, whether the old Restrictive Rule regarding episcopacy had not again been contravened.

Three members of the Judicial Council, M. A. Childers, J. S. French, and W. G. Henry, while they concurred in this decision, stated that they did so because "if an act of a legislative body is not clearly unconstitutional, the judicial body reviewing same should sustain its constitutionality. On the basis of that universal rule of construction, we concur in the decision set forth above." These three members, however, stated significantly: "We believe there is a conflict between these two provisions of the Constitution and that the provision of the *Discipline* denying retired Bishops the right to vote in the Council of Bishops is of doubtful constitutionality." [8]

Subsequently, at the request of Bishop John M. Moore, supported by briefs from Bishop Edwin H. Hughes and Bishop A. Frank Smith, the Judicial Council agreed to hear arguments for a review and rehearing of this case. Bishop John M. Moore appeared before the council in person at its session April 22, 1947, and the Judicial Council officially reports:

[6] *Discipline*, 1944, ¶ 437.
[7] *Judicial Decisions* (beginning April 26, 1940), pp. 99-100.
[8] *Ibid.*, pp. 100-101.

He presented an able and carefully prepared brief, was fully heard, and given every opportunity to present his arguments. After full consideration of the petition and arguments, all members being present and voting, it was voted to reaffirm without change the opinion and decision previously adopted.[9]

Thus the Judicial Council, 139 years since 1808 and 103 years since 1844, officially affirmed the right of the General Conference, now written at this place in the constitution, to fix as well as define the "powers, privileges, and duties" of episcopacy.

Under this provision also there seems little doubt that if a bishop shall impress a General Conference as being inefficient or unacceptable, that body may "provide for his discontinuance," or arrange for the Jurisdictional Conference to do so as it may determine.

Under the item above cited the General Conference of 1940 acted when it outlined by statute the duties of a bishop in The Methodist Church. These duties, as written in the *Discipline* by majority action of the General Conference, were so generally taken over from the *Discipline* of the two former Episcopal Methodisms, and had been for so long such an integral part of their organic law that they are of the essence of Methodist constitutional episcopacy itself. These powers, however, whether they be merely statutory, as the enactment of them by the General Conference of 1940 seems to imply, or constitutional, as may be affirmed by reason of their perennial presence in Methodist episcopacy from its origin, may be classified and discussed further as they appear in the present *Discipline*. They are (1) to preside in the conferences; (2) to form the districts; (3) to fix the appointments, including appointing deaconesses, to fix Quarterly Conference membership of ministers at school, and so forth; (4) to travel; (5) to oversee the spiritual and temporal affairs of the church; (6) to organize missions; and (7) to ordain.

There are many minor duties of the bishops, of course, but the above are considered the most important and distinctive and will be taken up in order.

As Conference President

The bishops "shall appoint the times for holding the Annual Conferences" [10] and have always had this right. In practice the individual bishop in charge of a conference announces the time of holding such conference, though as both bishop and conference are anxious to make this time

---

[9] *Ibid.,* p. 119.
[10] *Discipline,* 1944, ¶ 626.

agreeable to all concerned, each conference, either by resolution, "request," or long continued custom, in effect presents the bishop with a time schedule which most bishops take as practically determinative. The bishop, however, since he usually has more than one conference to preside over, must be allowed to fix his own program of visitation and the constitution gives him this right.

The bishop has the right to call special sessions of a conference if three fourths of the district superintendents agree; and the conference itself has the right to provide for adjourned sessions if it so decides. The place where an Annual Conference shall meet is decided by the conference, though a majority of the district superintendents, with the bishop's consent, may change such place "should it become necessary for any reason." [11]

The bishop has the right to adjourn an Annual Conference when in his judgment all the business has been transacted. Under former Methodist law (1804-1939), a bishop was compelled to allow a conference to "sit a week at least," meaning that he could not adjourn a conference against its will until after a week had elapsed. Conferences could, and frequently did, adjourn themselves with the bishop's consent, after much shorter sessions. There is no mention in the present *Discipline* of any regulation with reference to adjournment.

When in the chair at Annual, Jurisdictional, or General Conference, the bishop acts primarily as moderator, preserving order and conducting the business of the session as a responsible chairman always does. But the bishop, by reason of the peculiar organization of the Methodist system, has always been, and must today be, something more than a mere moderator who must wait for the house to act. He is compelled to call certain questions in open conference and to see that the answers are properly given and recorded. He feels responsible, and is indeed responsible, for many of the manifold activities of the conference session itself. The "church program," as a later age was to call it, is largely in his hands, and it is necessary to steer the sessions of the conferences—and sometimes of the General Conference itself, if he is presiding—along the necessary way. Strictly speaking, therefore, the bishop, as conference president, occupies a much more distinct place than does the chairman of a convention or the Speaker of the House. These men may wait upon the direction and intent of the body over which they preside in a way that no Methodist bishop may do when in charge of a conference. To be sure, the Methodist bishop, as well as the Speaker, must, in presiding, adhere

[11] *Ibid.,* ¶ 627.

strictly to parliamentary procedure and practice, but he must also keep the conference session moving through the minute questions and transacting all its other business. This combination of an apparently impartial and disinterested presiding officer, with an active and aggressive conference leadership, calls for the highest sort of tact and alertness on the part of the bishop. It is no wonder that Methodists have long appraised their bishops quite definitely by the way they "handle their conferences."

In acting as parliamentary presiding officer the bishop must decide questions of everyday order and procedure much more often than questions touching Methodist law. His ruling on a matter of parliamentary procedure is subject to immediate review and possible appeal by any member of the house. Indeed there have been several instances where the bishop, ruling on a matter of order or parliamentary procedure, was reversed by the house, though normally, as in any parliamentary body, the chair's ruling is apt to be sustained on the unwritten principle that the chair is really acting for the good of all. But because of Methodist disciplinary law the bishop must view all legislation and matters coming before him from a dual standpoint: that of its congruence with Methodist usage and law, and that of its parliamentary orderliness. When he rules as a parliamentary officer the house can be appealed to and possibly reverse him; when he rules as a bishop passing upon a matter of law the house, if it is in an Annual Conference, cannot estop, though it can appeal. Formerly such appeals went, in the case of the Methodist Episcopal Church, to the next General Conference; in that of the Methodist Episcopal Church, South, to the next meeting of the College of Bishops. Now in The Methodist Church they go to the Judicial Council.

An interesting question arose once in the Methodist Episcopal Church and might arise again. Did the bishop, who could not interpret law before the General Conference, have the right to refuse to entertain a motion which seemed to him to contravene the constitution of the church? That he could do so before an Annual Conference or Quarterly Conference seems clear enough. Indeed in 1860, the "Committee on Law Questions" of the General Conference had before it this question:

If a motion is made in an Annual or Quarterly Conference, which, if passed, would be a positive violation of *Discipline*, should the President put the motion and allow the *Discipline* to be set aside, or what should he do?

Answer. He should refuse to put the motion.[12]

This report was adopted by the General Conference of 1860, and

[12] *Journal*, 1860, p. 297.

while it dealt not directly with episcopacy (for a district superintendent or even a pastor might be sitting in the chair at a Quarterly Conference), yet it caused considerable discussion.

Bishop Stephen M. Merrill, a great authority on Methodist polity, supported the position that the bishop, even when presiding over the then all-powerful General Conference, ought to have the right to stay unconstitutional proceedings. He affirmed that as the bishop was expected to keep order as a parliamentarian, he must certainly keep order with respect to the weightier matters of church order and constitutional law.[13] Nevertheless Merrill's position was directly countered by the action of the Methodist Episcopal General Conference in 1912 when it adopted the report of its Committee on Judiciary touching this very question:

In deciding whether a question is in order, the Bishop must necessarily decide according to principles of parliamentary law, notwithstanding the statement that "questions of law shall be decided by the General Conference." But in view of the provision in the *Discipline* that a Bishop presiding in a General Conference cannot decide questions of law, he cannot pass upon questions of constitutional law, neither can he construe enactments made by the General Conference.

. . . .

It has been decided on numerous occasions in the House of Representatives that a Speaker cannot rule a resolution or proposed legislation out of order on the ground that it is in violation of the federal Constitution. From the days of John Quincy Adams to the present day . . . the Speaker has overruled the point on the theory that it was not the duty of the Chair to construe the Constitution as affecting any proposed legislation.[14]

This action on the part of the General Conference of the Methodist Episcopal Church in 1912 provided the ruling law upon this matter in that connection and remained such. In the Methodist Episcopal Church, South, this situation could not have arisen as the bishop's ruling would at once have been taken as the law upon this matter, though, of course, there might have been an appeal to the College of Bishops. In The Methodist Church, where the Judicial Council is the final determinant of law, the practice and procedure as followed since 1912 in the Methodist Episcopal Church is presumptively to be followed.

Bishops when serving as conference presidents have traditionally acted as the leader of the body in expressing the thought of the conference

[13] *Digest of Methodist Law* (1904), p. 79.
[14] *Journal*, 1912, p. 560.

upon current matters, showing courtesy to visitors, commending, as fathers in the church, the elderly ministers who superannuate, welcoming and giving counsel and advice to young ministers who are admitted, and at times leading the devotions or preaching the ordination sermon. The bishop's usual desire to "rest a day or two" after he has held an Annual Conference is well understood by his brethren.

FORMING DISTRICTS AND MAKING APPOINTMENTS

A pristine right of episcopacy has always been the forming of the separate districts within any one Annual Conference. This is so tightly tied up with the making of appointments that the one can scarcely be considered without the other, as the number and personnel of those who are to become district superintendents is always crucial in every slate of appointments. The present *Discipline* affirms the right of the bishop to form the districts, but qualifies this with two provisos: The bishop must consult with the district superintendents before he announces the formation or grouping of the separate districts; and each Annual Conference is to be allowed to determine for itself how many such districts it shall have.[15]

The power to determine the number of its districts was one given the Annual Conferences by the Uniting Conference. Until then, in both episcopal Methodisms, the bishop decided both the number and the geographical configuration of all districts. Theoretically these two matters, the number of the districts and the bounds of each, go together, so that if the bishop be expected and allowed to "form the districts," it might be expected that it would be necessary for him to be allowed to plan the number and extent of these as one operation. Indeed this was definitely held to be the law by the Methodist Episcopal Church in 1916.[16] But what theory may demand, practice since the Uniting Conference has managed to ignore—and with success. No active bishop of The Methodist Church has to date expressed any doubt or dislike for this particular arrangement, and all bishops seem to feel that it is quite satisfactory.

The fixing of the appointments is, of course, the great privilege and duty of the bishop. But episcopal duty in this regard is, as might be expected, carefully prescribed by the *Discipline*. Appointments can be made by the bishop only "after consultation with the district superin-

[15] *Discipline*, 1944, ¶ 431 (3).
[16] *Journal*, 1916, pp. 448, 553.

tendents";[17] and after all appointments are first read "openly to the cabinet." [18] Even then such appointments are not to be publicly and finally made until the district superintendents have been able to "consult with pastors when such consultation is possible." These last measures —the reading of the complete appointments to the open cabinet, and the pre-appointment consultation with the pastors—were adopted after long years of experience in the two episcopal Methodisms. Methodist Protestants may very properly say that the last—consultation with the pastors—was adopted after they had fought for it long ago and had made clear its value in their connection.

The bishop has the disciplinary right to appoint an associate pastor for a charge,[19] and deaconesses to work within his area.[20] He can fix the Quarterly Conference membership of those who are left without appointment to attend school.[21] He can organize missions[22] and make or change appointments of preachers between sessions of the Annual Conference "as necessity may require," and after he has consulted with "the district superintendents," presumably those whose areas are involved. He must appoint the district superintendents annually, but within the jurisdictions in the United States he may not appoint a minister as district superintendent "for more than six consecutive years, nor for more than six years in any consecutive nine years." [23]

The right of a bishop to appoint members of the Annual Conference to connectional or educational positions and the like has been long exercised, though carefully defined in every *Discipline*. A study of successive *Disciplines* through the years will make clear the great growth of such appointive positions outside the regular conference pastorate or eldership, and will at the same time show how carefully hedged about such appointive possibilities have been.

The present *Discipline*, in treating of this whole matter of connectional appointments, carefully distinguishes between two classes of such positions. The one consists of such persons as publishing agents, board executives, church editors, chaplains, and so forth, who may be appointed annually by direct action of the bishop. The other class of appointments consists of those who are supposedly less directly connected with the

[17] *Discipline*, 1944, ¶ 431.

[18] *Ibid.*, ¶ 432.

[19] *Ibid.*, ¶ 431 (4).

[20] *Ibid.*, sec. 5.

[21] *Ibid.*, sec. 6.

[22] *Ibid.*, sec. 8.

[23] *Ibid.*, ¶ 432 (3).

organic work of the church, such as agents for tracts, temperance workers, evangelists at large, and the like. Several classes of persons in this category are named in the *Discipline*. The appointment of persons in this class can be made by the bishop only on recommendation of the district superintendents, confirmed by a two-thirds vote of the Annual Conference.[24]

As the *Discipline* carefully prescribes what appointments the bishop may make, it is understood that he may make these appointments only, and none others. Indeed the General Conference of 1916 of the Methodist Episcopal Church so determined by affirming and adopting as law a ruling of the bishops of that church given in May, 1913:

Bishops should strictly construe the law in regard to special appointments of members of an Annual Conference and should make no special appointment that is not clearly authorized according to the *Book of Discipline*. Where a Bishop has made an appointment and subsequently is convinced that such an appointment is not clearly authorized, he should correct it at the earliest moment he can do so with propriety.[25]

ORDINATION

Ordination is a peculiar power possessed by the episcopacy, and "in every episcopal church upon earth, since the first introduction of Christianity, has been considered as essential to it," to quote Bishops Coke and Asbury. But these two men, the first representatives of Methodist episcopacy in this country, go on to say that the power to ordain is

singularly limited in our bishops. For they not only have no power to ordain a person for the episcopal office till he be first elected by the General Conference, but they possess no authority to ordain an elder or a travelling deacon till he be first elected by a yearly conference.[26]

This is a very great restriction as over against the independent action in conferring orders which every bishop in the chain of the historic episcopate has enjoyed. But the Methodist bishop, who has never laid claim to an order which would lift him above his presbyterial brethren, and whose own orders and superintendency took their origin not under the hands of the historic episcopacy but under those of a Methodist presbytery—John Wesley and his brother priests of the Church of England acting together—fittingly carries on the Methodist tradition by

[24] *Ibid.*, sec. 5.
[25] *Journal*, 1916, p. 516.
[26] David Sherman, *History of the Revisions of the Discipline* (1874), p. 351.

waiting upon Methodist conferences to give him authority likewise to ordain. He cannot ordain without this, and every bishop who ordains men to the office of elder or deacon is careful to state both in the ordination parchment given to the ordinand, and in his report to the conferring conference, by what authority he laid his hands upon that particular man.

In the Episcopal Address of 1844 the position was taken that the bishop, when ordination has been voted by a conference, "is under *obligation* to ordain the person elected, whatever may be his own judgment of his qualifications." [27] But John Emory, in his *Defense of Our Fathers*, held that the bishop not only had the right, but was expected to refuse ordination to one whose ordering should be challenged at that point in the ordination service where the bishop asks publicly "if there be any of you, who knoweth any impediment or crime . . . for the which he ought not to be received into this holy ministry, let him come forth in the name of God, and shew what the crime or impediment is." [28] This situation, however, could scarcely ever arise, and bishops are always happy when they can, by the august authority of the church vested in them, give, by the imposition of their hands and by prayer, the office of deacon or elder to those persons whom the empowering conference shall think to be worthy of the same.

A bishop by himself may ordain, and does ordain, to the office of deacon, the lowest ministerial order in The Methodist Church as well as in the Church of England and the Protestant Episcopal Church. The deacon was the almoner of the early church, and his status, while truly ministerial in the original meaning of that term, did not for some decades have the idea of a fixed, crystallized order. Certain Christian churches today hold the word "deacon" in the pristine sense of this early church office, and regard the deacon as a layman set apart for special duty. But in Methodism the office of deacon is that in which the ordinand is empowered to "execute the office of a deacon," is invested with the right to read the Scripture in the church, to preach the Word, and to assist the elder when he ministers the Holy Communion. All this is conferred by the bishop's ordination.

With the elder, or highest ecclesiastical order in The Methodist Church, a somewhat longer ordination rite is followed, equivalent to the office for the ordaining of a priest in the Church of England. The bishop must also, in conferring elders' orders, be joined by certain other elders present, who together lay their hands upon the head of the ordinand

[27] Collins Denny, A Manual of the Discipline (1931), p. 82.
[28] P. 65.

while the bishop prays: "The Lord pour upon thee the Holy Spirit for the office and work of an elder in the Church of God, now committed unto thee by the authority of the Church through the imposition of our hands." Immediately after this the ordinand is invested with the right "to preach the Word of God, and to administer the holy sacraments in the congregation."

At the ordination or consecration of a bishop, several bishops and certain selected elders join together. The imposition of hands and the investiture follow the traditional rite of episcopal ordination of the Church of England, as Mr. Wesley arranged this for his American superintendent. The presiding bishop in Methodism makes the report of the ordination or consecration to the electing conference and signs the ordination parchment.

Travel and Administration

The duty of a bishop "to travel" has always in Methodist minds been regarded as essential to superintendency itself. Francis Asbury set the pattern by going in person from place to place the better to oversee the work. Bishop John M. Moore states that the example of the English bishop who was constantly "on visitation" may have influenced Asbury, but the likelihood is that it was also practical necessity which made him go continually, superintending the work, preaching, teaching, encouraging, leading. Thus only could superintendency be "general." At any rate, subsequent years and succeeding bishops kept up the custom, so that when a bishop asked leave to retire, he asked it in terms of this one duty—that he be allowed to "cease to travel." Bishops in The Methodist Church today find this same duty resting heavily upon them. They "live out of a suitcase," not out of saddlebags; they cross rivers on Pullman cars, not on primitive ferries; but the obligation to move continually over their areas, preaching, dedicating churches, holding conferences, and leading their brethren in the program of the church always remains with them.

An enormous mass of administrative detail falls upon the present-day bishop. Said Bishop G. Bromley Oxnam:

Let me point out . . . the size of our episcopal areas. The sheer geographical responsibility makes adequate supervision impossible. I am charged with the administration of 1,438 churches. The institutions on whose boards I serve and whose meetings I should attend would take more than one hundred days out of each year if I did my duty.[29]

[29] William K. Anderson, ed., *Making the Gospel Effective* (1945), p. 187.

In addition to what Paul complained of as "the care of all the churches," the present-day bishop is called upon to act in a representative capacity over his area, and indeed over the whole church. He is expected to travel constantly, as has been said, and his program of episcopal visitation calls upon him not only to preach and dedicate churches in his own area, but to attend meetings, conferences, and commissions, as Bishop Oxnam suggests, not only those of his own connection but of other Protestant denominations. Bishops are put by the General Conference upon almost all the boards of the church. Formerly all were automatically members of the Board of Missions and the Board of Education. The custom has grown of electing one of the episcopal members as head of each such board or commission, and almost all the boards now have bishops as president and vice-president. In making up the membership of such boards or commissions, and in securing personnel for many of its own committees, the General Conference is accustomed to request that the nominations be made by "the bishops." As a consequence, the bishops at the sessions of the General Conference, spend much time in discussing and making up lists of nominees or, it may be, appointments. "And resolved that the bishops be requested to appoint the members of this commission," is a common way of ending motions setting up new commissions, committees, and church bodies of all sorts. This episcopal oversight of all such organizations secures church-wide representation upon the general agencies thus created, but takes much time on the part of the bishops. "We spend hours and hours," a bishop said, "in discussing nominations and trying to get the right men on the boards and committees which we are asked to appoint."

At General Conference sessions the bishops, in accordance with a time-honored custom, do not take part directly in the deliberations of that body and are careful not to appear to be sponsoring any individual piece of legislation, especially if such legislation be considered at all controversial. The Council of Bishops as a whole does report through its secretary at stated intervals such nominations as it may have been requested, or expected, to make, and the council likewise never hesitates to call to the attention of the conference any special matter which the bishops feel in duty bound to declare. But although individual bishops serve actively upon the general boards and are often prime workers in the legislative committees of such boards, and are otherwise wholeheartedly in support of some special measure at General Conference, episcopal propriety demands that the bishops keep completely out of the actual passage of legislation. This is in part due to the fact that, as the bishops are the constitutional presidents of the General Conference, they should not, and may not, be partisan in the least when acting as presiding officers. But this sudden quiescence during the sessions of the General Conference of a great group of men who are in person and in actuality the normal leaders of the church upon every other occasion, causes some questioning as to whether their very real ability and counsel might not be better used at the quadrennial seasons.

In administering their own areas the bishops take very seriously the heavy duty of stationing the preachers. Present-day bishops feel that the opportunity now given to pastoral relations committees, and to preachers themselves, to declare their wishes in regard to appointments is a helpful thing. It is recognized that a somewhat anomalous situation can result, and is resulting, in certain conferences where congregational pressure and pastoral desires are the determining factors in many pulpits, while in other places the congregation yet looks to the appointive powers for the needed appointment. Certain contemporary bishops deplore the trend toward congregationalism, while others think it is "no worse"—as Bishop Edwin H. Hughes put it—than it was years and years ago. All bishops feel that, as the responsibility for making appointments rests upon them, they must carefully and wisely assume this truly great burden. Many feel that where a happy mixture of congregational and pastoral assent to episcopal appointment can be realized, the situation is almost ideal. Methodism is still the envy of other churches in being able to put a man in every place and have a place for every man. The itineracy has also the advantage of being able to "carry" and place older men whose diminishing powers put them at a disadvantage or retire them altogether in a "called" ministry.

In their relation to the district superintendency the bishops today take the same position which the church has always held regarding this— that it is in effect an essential part of the episcopal administration. Bishops, therefore, continue to insist upon their right and obligation to name their own district superintendents. No bishop today believes in the elective presiding eldership, though there are certain bishops who, from time to time, ask their conferences to nominate, by a ballot meant for the bishop alone, men whom the conference members feel might make good district superintendents. The few bishops who follow this practice are aware of its danger and guard against it by giving no advance notice of such an advisory ballot and by maintaining silence to all concerning the result of the ballot itself. All bishops feel that the bishop himself should directly appoint the superintendents under our present law.

90

While the division of the episcopacy by the jurisdictional grouping is not looked upon with favor by many bishops, all recognize that, as this is fundamental to the Plan of Union of The Methodist Church, it should be respected and made to fulfill its utmost usefulness. All agree, however, that there should, and must be, a well-wrought plan of travel on the part of the bishops so that episcopal visitation and presidential supervision within the limits set by the constitution shall be continued beyond the bounds of any one bishop's jurisdiction. The old lesson which Tigert stressed, when he showed how the Northern bishops never went south of Philadelphia or the Southern bishops north of Baltimore, before the fateful day of 1844, is one which no general superintendency can afford to overlook. Therefore for the bishop of the Philadelphia area to be invited to visit the Western Jurisdiction and hold conferences, for instance, and for the bishop of the Birmingham area to be invited to Michigan, and vice versa, are moves which the bishops feel will make for better understanding, as well as for a more general superintendency.

It is not commonly appreciated that the bishops are the natural spokesmen and leaders of the church at other times than when the General Conference is meeting. In the former Methodist Episcopal Church, South, the College of Bishops was frankly entrusted with the duty of making pronouncements upon "great social questions of national and international importance," and other groups and bodies were discouraged if not forbidden to give out statements in the name of the church.[30] At present, boards, commissions, and various organizations within the framework of The Methodist Church issue their official and semiofficial resolutions, papers, commitments, and the like, and these quite often are featured in the public press. But the Council of Bishops, by virtue of its unique status, acting as the corporate general superintendency, can, and should, take the lead in public affairs and in all matters affecting church-wide interest, to a far greater extent than any board or commission is able to do.

Upon the entry of the United States into the Second World War in 1941, the Council of Bishops issued a statement which was at once given to the church and to the world. Such a statement, whether its particular pronouncements were considered wise or not, was entirely proper and indeed necessary on the part of the Council of Bishops, for that organization has been directed by the constitution to plan for the general oversight, and for the promotion of the temporal as well as the spiritual aspect of the entire church. The council must not fail, there-

[30] *Discipline*, 1938, ¶ 137-a.

fore, to continue to exercise the role of leadership with which the church has entrusted it.

In conclusion let it be said that the present-day bishop of The Methodist Church is first and foremost an overpastor of many brethren and the president of those conferences put under his care. If he does not give such conferences his presidential and residential supervision, no one else will. By so much as other duties take him away from administering his own area, and caring for his own preachers and churches, by that much is this important function of the church's ministry lessened or lost. In a noble statement to the Commission on Church Union in 1918, Bishop William Fraser McDowell said: "When I hear men talk about the bishops being the chief ministers and chief pastors, I always think, not of the word 'chief,' but of being chief 'minister,' chief 'pastor' to my brethren."

Beside the primary duty of manning his area and directing its program, the bishop is an officer of the general church, one who must see far past jurisdictional boundaries, even if he is not permitted to supervise work beyond them. He has a representative, church-wide, and world-wide mission to perform, and finds many times that he is called upon to represent universal Christian brotherhood as well as his special ecclesiasticism. Traveling, speaking, writing, superintending, presiding—on he must move, following the same long trail, though with different means of transport, as that followed by Asbury. The Methodist Church is an episcopal church in a very real sense, and the bishops are yet "set apart" for a profoundly important work.

PART TWO

The Conference System

VI

THE FIRST CONFERENCES

It is desired . . . That we may meet with a single eye, and as little children who have everything to learn; That every point may be examined from the foundation; That every person may speak freely whatever is in his heart; and That every question proposed may be fully debated, and bolted to the bran.
—John Bennett's Minutes, 1744

JOHN WESLEY CALLED THE FIRST METHODIST CONFERENCE IN 1744. To this came, at Wesley's summons, the Rev. Charles Wesley, the Rev. John Hodges, rector of Wenvoe, the Rev. Henry Piers, vicar of Bexley, the Rev. Samuel Taylor, vicar of Quinton, and the Rev. John Meriton, of the Isle of Man. All these men, as well as Wesley himself, were ordained clergymen of the Church of England—"priests of the church," as they would have put it.[1]

The clergymen discussed the advisability of admitting to their conference certain lay preachers who had also evidently been notified of the meeting. "After some time," Wesley explains, "I invited the lay preachers that were in the house to meet with us." This radical and momentous step admitted to the conference four lay preachers whose names often figure in early Methodist annals: Thomas Maxfield, Thomas Richards, John Bennet, and John Downes.[2]

This historic 1744 conference had within it the germ of every succeeding conference in its reliance upon official question and answer, open debate, majority rule, and the careful preservation of the "minutes" in written form. Subsequently other conferences were called by Wesley until in time a further development and final fixture of these institutional features occurred. From the beginning the conference exercised that right which is inherent in every autonomous body—to act as the judge of the qualifications of its own members.

Men were first admitted to the conference fellowship informally, then in accordance with fixed tests, as the organization grew and the inevitable crystallization set in.

[1] *Wesley's Works*, American ed., V, 191.
[2] Thomas B. Neely, *The Governing Conference in Methodism* (1892), pp. 4-5.

In due time, as conference succeeded conference and year followed year, the regular pattern of work became fixed and codified in what were called after a time the "large minutes." These became the definitive pattern for early Methodist discipline, and when American Methodism was organized into a church in 1784, the "large minutes" of British Methodism, a sort of revised statutes of successive conference actions, were taken as a guide and directive.

Attention has been called to the fact that English Methodist conferences had no authority save an advisory one, and that Wesley, while he lived, was the dominant and controlling power. He was, of course, supported in his disciplinary measures by the actions which succeeding conferences took, but it was Wesley who managed the conferences and set his seal upon the whole of the Methodist discipline as it gradually evolved. "He was the Church in a more emphatic sense than Louis XIV was the State," observed Bishop Neely.

At Wesley's death the English conference, although legally established, was at best an introverted, truncated body as far as its own privileges and rights were concerned. It soon became divided over the question as to its right to ordain ministers and to make rules for ordination. It had a strong party whose members were determined that there should be no outward break with the Establishment; it had an equally powerful group who felt that Methodism should set itself free from the dominance of the Church of England and live a life of its own. It was many years, well into the nineteenth century, before British Methodism really found itself. Meanwhile, of course, it followed in its own life and practices the august rules and iron discipline which, under its founder, it had evolved through the remarkable early years of the Methodist Movement.

But in America there was a different story. From the first, Methodist conferences on these shores felt themselves competent to manage their own affairs to a degree unknown in Britain. The question-and-answer pattern of transacting business was, of course, kept according to the practice of the "large minutes," but the conference answered the questions which the conference asked. Indeed at one notable American conference, that held in Fluvanna County, Virginia, in 1779, the preachers who gathered voted that they ought to have, and should have, the right to administer the sacraments of the church, ordination or no ordination.[3] This was breaking with the past with a vengeance, but the American Revolution had made it all but impossible at the time to find Church of

[3] John J. Tigert, A Constitutional History of American Episcopal Methodism (rev. ed., 1904), pp. 106-7.

England clergymen who could, or would, take care of this matter. Subsequently the heavy hand of Francis Asbury fell on the Fluvanna Conference and all its ways and works, and Asbury saw to it that a later conference held in Baltimore should undo the move of the Virginia brethren. But that there was a spirit of almost total independence alive in the colonial Methodists became more and more manifest, even apart from the political and military conflict.

When Asbury himself, after the Revolution, made the epochal move of calling the preachers to come together in a conference to decide whether or not he should accept Wesley's ordination, the move was not one to give surprise on this side of the ocean. That it surprised Wesley, when he heard of it, there is no doubt, though there is no record of his ever objecting. He had sent Coke to ordain Asbury with no more by-your-leave of American Methodists than he had asked of English bishops when he had ordained Coke. Ordinations were always managed that way, the English bishop being beholden not to conferences or convocations but to his own conscience that he should "lay hands suddenly on no man." But Asbury, before he would accept the ordination Wesley planned, desired the voted consent of his preacher-brethren. These, he insisted, must be assembled and consulted on the matter. The calling of the conference, which met at Baltimore in Christmas week of 1784, was therefore entirely due to Francis Asbury. "This Conference had not entered into Wesley's platform or Coke's. In Asbury's platform, however, it was the chief plank." So held Bishop Tigert.[4]

Bishop Neely put it even more strongly:

The suggestion conceded power to the Conference such as it never possessed before. . . . Even if his [Asbury's] purpose was to strengthen his own personal power, its effect was the destruction of supreme personal government on the part of Wesley, Coke, Asbury, or any other individual. It destroyed personal government and placed the governing power in the Conference.[5]

Thus it came about that, at the conclusion of the organizing Conference of 1784, the sovereignty, so far as American Methodism was concerned, had definitely passed from England to America and from John Wesley to the American Methodist preachers acting in conference. Although Asbury and Coke were to define and defend the Methodist episcopacy which Coke had brought over in person, and which Asbury and Coke together assumed for the new church, and although the con-

[4] *Ibid.*, p. 192.
[5] *Op. cit.*, p. 252.

stitutional status of Methodist episcopacy was to be maintained from that day to this, there has never been any question but that in the pristine Methodist Episcopal Church the real sovereignty lay in the personnel of the preachers. Whether these met in a general convention, as the Christmas Conference is usually asserted to have been, or in an irregular General Conference, or in that imaginary, unitary Annual Conference of all preachers everywhere—wherever they were, the preachers were the authority for the church, its ultimate sovereign power. These preachers could have met in conference or convention at any time before 1808 and have done away their church or changed any of its forms had they so chosen. They were absolute and final in all matters touching what they would have called their "connexion." And to this day, while the church has seen fit since those early years to place laymen as well as preachers in the Annual Conferences, all traveling preachers, being *ipso facto* Annual Conference members, yet enjoy the right inherent in such membership— that is, to be sovereign constitutional electors and directors of their church.

There has always been some confusion in Methodist records in regard to early "general" conferences as over against the growing and dividing "annual" conferences.[6] At Baltimore, in 1784, the preachers who met in the organizing conference were to all intents and purposes American Methodism in session. The number was comparatively small—"three score and more," said one recorder; "less than eighty," another. But these men represented the connection completely as they met at this memorable gathering.

The early Methodist preachers made the attempt for some years to preserve a sort of fictional and theoretical unity, so that when one "conference" acted all were presumed to be acting or at least to be involved in the action. "Until the appointment of stated or regular General Conferences," says Stevens, referring to this early period, "the Annual Conferences continued to be considered local or sectional meetings of the one undivided ministry, held in different localities for the local convenience of its members, every general or legislative measure being submitted to all the sessions before it could become law." [7]

[6] Collins Denny, A Manual of the Discipline (1931), p. 39.
[7] Abel Stevens, A Compendium History of American Methodism, p. 195.

VII

THE GENERAL CONFERENCE

There shall be a General Conference for the entire church with such powers, duties, and privileges as are hereinafter set forth.

—Constitution, Div. II (1)

In 1808 the members of the several Annual Conferences, not as conference members but as Methodist preachers, transferred to a representative General Conference almost the whole of their connectional power. The origin and formation of this first representative General Conference has been narrated in a preceding chapter. By the time the "turn of the century"—1800—had come, it was proving impracticable, if not impossible, for the scattered and rapidly increasing ministry of the church to meet regularly and legislate satisfactorily. The idea of a representative General Conference took shape in the minds of the church leaders and in due time was put into effect, but not without struggle, discussion, and debate.

Before this plan was adopted there was for a time an ill-fated scheme of control known as "The Council," which Asbury devised and for which he hoped much. It was, in effect, Asbury's selection of a small group of men who had, as David Sherman expressed it, "powers similar to those of the General Conference." [1] As the council was composed of bishops and presiding elders (who were made so by the bishops), it was a continuing rule of episcopacy. Complaints arose at once from the first session of the council—in Baltimore, in December, 1789—to its speedy death by common consent two years later. It was too much of an oligarchy and Asbury himself requested that it might be named no more.

The General Conference of 1792, with the debacle of the ill-fated council before it, decided definitely and positively that hereafter the General Conference alone should be empowered to make rules and regulations for the church. Thus, formal recognition was given to the General Conference as the sole lawmaking body in Methodism. Its power

[1] *History of the Revisions of the Discipline* (1890), p. 297.

99

in this regard has never since been questioned and is basic in all Methodist history and law.[2]

Jesse Lee is given credit for first suggesting the idea of a delegated General Conference, and did so before the Conference of 1792 had convened. But it required sixteen years more of growth and discussion before Lee and his compeers could see the plan adopted and put into effect.

The whole situation having to do with the creation of a delegated General Conference was full of drama, and every move was important as these moves unfolded in 1808. Bishop Neely's authoritative and comprehensive study of the origin of this conference makes it clear that nothing was done without a struggle. But when at last the regulations calling for a quadrennial General Conference had finally been adopted, the historian must admit that a statesmanlike move of the greatest import had been ably accomplished.

The General Conference then created was invested with sweeping powers. Every right and power not specifically denied to it was frankly delegated to it by the creating ministry. In this respect the General Conference differed from the Congress of the United States. That body has only such powers as are granted to it; the General Conference had all powers not denied to it. It had "full power to make rules and regulations for the Church under the following limitations and restrictions." The "limitations" came to be called in Methodist records "the Restrictive Rules," and from that day to this they have played a leading part in all Methodist history.

As these rules themselves were much debated, and as one of them— that having to do with the ratio of representation—was greatly modified through the years and finally done away in 1939, and as all of them have been under attack from time to time, attention must now be given to the meaning and import of the restrictions in question. They are in the language of 1808, for, though slightly modified through the years, they are today substantially the same except the second rule.

The First Restrictive Rule ran:

The general conference shall not revoke, alter, or change our articles of religion, nor establish any new standards or rules of doctrine contrary to our present existing and established standards of doctrine.

This is the first and great rule protecting the doctrines and Articles of Religion of the Methodist Church. Above all other reasons given by the

[2] *History of the Revisions of the Discipline* (1874), p. 28.

fathers of 1808 for the organization of the General Conference was that "our body of doctrine and Methodist principles" might be preserved and kept inviolate.[3] The General Conference which they therefore created was not allowed to touch or alter in any degree the Twenty-five Articles (which were the formal doctrinal expression of the church); nor could any new standards or contrary rules of doctrine be established. The effect of this restriction was to lock up all existing Methodist doctrine and standards of doctrine and place these forever beyond the reach of any General Conference. In practice this has meant that no Article of Religion and no formal expression of the church's faith can be amended by a General Conference. So whenever a "standard of doctrine" has been claimed in connection with some proposed action by a General Conference, that body moves with extreme caution. Curiously enough, the Ritual of the church, packed full as it is with doctrine of the highest import, has been amended from time to time by successive General Conferences and their appointed commissions with no challenge from anyone. Such amendment and revision, however, has never been open to attack on the ground that the revision in question has established a "new" standard, or a rule of doctrine "contrary to" the existing and established standards of 1808. Most ritualistic revision has been motivated by the desire to get certain objectionable phrases or ceremonies out, rather than to get something new in.[4]

Methodist standards, with the exception of the Articles of Religion, have been somewhat indeterminate. Even Mr. Wesley's *Sermons* and *Notes on the New Testament*—Methodism's traditional canon—have always been affirmed to "contain" Methodist doctrine, not to be that doctrine in themselves.

There may be a question as to whether in the First Restrictive Rule "any new standards" or "rules of doctrine contrary to our present existing and established standards" are two co-ordinate expressions. Or does the latter expression, "rules of doctrine contrary," and so forth, modify and explain what "new standards" are? If the latter point of view is held, then a General Conference might or may establish a "new" standard so long as this new standard does not become a rule contrary to the present existing and established standards. If the above expressions, however, are co-ordinate, then nothing whatever in the way of doctrine which might be considered "new" could, or can ever be, put into Methodist discipline and practice by a General Conference.

[3] Thomas B. Neely, *The Governing Conference in Methodism* (1892), p. 351.

[4] Nolan B. Harmon, *The Rites and Ritual of Episcopal Methodism* (1926), pp. 65-67.

The Second Restrictive Rule was:

They shall not allow of more than one representative for every five members of the annual conference, nor allow of a less number than one for every seven.

This regulation governing the proportion of representation in the General Conference was destined to suffer more change than any other of the Restrictive Rules and finally to be done away altogether. Its purpose, of course, is clear, but as the church grew, the limits of representation were necessarily changed, with conferences growing larger and larger and thus widening the basis of representation. As each change in this rule, or the substitution of new figures determining representation, entailed a constitutional change and meant that the new figures must be submitted to all the Annual Conferences for approval, an awkward situation continued to result. Lay delegation as called for by the Methodist Episcopal Church in 1872 also forced a change in this rule, and it was necessary to amend it in order to allow the layman to become a part of the General Conference. So it was that this particular rule, which was never meant to be more than directive in a statutory way, blocked action on the part of the growing church at many points. Therefore in 1900, when the Methodist Episcopal Church adopted a formal, well-wrought constitution, it decided to do away entirely with this rule defining limits of General Conference representation, though these limits were definitely specified elsewhere in the constitution but not in this time-honored place. In place of this rule a regulation was inserted which dealt with Annual Conference limits, not those of the General Conference:

The General Conference shall not organize nor authorize the organization of an Annual Conference with less than twenty-five members.

The situation which seemed to call for this constitutional restriction of 1900 was one which fundamentally was felt quite keenly at the time the Methodist Episcopal Church was writing its then new fundamental law. However, when the united church came into being in 1939 and the Plan of Union was formulated, the Second Restrictive Rule of 1808 did not appear in its traditional place, nor was this Methodist Episcopal regulation of 1900 kept. Its matter and meaning were transferred to the section of the constitution dealing with the General Conference and now appear as Article I of Section I:

The General Conference shall be composed of not less than 600 nor more than 800 delegates, one-half of whom shall be ministers and one-half lay members, to be elected by the Annual Conferences.

After thus dropping or changing the Second Restrictive Rule, the five other Restrictive Rules of 1808 were kept in their time-honored place in the present constitution, but the former third rule became the second, the fourth became the third, and the other figures were changed accordingly.[5]

The omission of the old second rule was wise, as the proportionate representation which may be allowed Annual Conferences can, and will, now be worked out within the prescribed limits by the General Conference itself, with such changes from time to time as may be deemed advisable.

As has been made clear, the General Conference, under the six historic restrictions, enjoyed enormous power in directing the affairs of the two Methodist Episcopal Churches. It had the power of electing bishops and connectional officers, and of managing through its committees and through the boards, whose members it elected, all the actions and program of the church. It was absolutely supreme as a lawmaking body, and, in the Methodist Episcopal connection, was also the interpreter of that law and final arbiter of all matters relating to the fundamental law of the church.

The Third Restrictive Rule read:

They shall not change or alter any part or rule of our government, so as to do away Episcopacy or destroy the plan of our itinerant general superintendency.

This restriction has been discussed in the former chapter treating of the episcopacy. It was amended by the Methodist Episcopal Church in 1856 so as to allow for missionary bishops, and such bishops were elected under it. But at union in 1939 the language adopted for The Methodist Church was that of the rule of 1808 and so stands today. The Methodist Episcopal Church, South, never amended this rule at all, and the Methodist Protestant Church had no bishops and strictly speaking no restrictive rules as such.

The Fourth Restrictive Rule read:

They shall not revoke or change the general rules of the United Societies.

This refers to the regulations and rules of the Wesleyan Societies when they were *societies*. The "General Rules" were not primarily doctrine, though they were posited on doctrine and fundamental Christian beliefs. They were, in effect, rules for practical conduct, and emphasized

---

[5] Constitution, Div. II, Sec. 2.

in a heavy and objective way certain outward actions as definitive for, and obligatory upon, all Methodists.

It must be remembered that the General Rules were written for those who already belonged to the Church of England, most of them, though doubtless there were some Methodists who had other or no definite church affiliations. The Wesleyan Societies in Britain were open to all who would promise to conform to these outward regulations as an "evidence of their desire of salvation." Wesley himself wrote them and put in this concluding word: "These are the General Rules of our societies; all of which we are taught of God to observe, even in his written Word, which is the only rule, and the sufficient rule, both of our faith and practice. And all these we know his Spirit writes on truly awakened hearts." [6]

The General Rules, as an integral whole, were transferred to America and were taken as belonging among the Methodist standards, though they manifestly deal primarily with conduct rather than with doctrine. They were made sacrosanct by the General Conference of 1808 when it formally wrote this Restrictive Rule, and have since been held not only in historic appreciation but have been applied in so far as was considered possible to everyday life. In the Methodist Episcopal Church and Methodist Episcopal Church, South, every minister for years and years was required to read the General Rules at least annually to his people or "see that they be read." Among all Methodists, however, succeeding generations have nullified or overlooked certain regulations considered minor, such as the wearing of gold and costly apparel. Nevertheless, these rules are in The Methodist Church today where they were in the Methodist Church of the past, written into its fundamental law and beyond the reach of anything but a constitutional change.

The Fifth Restrictive Rule read:

They shall not do away the privileges of our ministers or preachers of trial by a committee, and of an appeal: Neither shall they do away the privileges of our members of trial before the society or by a committee, and of an appeal.

This is the guarantee for the right of fair trial and has never been in question in the Methodist connection. This right is so fundamental to English-speaking people that we who are far removed from 1808 can scarcely appreciate the reason for the writing of such a regulation into the fundamental law of the church at that early date. The regulation speaks for itself and stands today in its time-honored form.

[6] *Discipline,* 1944, ¶ 98.

The Sixth Restrictive Rule read:

They shall not appropriate the produce of the Book Concern, or of the Charter Fund, to any purpose other than for the benefit of the travelling, supernumerary, superannuated and worn-out preachers, their wives, widows and children.

The "produce" in this rule—defined as the profit of the Book Concern—was in 1808 the only property, beside the Chartered Fund, which the General Conference might have been able to utilize. It was deemed wise in an era when other causes might claim support, to hold the General Conference to the principle of utilizing the profit of the Publishing House for the conference claimants only. The Publishing House was, of course, not founded to make money for such conference claimants but for "the advancement of the cause of Christianity by disseminating religious knowledge and useful literary and scientific information in the form of books, tracts, and periodicals." [7] The money which the Publishing House, or Book Concern, might make was to be appropriated by the General Conference, or its agents, only for the cause of the superannuated preachers, their widows, and orphans. This was the plan put into effect by John Dickins, Ezekiel Cooper, and the Book Concern in the early years of American Methodism and followed ever after.

It is to be noted that the regulation affecting the produce of the Publishing House was one specifically enjoined upon the General Conference itself. In practice, the Publishing House has determined through its duly established management the amount of its net produce, after accounting for its entire business program. It has necessarily put back into its operations such funds as it felt would improve the business or take care of expenses, and then, in accordance with the General Conference regulation, has divided its produce among the respective conference claimants. Since the church has denied to the General Conference the right to apply the produce of the Publishing House to any cause other than the one stated in this rule, no publishing agent, book committee, or board of publication has ever felt that it, or he, would have the right to use this money in any other than the way the church has said the General Conference must use it.

PRESENT RESTRICTIVE RULES

Such are the Restrictive Rules which before union acted as the only check upon total General Conference sovereignty. These rules were kept

[7] *Ibid.,* ¶ 1102.

in the Plan of Union, as has been said, and are now written into the constitution of The Methodist Church. At the risk of some repetition they are repeated here in the language of the present constitution:

1. The General Conference shall not revoke, alter, or change our Articles of Religion, or establish any new standards or rules of doctrine contrary to our present existing and established standards of doctrine.
2. The General Conference shall not change or alter any part or rule of our government so as to do away episcopacy, or destroy the plan of our itinerant general superintendency.
3. The General Conference shall not do away the privileges of our ministers or preachers of trial by a committee and of an appeal; neither shall it do away the privileges of our members of trial before the church, or by a committee, and of an appeal.
4. The General Conference shall not revoke or change the General Rules of the United Societies.
5. The General Conference shall not appropriate the produce of the Publishing House, the Book Concern, or the Chartered Fund to any purpose other than for the benefit of the traveling, supernumerary, superannuated, and worn-out preachers, their wives, widows, and children.[8]

While these rules are now given an honored place in the constitution of The Methodist Church, they are not by any means as important as once they were. In early days the section of the *Discipline* treating of the General Conference and giving full power to that body under the Restrictive Rules, sufficed to make these rules themselves practically the sole arbiter and definition of constitutionality. Today, with a full-orbed constitution adopted which covers all manner of structural detail and which establishes constitutionally many other agencies beside the General Conference, these rules, since they regulate the General Conference only, sink somewhat into the background. They have a historic and adjectival significance and will, of course, be kept, but they are not today the prime definitive force which they were from 1808 on in the former churches.

GENERAL CONFERENCE LIMITATIONS

Beside the Restrictive Rules, which have been discussed and which have always limited and defined General Conference powers, the Plan of Union further limits the General Conference in certain important ways. There is the statement that the General Conference shall have full legislative power, but this is qualified by the phrase "over all matters distinctively connectional." This constitutional warrant does not deny the

[8] Div. II, Sec. II.

General Conference legislative power over special or jurisdictional matters, but it does not affirm it. Also, in order to make clear and define the connectional power of the General Conference, there are today fourteen constitutional sections which treat of and enjoin certain general and special duties. It was evidently the desire of the framers of the constitution of The Methodist Church—the Joint Commission on Union—to outline in a comprehensive way all the duties of the General Conference. The present provisions, therefore, are a contrast to the situation created by the old Restrictive Rules. Before union the General Conference could do all things except those forbidden it; now it is definitely told what it can do in the following fourteen definitive instructions:

The General Conference shall have full legislative power over all matters distinctively connectional, and in the exercise of said powers shall have authority as follows:

1. To define and fix the conditions, privileges, and duties of church membership.
2. To define and fix the qualifications and duties of elders, deacons, supply preachers, local preachers, exhorters, and deaconesses.
3. To define and fix the powers and duties of Annual Conferences, Mission Conferences, and Missions, and of District, Quarterly, and Church Conferences.
4. To provide for the organization, promotion, and administration of the work of the church outside the United States of America.
5. To define and fix the powers, duties, and privileges of the episcopacy, to adopt a plan for the support of the bishops, to provide a uniform rule for their superannuation, and to provide for the discontinuance of a bishop because of inefficiency or unacceptability.
6. To provide and revise the Hymnal and Ritual of the church and to regulate all matters relating to the form and mode of worship, subject to the limitations of the first Restrictive Rule.
7. To provide a judicial system and a method of judicial procedure for the church, except as herein otherwise prescribed.
8. To initiate and to direct all connectional enterprises of the church, such as publishing, evangelistic, educational, missionary, and benevolent, and to provide boards for their promotion and administration.
9. To determine and provide for raising the funds necessary to carry on the connectional work of the church.
10. To fix a uniform basis upon which bishops shall be elected by the Jurisdictional Conferences and to determine the number of bishops that may be elected by Central Conferences.
11. To select its presiding officers from the bishops, through a committee,

provided that the bishops shall select from their own number the president for the opening session.

12. To change the number and the boundaries of Jurisdictional Conferences upon the consent of a majority of the Annual Conferences in each Jurisdictional Conference involved.

13. To establish such commissions for the general work of the church as may be deemed advisable.

14. To enact such other legislation as may be necessary, subject to the limitations and restrictions of the Constitution of the church.[9]

These several powers and duties of the General Conference are outlined specifically, so some authorities hold, in order to make clear what matters are "distinctively connectional." The expression, "and in the exercise of said powers shall have authority as follows" is clearly an attempt to outline and define, and therefore the above provisions *limit* the power of the General Conference.

But other Methodist authorities hold that these provisions are put in to illustrate and indicate in a general way what may be taken as "matters distinctively connectional." They also affirm, and with some validity, that the fourteenth item opens the door for any sort of action which does not directly contravene the constitution at some other point.

A most important item in this regard also is the constitutional reservation of rights on the part of the Annual Conferences. As the "basic body in the church," the Annual Conference has "reserved to it . . . such other rights *as have not been delegated to the General Conference* under the Constitution." [10] This is a most important and far-reaching reservation, and throws into sharper focus the list of powers now specifically given to the General Conference.

There is one right which neither the General Conference nor Annual Conferences possess under the constitution, namely, to alter the number, names, and boundaries of the Annual Conferences. This is a power reserved to the Jurisdictional Conferences in the United States and to the Central Conferences outside the United States.[11] The framers of the present constitution might have noted this exception when they reserved to the Annual Conferences *all* rights not given to the General Conference.

It is thus clear that the constitution of 1939 of The Methodist Church is very different from that of 1808. Before 1939 the General Conference had all powers not specifically denied it. In 1939 it was given full legisla-

[9] Constitution, Div. II, Sec. I, Art. IV.
[10] *Ibid.*, Sec. VII, Art. II.
[11] *Ibid.*, Sec. VIII, Art. IV.

tive power but only over connectional matters, which matters were carefully outlined in thirteen specific paragraphs. The fourteenth paragraph does open the door to wider action by allowing the General Conference to enact "such other legislation as may be necessary, subject to the limitations and restrictions of the Constitution of the church." What this "other legislation" may be, is necessarily left open—wide open, some able authorities hold.

The old Restrictive Rules, as these have been slightly amended (and with former second rule omitted), are inserted in the constitution of the present church, but they follow the positive directions just shown, and, as has been indicated, simply regulate negatively the General Conference, which is itself treated in only a part of the constitution.

No power has been given to the General Conference to elect any bishops or general church officers, except members of the Judicial Council, minor boards, and certain members of boards. It "selects," not "elects," its own presiding officers from the bishops, through a committee. The bishops have no control over the personnel of such presidency except at the opening session of each General Conference.[12] The General Conference does, of course, elect its own officers, secretaries, committees, and the like, and elects the members of the Judicial Council according to well-drawn regulations.

It is to be noted also that all judicial power has been taken from the General Conference and is now vested in the Judicial Council. The conference cannot now pass upon any question of ecclesiastical or Methodist law. It can, however, determine its own parliamentary practice and parliamentary law, and may sustain or reverse the ruling of its chairmen in this field, when properly appealed to.

[12] *Ibid.*, Sec. I, Art. IV (11).

VIII

CONSTITUTIONAL CHANGE AND AMENDMENT

*Amendments to the Constitution may originate in either
the General Conference or an Annual Conference.*
—Constitution, Div. II, Sec. III (1)

THE PROCESS OF AMENDING THE CONSTITUTION OF THE METH-
odist Episcopal Church, or churches, has been so closely interwound with
the formation of the delegated General Conference and subsequent General Conferences that it is best studied in connection with these.

It was evidently in the minds of the fathers of 1808 that the "restrictions" which were then put by the creating church upon the General
Conference might themselves, in process of time, become onerous or
obsolete. And since there was no possibility under these restrictions
of any General Conference doing anything to modify them, a method
was provided by which the restrictions might be altered should need
arise, but only by the creating power itself: "Provided nevertheless, that
upon the joint recommendation of all the annual conferences, then a
majority of two-thirds of the general conference succeeding, shall suffice
to alter any of the above restrictions." [1]

Up to this point, as has been made clear, the sovereignty in the Methodist Episcopal Church had resided beyond question in the entire body
of traveling ministers. These ministers were now turning over their
power, under certain restrictions and stipulations, to the quadrennial
General Conference which they were creating. If the restrictions and
stipulations which they insisted upon, as a prerequisite to giving up their
rights, should be thought worthy of change or alteration in future, they
intended to be the originators and proposers of such alteration. But they
referred to themselves in this connection not as a body of traveling
ministers, but as "the Annual Conferences." Action in case of a proposed amendment was to come from these "conferences." Furthermore,
every conference had to concur in any recommendation counseling
change, and a majority of one in any Annual Conference could block
the unanimous recommendation of all the members of all the other

[1] *Discipline*, 1808, p. 16.

conferences. The brethren of 1808 certainly intended that their restrictions should restrict.

This almost immovable situation became embarrassing when the growth of the church began to demand a change in the Second Restrictive Rule. That rule, it was clear, should be amended so as to keep the General Conference from being too large, as would have been the case if one delegate were allowed for every five conference members. But to amend the rule required unanimous action of all the Annual Conferences, action which the General Conference itself could not propose. This awkward situation was resolved after some years by the passage of an amendment which was itself a method of amending the Restrictive Rules.

The General Conference, as has been said, had no power to do this or even to propose a change. But in 1828 it cut the Gordian knot by "suggesting" to the several Annual Conferences

the propriety of recommending to the next General Conference so to alter and amend the rules of our *Discipline*, by which the General Conference is restricted in its powers to make rules and regulations for the Church, commonly called the Restrictive Rules, as to make the proviso at the close of said Restrictive Rules, No. 6, read thus:—

Provided, nevertheless, that upon the concurrent recommendation of three-fourths of all the members of the several annual conferences who shall be present and vote on such recommendation, then a majority of two-thirds of the General Conference succeeding shall suffice to alter any of such regulations excepting the first article.

And, also, whenever such alteration or alterations shall have first been recommended by two-thirds of the General Conference, so soon as three-fourths of the members of the annual conferences shall have concurred with such recommendation, as aforesaid, such alteration or alterations shall take effect.[2]

The General Conference adopted this proposal and, by inference at any rate, implied that the bishops should see that this matter was brought to the attention of the several Annual Conferences.

This was done and the conferences in due time concurred, although for years there was a question regarding the action of the Illinois Conference, which was doubtful or unrecorded.[3] Nevertheless it was reported to the General Conference of 1832 that the measure had properly passed

[2] *Journals*, I, 353-54.
[3] Thomas B. Neely, *The Governing Conference in Methodism* (1892), pp. 402-3.

all the conferences, and forthwith it was written into the book of *Discipline*.

There are one or two minor variations between the language of this proviso as the *Discipline* of 1832 and as all subsequent *Disciplines* show it, as over against the exact language which the General Conference of 1828 passed and asked the conferences to vote upon. "Any of such regulations" became "any of the above restrictions"; "members of the Annual Conferences" became "members of all the Annual Conferences"; "shall have concurred, as aforesaid, with such recommendation, such alteration or alterations shall take effect" became "shall have concurred as aforesaid, such alteration or alterations shall take effect." Bishop Neely states that these alterations "are more interesting than material in a legal sense," since the General Conference of 1832 accepted this form as final. But Bishop Neely also asks the pertinent question: "Who presumed to alter the proposition of 1828 even in the slightest particular?" [4]

This entire constitutional change was at the instance of the able and useful Wilbur Fisk, with William Winans, of Mississippi, in strong support. It did several valuable things. It allowed the General Conference, as well as the Annual Conferences, to initiate constitutional changes; it recognized the entire body of ministers, not their conference organizations, as the sovereign power; and it forced these ministers to "be present and voting" to qualify as electors. "Three fourths of all the members of the Annual Conferences, present and voting."

This amendment of 1832 also made a distinction between the "first article"—universally understood to be the First Restrictive Rule—and the other rules. The first rule referred to doctrine and specifically excepted Methodist doctrinal standards from any action by the General Conference. Before 1832 any of the restrictions of the famous six could have been abrogated or changed by joint and unanimous action of all the Annual Conferences. After 1832 the last five rules could be amended by the process which has been indicated, but the First "Article" could not be. It remained under the almost immovable regulation of 1808, so Bishop Tigert held. Doctrine was almost completely sacrosanct. Bishop Neely suggested as late as 1892 that the only way for the church to alter any of its doctrinal statements or standards would be first to amend the proviso of 1832 by striking out the words "except the First article," and so get this out by constitutional action, then make the proposition to alter the particular doctrinal affirmation or matter which the church

[4] *Ibid.,* p. 405.

112

might wish to alter, and alter that by another constitutional vote.[5] Bishop Tigert, however, held that this process was of "doubtful validity" and that the old 1808 provision requiring joint recommendation of all the conferences and two thirds of the General Conference succeeding was necessary.[6] Needless to say, no serious move was ever made to alter standards of doctrine, and the language of 1832 remained in the respective *Disciplines* unchanged until church union in 1939. In the *Discipline* of the Methodist Episcopal Church, South, however, the regulation giving the bishop power to declare unconstitutional any act of the General Conference was added and inserted at this particular place.

In 1939, when the present constitution of The Methodist Church was adopted, the time-tested method and process of amending constitutional matters was continued and written into the constitution itself. The First Restrictive Rule was again kept beyond the reach of ordinary constitutional process, but not as far beyond that reach as it had been:

Amendments to the Constitution shall be made upon a two-thirds majority of the General Conference present and voting and a two-thirds majority of all the members of the several Annual Conferences present and voting, except in the case of the first Restrictive Rule, which shall require a three-fourths majority of all the members of the Annual Conferences present and voting. The vote, after being completed, shall be canvassed by the Council of Bishops, and the amendment voted upon shall become effective upon their announcement of its having received the required majority.[7]

This allows the present church, by a slightly more difficult process, to alter its fundamental law as touching, so I hold, either the language of the First Restrictive Rule, or any matter which falls under the protection of that rule. The present words "except in the case of the first Restrictive Rule" are rather broad but are clearly intended, or so it appears, to refer to any amendment or proposed amendments having to do with doctrines or standards of doctrine. Such standards are not now as far beyond the reach of regular constitutional process as they were formerly, but change or revision is made more difficult by the demand that three fourths of all Annual Conference members present and voting must today concur either in proposing such an amendment or in passing it once it is before them. Other amendments not falling under the "case of the first Restrictive Rule" require only two thirds of the Annual Conferences' vote for

[5] *Ibid.*, p. 407.
[6] John J. Tigert, A *Constitutional History of American Episcopal Methodism* (rev. ed., 1904), p. 404.
[7] Constitution, Div. II, Sec. III (2).

concurrence. It is thus seen that the present method of amending the constitution of The Methodist Church, and the Restrictive Rules in particular, is slightly less difficult than was the case before union, and the method of amending now allowed "in the case of the first Restrictive Rule" is more liberal than it was under the old constitutions of the former churches. Now it requires two thirds of a General Conference plus three fourths of the Annual Conferences, or vice versa.

There was for many years a spirited discussion among Methodist constitutional authorities as to the exact matter of the constitution of the church. The word "constitution" was used somewhat loosely by the fathers of the past, but it agreed from the study of such authorities as Bishops Joshua Soule, S. M. Merrill, T. B. Neely, J. J. Tigert, and Collins Denny that the whole section of the *Discipline* creating and setting up the General Conference ("Of The General Conference"), as well as the restrictions and provisos relating to the amending of those restrictions— all of it was truly constitutional and could be amended only by the due process therein provided. Indeed the General Conference of the Methodist Episcopal Church in 1892 decided by the adoption of the so-called "Goucher substitute" that the constitution of the church was in substance the section of the *Discipline* of 1808 "together with such modifications as have been adopted since that time in accordance with the provisions for amendment in that section." [8]

To settle this matter and to provide a formal document about which there could be no question, the Methodist Episcopal Church adopted a rather brief well-integrated constitution in 1900. This instrument was frankly recognized as a verbal alteration and positive restatement of Methodist fundamental law, and as such was referred to the Annual Conferences for their adoption. The necessary processes having been followed out, in due time this constitution was adopted and appeared first in the *Discipline* of 1900. It remained unaltered until 1939 when the Plan of Union, or constitution of The Methodist Church, was adopted in the same way.

The Methodist Episcopal Church, South, held to the old 1808 General Conference section of the *Discipline*, and the amendments which had been added thereto by constitutional process, as its fundamental law. The General Conference of 1930 considered a well-drawn constitution, and reviewed and amended it item by item with the intent to adopt it by the necessary two-thirds majority and send it down to the Annual Conferences for their action. But the document failed to get the neces-

[9] *Journal*, 1892, pp. 206, 228.

sary two-thirds majority and so came to nothing, except for the Judicial Council feature which was separately passed, referred to the Annual Conferences, and adopted.

The Methodist Protestant Church began with a written constitution. The *Discipline* of that church was always entitled *The Constitution and Discipline of the Methodist Protestant Church*. It was amended from time to time by its own well-stated processes, the most important change being that of 1920 when an executive committee was created which had many of the powers of the General Conference ad interim.

The present church frankly adopted a Plan of Union by constitutional process in each of its three constituent churches, and thereby established a written constitution for The Methodist Church. In the *Discipline* of 1944 the Plan of Union appears under the title "The Constitution," and the Plan of Union refers to its own provisions, in certain instances, in the words "as provided in the Constitution," or "under the Constitution." [9] Also under Section III (Amendments), it is clear that all such are amendments "to the Constitution," and are to be made in the time-honored way. Not a word or a line in the Plan of Union adopted and put into effect by The Methodist Church at the time of union can therefore be altered except by constitutional process. The Plan of Union became, and now is, the constitution of The Methodist Church.

[9] Div. II, Sec. VII, Art. II. *Vide Journal*, 1939, Uniting Conference, Declaration of Union, p. 399.

IX

LAY REPRESENTATION

The General Conference shall be composed of not less than
600 nor more than 800 delegates, one half of whom shall be ministers and one half lay members, to be elected by the Annual
Conferences.

—Constitution, Div. II, Sec. I, Art. I

AN EPOCHAL CHANGE WAS MADE IN THE STRUCTURAL ORGANIZATION OF
the Methodist Episcopal churches when lay representation came about in
both Annual and General Conferences. This embodied the old principle
for which the Methodist Protestant fathers had waged their fight, and
upon which, to a great degree, they had formed their church. After their
withdrawal in 1828, the Methodist Episcopal connection for a few years
heard little more within its own fold concerning lay representation. But
the principle was a valid one, and the years began to show the incon-
gruity of a Protestant church composed of millions of loyal members and
living in a democratic country who had no voice whatever in the management of their own beloved organization.

As early as 1840 "certain abolitionists," as Dr. James Porter called
them in his *History of Methodism*, renewed the call for lay representation. But the General Conference of that year took the findings of a
committee which it appointed, and declared that was "not expedient to
change the form of our church government in any of the matters suggested." [1] By 1852 the protagonists of lay representation had got little
farther when another committee, chairmanned by Dr. Matthew Simpson,
later bishop, reported it "inexpedient so to alter the economy of our
church as to introduce lay representation into the General and Annual
Conferences." [2] Only three votes were cast against the Simpson report.

In 1860 the bishops of the Methodist Episcopal Church referred to
the matter in their Episcopal Address but did not make any recommendation. The conference itself, however, appointed a committee again, and
this committee recommended that the matter be submitted to the Annual Conferences and to all "male members" of the church who were

[1] Journals, II, 75.
[2] Journals, III, 147-48.

over twenty-one years of age. This last somewhat irregular proceeding was carried out and, according to the report by the bishops in 1864, showed that 28,884 "male members" were in favor of lay representation; 47,885 against it. The preachers, or conference members, registered 1,338 for; 3,069 against.[3] Thus it lost again.

The *Methodist*, founded in 1861 and published at New York, became an organ of those who wanted lay representation. It was ably edited by G. R. Crooks, and its influence was enormous in ultimately securing the adoption of this change in the Methodist Episcopal Church.

In 1868 there was considerable agitation in the General Conference over the result of this ballot. Sentiment favoring lay representation had apparently grown during the balloting, for the conference appointed a committee again, but this time with frank instructions to prepare a "plan." [4] The plan, drawn up pursuant to this mandate, dealt solely with lay representation in the General Conference, not in the Annual Conferences, and called for two lay delegates to represent each Annual Conference in the General Conference. These two were to be chosen by an "electoral conference" of laymen, who should in turn be elected to such electoral conference by the respective Quarterly Conferences.

Meanwhile, in a vigorous tract for the times, James Porter in 1867 attacked the proposal for lay delegation under the title "Lay Representation in the Methodist Episcopal Church Calmly Considered." That Dr. Porter felt the weight of the old contention that laymen have no voice at all in the management of the church is indicated by his attempted rebuttal of this argument. He affirmed: (1) That the minister had no more control over matters of doctrine and doctrinal standards than have the people (because the First Restrictive Rule blocked any change in doctrine). (2) That in matters of education and church-related colleges, the laity on boards of trustees, and not the ministers, are in positions of authority. (3) That in managing as well as in subscribing the benevolences of the church, the lay voice through lay representation on committees and in administrative work is vastly important.

But in spite of Dr. Porter and his not very impressive arguments, the time had come for the Methodist Episcopal Church to admit laymen to its conferences and councils. The 1868 General Conference directed that its plan for lay representation be put before all the members of the church, lay as well as clerical, for approval or disapproval.

[3] *Journal*, 1864, p. 278.
[4] *Journal*, 1868, pp. 264-65.

There shall be held a general election in the several places of worship of the Methodist Episcopal Church, at which all members in full connection and not less than twenty-one years of age, shall be invited to vote by ballot "For Lay Delegation" or "Against Lay Delegation." [5]

As it turned out, a majority of those who voted in the church polling places during the quadrennium were for lay representation—by a two to one vote. But this vote was advisory only. The ministerial ballot on the actual written plan, whereby the Second Restrictive Rule was to be altered so as to admit laymen, was the deciding factor. This vote, according to Bishop Simpson reporting to the General Conference of 1872, stood: for the proposed change, 4,915; against it, 1,597. After prolonged discussion the General Conference adopted a formal motion to concur with the action of the Annual Conference members in altering the Second Restrictive Rule as provided, and the constitutional majority was at once given.[6]

This might have been expected to settle the matter but grave questions were at once raised concerning the difference in language between the resolution passed by the Annual Conferences and that adopted by the General Conference. There was also injected the argument that the lay people of the church had voted for the principle of lay representation, not upon a definite plan, as had the preachers. Meanwhile certain lay delegates had actually been elected and had come to the General Conference with the expectation of being seated. A resolution to seat them, however, was coupled with a statement that it was "understood that the General Conference, as thus constituted [i.e., according to the "plan" held to be adopted] may at any time alter or amend the same, and cause such alteration or amendment to take immediate effect." [7] This collateral argument was reversing the sovereignty of the church with a vengeance and would, if agreed to, as Bishop Neely explains, "put only the Restrictive Rules beyond the sole control of the General Conference." [8] This "Kynett resolution" was therefore wisely laid on the table. Subsequently, however, after the parliamentary language and situation had been straightened, the lay delegates who were present and who had the proper credentials were seated as members of the conference.

The plan of lay representation as adopted by the General Confer-

[5] Thomas B. Neely, *The Governing Conference in Methodism* (1892), p. 424; see also *Discipline*, 1868, Appendix.

[6] *Journal*, 1872, pp. 44-46.

[7] *Journal*, 1872, p. 43.

[8] *Op. cit.*, p. 429.

ence of 1872 provided for two lay delegates from each Annual Conference, except where a conference had only one clerical delegate, and in such cases only one lay delegate was allowed. Lay and clerical members were to deliberate as one body but vote separately, if such separate vote should be called for by one third of either order. In such cases both orders had to concur to complete the action.[9]

General Conference lay delegates were to be elected by an electoral conference of laymen, which was to assemble on the third day of the session of the Annual Conference held previous to a General Conference. The electoral conference was to be made up of one layman from each circuit or station, and each must be over twenty-five years of age, and must have been a member of the church for five years.

Thus was lay representation in the General Conference introduced into the Methodist Episcopal Church. The above provisions continued with slight modification until 1900 when that church adopted a constitution. The election of lay delegates was at that time put in the hands of a regular lay conference which was then established. This lay conference, as established in 1900, was something more than the old lay electoral conference which met only once every four years. It was in effect a parallel conference to that of the ministers, and was established for the purpose of "voting on constitutional amendments," considering and acting upon matters relating to lay activities, and such other matters as the General Conference might direct. One lay member from each pastoral charge was to be elected to the lay conference by the suffrage of all the lay members who were over twenty-one years of age. Clerical and lay members were to meet in united sessions for certain parts of the joint program, and to divide into separate bodies to carry on the specific task committed to each.[10]

It is thus clear that lay delegation came about slowly and by two successive moves in the Methodist Episcopal connection. One move in 1872 admitted laymen to the General Conference; another in 1900 admitted them collaterally to the Annual Conference by establishing in parallel with the Annual Conference a lay conference. But members of the lay conference were never actually members of the Annual Conference, either in name or in actuality.

Bishop Neely, commenting upon all this, said:

The admission of laymen to the General Conference has been pronounced the most remarkable instance of the voluntary relinquishment of power to

[9] *Journal*, 1872, pp. 44-46.
[10] M. E. Constitution, Div. III, Art. IV.

be found in the history of the world. The clergy were under no compulsion to give up the authority they had from the beginning, and yet they voluntarily admitted the laity into the supreme legislative body of the Church to share with them the vast powers of the General Conference.[11]

In the Methodist Episcopal Church, South

In the Methodist Episcopal Church, South, lay representation came at about the same date as in the Methodist Episcopal Church, but in both the Annual and the General Conferences. In 1866, that critical and revolutionary year for Southern Methodism, a special committee was created to report at the General Conference upon the matter of lay representation. The committee recommended it in a provision that would admit laymen to the General Conference in equal numbers with ministers; and recommended that four lay representatives should be elected to each Annual Conference from each presiding elder's district; and that these four be elected by the newly established District Conference. It was further provided that one of the men might be a local preacher. It was specifically stated that the lay members were not to vote upon ministerial qualifications or character. Dr. Holland N. McTyeire, later bishop, brought in the report for the committee.

Strong opposition immediately developed. Dr. John C. Keener, later bishop, endeavored to refer the committee's report to the Annual Conferences for their action, but to this it was objected that the Annual Conferences had been discussing this matter for some time and that the special committee was embodying the best common judgment to that date. Another blocking move was made by N. H. D. Wilson, of the Baltimore Conference, who stated that he wished no restrictions at all upon the lay delegates; that they be allowed to vote on ministerial qualifications and everything else, just as did other members of the conference. All substitute motions, however, were laid upon the table.

In the debate which then developed considerable attention was called to the fact that the laymen were not to be allowed to participate in voting upon ministerial qualifications. Dr. Keener renewed his attack upon the whole proposal, saying that the responsibility of the church had proceeded always from an ordained ministry: "The Apostle Paul says you have ten thousand instructors in Christ but not many fathers." Dr. Keener, yielding somewhat, finally said he would agree to allow two laymen from each presiding elder's district, but not four.

Dr. McTyeire defended his report by saying that it was "a compro-

[11] *Op. cit.*, p. 134.

mise," and that he felt that four lay delegates from each district, who would not be allowed to vote upon ministerial qualifications, would give the laity of the church the representation it would need in the Annual Conferences. Whereupon Leonidas Rosser, of Virginia, arose and spoke vehemently against the whole proposition: "If the laity had had the inalienable and original right to create the ministerial office . . . I would then concede that the laity have a right to legislate for me as a minister of God. I will never consent that any layman, though he be as pure as an angel, shall decide upon my ministerial character." The Rev. Guilford Jones offered the objection that "you cannot get intelligent laymen to come to our General Conference"—that prominent laymen were all busy and would never take the time to attend. Dr. A. L. P. Green spoke for the report. H. H. Montgomery offered an amendment providing that the lay delegates at the General Conference should be one half the number of the clerical delegates, not equal to them. This amendment, however, was voted down and the house adopted the McTyeire report by a good majority.[12]

In the Methodist Episcopal Church, South, the ratio of lay representation in the Annual Conferences was changed later (in 1914) to provide for eight delegates from each presiding elder's district; and then in 1926 it became one lay delegate for every 800 church members. This last was an endeavor to provide for lay representation on a numerical basis, and it had the effect of giving the larger churches an opportunity to claim—or seek to elect through the District Conference—more than one delegate. This principle was done away by the Plan of Union, in which one delegate from each pastor's charge, irrespective of the size of that charge, was provided for. So the law now stands.

LAY RIGHTS FOR WOMEN

Paralleling the demand for lay representation, or perhaps following its successful implementation, came the movement for equal lay rights on the part of women members of the respective Methodist churches. In 1888 at the General Conference of the Methodist Episcopal Church, five women were elected members by as many lay electoral conferences—among them Frances E. Willard, who had been elected by the Rock River Conference. Prolonged debate ensued as to whether women were eligible to sit in electoral conferences or in the General Conference. As it turned out, the women who appeared at the conference in 1888 were

[12] *Journal*, 1866, p. 109.

not seated, but this rebuff stirred the church during the ensuing quadrennium.

In 1892 no women appeared as delegates, though two had been elected as alternates. The Committee on Judiciary, however, in giving an official definition to the words "laymen" and "lay delegates," reported that these words applied to men only. This ruling caused a storm, and Dr. J. W. Hamilton, later a bishop, moved to submit to the Annual Conferences an ingenious proposition to amend the second Restrictive Rule so that this rule would state positively concerning lay delegates that "said delegates must be male members," with the purpose that, when this amendment failed, the original wording might be interpreted as making no sex discrimination.

This amendment caused much confusion during the quadrennium, and a number of Annual Conferences refused to vote on it at all. Thereupon the Colorado Annual Conference proposed an amendment which affirmed directly that "delegates may be either men or women." This Colorado amendment was defeated by a very slim margin.[13]

Four women were elected delegates to the General Conference of 1896, and at this conference a stormy debate came on with reference to the eligibility of women. A "compromise" plan was finally worked out, but in the meantime the four women who had been elected delegates and whose names appear on the official roll had withdrawn directly or indirectly from sitting in the conference. However, their expenses were paid like those of all other delegates.

The matter was again held in abeyance as the proposed new constitution for the Methodist Episcopal Church was about to be voted on, and this document itself granted "equal laity rights to women." In 1900, therefore, when the constitution was accepted by the church, all measures for which the women had been contending were successfully obtained. Ordination of women was a question which arose later, and is somewhat apart from laity rights as such.

In the Methodist Episcopal Church, South, a somewhat similar course was pursued regarding conference rights for women, but here also constitutional action was required before the end was attained. In 1914 there was a heated debate over a memorial asking that women be allowed to become stewards and to hold other representative positions in the church. The General Conference sustained the committee which refused to concur in the memorial. But in 1918 the General Conference

[13] James M. Buckley, *Constitutional and Parliamentary History of the Methodist Episcopal Church* (1912), p. 311.

approved the same proposal by a large majority. At this the bishops of the Southern church laid down an episcopal check, holding that the General Conference had exceeded its powers and contravened the constitution of the church by this enactment.[14] Whereupon the General Conference passed the measure again by the constitutional majority and sent it down to the Annual Conferences. These gave an overwhelming vote in favor of the proposal (4,280 to 467), and at the General Conference of 1922 the bishops reported that "lay rights for women" had been written into the constitution.[15]

In both the Methodist Episcopal churches, as well as in the Methodist Protestant Church, women thereafter were elected from time to time to all and every conference. Needless to say, they were able and efficient members, as have been the women delegates elected to the Annual and General Conferences of The Methodist Church. In the present church, of course, women members have all the rights of laymen and are eligible for license to preach and ordination. They cannot, however, be admitted to the traveling ministry.

[14] Journal, 1918, p. 145.
[15] Journal, 1922, p. 62.

X

ORGANIZATION AND PROCEDURE

*The General Conference shall meet in the month of April
or May once in four years.*
— Constitution, Div. II, Sec. I, Art. II

THE PRESENT GENERAL CONFERENCE DOES ITS WORK PRINCIPALLY
through committees which in turn report their recommendations and
resolutions to the Conference for final action. Certain important committees are today very large since every Annual Conference delegation is
directed to place upon each of the major legislative committees two persons, one clerical and the other lay. At the first two General Conferences
of The Methodist Church the rules of organization adopted by that
body provided for two series of committees, one legislative, the other administrative. There were approximately twenty-five committees—adding
both series. The conference created the following general committees
in order: (1) Membership, Lay Activities and Temporal Economy; (2)
Ministry; (3) Education; (4) Missions and Church Extension; (5) Publishing Interests; (6) Conference Claimants; (7) Conferences; (8) State
of the Church.[1]

Upon these committees, which were the first eight legislative committees, each Annual Conference was required to place one clerical and one
lay delegate, to be chosen by the respective Annual Conference delegations, and their names reported in advance so that a proper committee
roll could be prepared.

The other legislative committees and all the administrative committees were provided for, but with no requirement that there be two representatives from each Annual Conference. These committees differ in
size, and there are different methods of nominating their members, and
so forth. Almost all the administrative committees were created upon
nomination of the Council of Bishops, though some were made by
appointment or nomination from the separate jurisdictions, while the
"Committee of Chairmen" (that is, the chairmen of the separate committees) naturally would be an ex officio creation of the several committees' own action.

[1] *Journal*, 1940, p. 134.

Each General Conference committee organizes under carefully prescribed rules and elects a chairman, vice-chairman, and secretary. Each has before it, after organization, all memorials, resolutions, and the like, relating to its special subject, as these have come to the General Conference and ask or suggest legislative amendment or revision. Such recommendations for specific action as the bishops may make in the Episcopal Address with which they traditionally open each General Conference are usually referred to the "appropriate committee."

In practice the large committees often break into subcommittees, and even into smaller ones when this seems desirable. Memorials, that is, formal requests for definite action, pour in upon the present-day General Conference and come from all sorts of organizations and groups throughout the church. Memorials may even come from an individual in certain instances if such a person can present in proper form what is patently a well-wrought plea. All memorials which are received are referred to the proper committee and are to be acted upon by that committee; and either "concurrence," or "nonconcurrence" may be voted regarding each one, or such action taken as may be decided by the committee. Memorials concurred in, as well as those nonconcurred in, are furnished in quadruplicate to the secretary of the General Conference, who in turn gives them to the clerk of the calendar who sees that they are printed in the *Daily Christian Advocate* (the paper and work sheet of the conference) in the order in which he receives them. Reports on memorials nonconcurred in are printed just as are those indicating concurrence. However, when a proposal receives nonconcurrence, unless there is a minority report, or unless some person is able to call the matter up from the floor, or propose its substance as an amendment to another report, it gets nowhere. Former practice was to have a blanket report covering all nonconcurrence memorials at one time.

Each memorial concurred in, as well as other formal resolutions and reports, is given a calendar number. Thus when the General Conference, after the committees have begun to report, can "take up the calendar," the legislative wheels really begin to move. As reports are called for, the chairmen of the respective committees present them, or have some other person do so for the committee. If there is a minority report this is presented at the time and as a substitute for the report of the majority. Any pending report is, of course, subject to amendment. The house determines what its action shall be, and this is recorded in the conference *Journal* and later goes into the *Discipline* itself when actual legislation is accomplished.

The above paragraphs furnish in brief outline the practice of the General Conference in the actual process of managing its own work in providing laws and regulations for the church. Within these few pages it is impossible to cover the manifold activities of this great body or even to sketch in bare outline its multitudinous duties. Sufficient has been written, however, to make it clear that this is a truly representative body and that its legal processes, vast as they are, are flexible enough to allow for every type of expression and desire on the part of Methodist people. Reference may be made to a copy of the General Conference *Journal* or files of the *Daily Christian Advocate* to appreciate more fully these processes.

Committees on Episcopacy

Significantly enough, the General Conference of The Methodist Church has no Committee on Episcopacy. All matters affecting the bishops in the present General Conference are taken care of by the Committee on Ministry. But in the former Episcopal Methodist churches the Committee on Episcopacy was the prime committee of the church. Created by the General Conference during the early years of the Methodist Episcopal Church, it became in episcopal Methodism, long before the break of 1844, the most important committee at any General Conference session. Upon it, by common custom, the leaders of each conference delegation served, and to it were referred—in some instances, with complete power—all matters affecting the bishops. It examined the character of each one, determined who were to be continued "effective," recommended those who were to be allowed to "cease to travel," recommended the number of new bishops to be elected, fixed during later years the salaries of the active bishops and the allowance of retired ones, and fixed, or had great weight in fixing, the areas where each bishop was to serve for the ensuing quadrennium.

In the Methodist Episcopal Church, South, the Committee on Episcopacy could only recommend to the bishops regarding the area in which each bishop should serve during the coming quadrennium. In the Methodist Episcopal Church, however, after a long series of General Conference enactments that body was able at length, through its Committee on Episcopacy, to make its will practically accepted in this regard.

In The Methodist Church today the plan of "presidential and residential" supervision is referred to by the General Conference in connection with the episcopal supervision of mission lands, but since the bishops are now amenable to their respective Jurisdictional Conferences, the

General Conference assumes no power to assign or legislate regarding specific areas. The bishops of each Jurisdictional and Central Conference, as has been shown, arrange the plan of episcopal supervision of the Annual Conferences, Mission Conferences, and Missions within their respective territories.[2] However, a Jurisdictional Conference's standing Committee on Episcopacy enjoys many of the great powers of the old Committee on Episcopacy of the two episcopal Methodisms. It can station the bishops individually, though it may not define their Annual Conference areas.[3] It can, of course, recommend concerning such areas, and the final plan of episcopal supervision must be reported to the Jurisdictional Conference itself for its records.

The lack of a Committee on Episcopacy in the General Conference, and that body's inability to elect bishops or to elect general church officers, or to do many things which it might do in its former days, makes it clear that the General Conference today is not the sovereign power which once it was. The jurisdictions of the church and the Judicial Council have both, as new institutions, taken over a great share of the former omnipotence of the General Conference. But with all that, the General Conference is today a vast and impressive lawmaking body.

What it has lost in relation to its past supremacy in the three uniting Methodist churches, it has gained by becoming dominant over their combined might; and, although shorn of some of its former strength by the Plan of Union, the General Conference of The Methodist Church is today, as it always has been, the most powerful organization in that church, and one of the most potent ecclesiastical organizations of the whole world.

[2] Constitution, Div. III, Art. IV.
[3] Discipline, 1944, ¶ 532.

XI

THE ANNUAL CONFERENCE

*There shall be Annual Conferences as the fundamental
bodies in the church, with such powers, duties, and privileges
as are hereinafter set forth.*

—Constitution, Div. II (4)

AFTER 1784, AS YEARLY MEETINGS GREW IN SIZE AND AS METHODISM
spread, the Annual Conference, as an organic unity in its own geographic
and unitary right, appeared. But the line between early Annual Conferences held in one special region, and what were called "general conferences" of the whole church, is necessarily difficult to draw. Indeed it is
hard to decide in the case of certain conferences held after 1784, whether
they were "general," as the Christmas Conference of 1784 was said to be
general, or were simply the "annual meeting" of such preachers as might
be able to attend. The whole epoch, with its various conference meetings, minutes, and lack of minutes, provides a field for speculation as
well as knowledge.

But after a time, certainly after 1792, the development of the Annual
Conference begins, not merely as a geographical unit but as a solid,
irreducible entity in its own right. "The conference" soon came to mean
to every preacher something more than an annual gathering. It was an
association of brethren who served in a definite region and felt themselves bound together in the most sacred task given to men on earth.
Each man knew himself called to his work, and knew that he was asso-
ciating also with a chosen group.

Certain novel features of Annual Conference structure may here profitably be noticed.

The Annual Conference from the first has been the minister's church.
His name is on its roll and before its bar he stands for appraisal by his
brethren, for blame or praise. At its sessions he gets his assignment for
work, and when he is retired it is upon its roll that his name is kept as an
honored superannuate. Once a year the name of each conference member
is read in open session of the conference, or checked over carefully, that
the character of each may be examined and passed. If there are any
charges to be made against any one, the character of the man in ques-

128

tion is "arrested" or held up until the judicial processes of the church, working through that man's conference peers, can be properly brought to bear. The usual preacher enters the conference as a youth and remains in it for life. Its fellowship becomes increasingly dear to him with the passage of time, and as the different conferences develop their own special attitudes of thought, and those inconsequential but characteristic ways of doing things, which speak of a corporate individuality, the members themselves seem to partake of the same characteristics which enwrap all.

The fellowship of the conference brotherhood becomes something exceedingly precious to the preachers who compose it. They should, and usually do, jealously guard its portals, and while the form of admission may grow routine, every conference expects its committee on admissions, now technically known as the Committee on Conference Relations and Ministerial Qualifications, to give much more than perfunctory attention to the candidates who come seeking entrance.

As time passes each minister gets to know the special field of labor and type of appointment his conference serves, the history of its past, the men who have labored before him, as well as those who are his comrades in the work. When he gets too old for active service or is incapacitated in some physical way, he becomes a pensioner on the conference roll, receiving whatever the general church and his own conference feel able to give him in the way of a stipend. When he dies his name is reverently called at the ensuing session of the conference and a brief tribute read concerning his life and labors. For all these reasons the Annual Conference comes to be in the mind of the individual minister the prime organization to which he can give his life, and through which he expresses his ministry.

Membership in an Annual Conference gives to each minister two great privileges and powers which are fundamental in Methodist polity. These powers are: The right to pass judgment upon all who seek membership in the conference itself, which means admission to the traveling ministry and usually to the ministerial orders of the church; and the power of exercising the sovereignty of the church whenever a constitutional change or move is pending. This last is also a privilege of lay members of the Annual Conference. Lay members, however, are not allowed to vote on admitting ministerial members.

Ministerial conference members have from the first been able to vote upon the qualifications of new members, and to act therefore as the gatekeepers of the ministry. This right we have seen to inhere in the first gathering of Methodist preachers, when the group which had been called together by Wesley decided to admit laymen to their company. It is the inalienable right of every organized body to judge of the qualifications of its own members, and this right has therefore always been claimed by every ministerial brotherhood. While the Methodists were no more than a society within the Church of England, admission to conference membership entailed nothing more comprehensive than that the candidate for admission should be examined according to the form prescribed by Wesley, in which certain questions were asked of the candidate touching his faith, his gifts, and his attitude toward Methodist rules and practices. The questions formulated for this purpose by John Wesley are yet asked of all ministers who are admitted into "full connection" in the Methodist ministry. They remain today the distinctive Methodist test for admission to the Methodist preacherhood.[1]

But when Wesley first proposed these questions to candidates for his ministry, it was assumed that such persons had already given proof of their devotion to the articles of the Christian faith, and were therefore good churchmen. It was not then anticipated that such persons, who rated as laymen (even perhaps in Wesley's mind), would ever be called to orders in a church, and indeed most of the preachers of Wesley's England never could have been. But before a Methodist "preacher" could stand before his brethren and be given their hand of fellowship and be empowered to preach the gospel as one of them, he must certify that he had faith in Christ, and that he was "expecting"—that was a cardinal Methodist test—to be made "perfect in love in this life." He also had to certify, among other things, that he was not embarrassingly in debt, and that he both knew and believed in "the Methodist doctrine." Answers of a proper sort having been given, the man was admitted.

But when Methodism in America became a church in 1784, something more was called for—an ordained ministry, not merely a specially admitted Methodist preacherhood, living under the aegis of another ecclesiasticism. Therefore Wesley provided, in the Sunday Service, forms for ordination which perpetuated two orders of ministers in the Methodist Episcopal Church. These orders, as far as outward vows and investiture are concerned, were almost exact replicas of the two lower orders of the Church of England. They are the Order of Deacons, and the Order of Elders (which latter is called the Order of Priests in the Church of England).

In accordance with this plan the Christmas Conference chose certain

[1] *Discipline*, 1944, ¶ 1923.

men to be ordained "elders." The actual ordination of the chosen men followed an election by the conference, though the ordination itself was according to the rite sent over by Wesley for that purpose. From that day to this, Methodist conferences—at first general, then annual—have assumed and exercised the right to elect men to orders, as well as to elect them to membership in the conference body itself. Election to orders by a conference must precede the actual ordination by a bishop; and every bishop is careful to state in the parchment of ordination given to the ordinand the name of the empowering authority which has given him the right to ordain.

This is a tremendous power which the Annual Conference in Methodism has always enjoyed and which it enjoys to this day. It is conceivable that any General Conference, as having full powers over all connectional matters (and the General Conference before 1939 had all powers not denied to it), could do as did the Christmas Conference—elect men to orders. But such a proceeding would be impracticable, if not disallowed, by force of Methodist common-law practice.

During the First World War the General Conference of the Methodist Episcopal Church, South, gave the right to its War Work Commission to select and certify properly qualified young men for the army and navy chaplaincy, and it empowered bishops to ordain such men for military or naval service. Also, under the so-called "missionary rule," the General Conference of the Methodist Episcopal Church empowered the Board of Missions to certify proper persons for ordination.[2] This was done in order that these men might proceed to the mission field without completing the four years' travel which a home conference usually requires before elders' orders are given. This rule and practice has wisely been continued in The Methodist Church, though with special provisions regarding it.[3] But these are special cases and no General Conference has ever taken from the Annual Conference its fundamental right to judge as to who shall be admitted to the ministry and orders of the church.

By constitutional enactment "lay members may not vote on matters of ordination, character, and conference relations of ministers."[4] This regulation grew out of the polity of the former Methodist Episcopal churches, in which it was made a part of their law when the laymen were first admitted to conference membership. In the Methodist Episcopal Church, since the ministers composing the Annual Conference sat

[2] *Discipline*, 1936, ¶ 533 (6).
[3] *Discipline*, 1944, ¶ 393 (5); 402 (6).
[4] Constitution, Div. II, Sec. VII, Art. II.

entirely apart from the laymen in the lay conference, matters of ministerial qualifications were referred only to the former group. But in the Methodist Episcopal Church, South, lay and clerical members sat indiscriminately together (as they do now in The Methodist Church) and it was impracticable and time consuming for the presiding bishop to attempt to separate the two orders when a vote was to be taken on admitting a young minister or to superannuate some elderly veteran. Some bishops would carefully call the attention of the body to the fact that only ministerial members were supposed to vote on such matters, but quite often the bishop, in taking care of routine proceedings, simply put the question to the whole conference with no one objecting. In fact in 1902 the College of Bishops in an episcopal decision affirmed: "The right to vote includes the right to speak, and the lay members of the Annual Conference can vote on the question, 'What traveling preachers are elected elders?' "

In The Methodist Church, as "matters of ordination" as well as of ministerial "character" are by definite constitutional law not to be voted on by laymen, who are actually members of the Annual Conference as they were in the former Methodist Episcopal Church, South, and the Methodist Protestant Church, something of the same problem which faced the Southern bishops is presented today. The Uniting Conference, in an effort to clarify this, directed that an Annual Conference "may order an executive session of the ministerial members to consider questions relating to matters of ordination, character, and conference relations." [5] But when the Southern California–Arizona Conference, on June 22, 1945, ordered an executive session under this provision, and excluded the lay members of that conference from such executive session, an issue was made of the constitutionality of the proceeding. Subsequently the conference, by unanimous vote, appealed to the Judicial Council to rule upon the legality of such executive session and the right of the General Conference to empower an Annual Conference to divide its own basic membership so as to hold an executive session under Paragraph 646 of the *Discipline*.

The Judical Council held that this matter was not properly before it for adjudication as no Annual Conference has the right to appeal to the Judicial Council concerning an action of the General Conference. Subsequently, however, the Council of Bishops made the appeal at the request of the Southern California–Arizona Conference. The Judicial Council in a long and reasoned opinion then sustained the language

[5] *Discipline*, 1944, ¶ 646; *Journal*, 1939, p. 455.

of Paragraph 646. It held, in brief, that the Annual Conference, with both laymen and ministers voting, was competent to call for an executive session of ministers if it so pleased, especially since the duty of passing on ministerial qualifications was entrusted to the ministers by the constitution. To this there was a strong dissenting opinion by H. R. Van Deusen and W. G. Henry.[6]

There is one exception to the right of an Annual Conference to control its own admissions. That is the case where a bishop transfers a minister from one Annual Conference into another. The orders and the ministerial standing of the transferred man are the responsibility of his original conference; that is, by virtue of his original admission and ordination he must be, and is, a conference member and usually an ordained elder of the church. But since the Methodist ministry is a "connection," each conference is served by, and serves all others, through its ministerial brotherhood. A bishop, therefore, who transfers a man into a conference is not under obligation to the receiving conference to allow that conference the right or power of approving or disapproving the transferred man. He assumes, and the conference assumes, that a member of any one conference is potentially a member of all, and unless there be charges pending against the character of a minister, he is subject to transfer, and by Methodist common law is received as a regular member of the conference to which he has been transferred.

As Electors

The other inherent right of each member of an Annual Conference is to act as an elector of the church. The General Conference, which makes laws for the church, is composed of persons elected to it by Annual Conference members, and when any constitutional change is pending the Annual Conference members determine whether such change shall be. Both clerical and lay members of the Annual Conference enjoy this privilege, though clerical members, being conference members for life, are *ipso facto* permanent electors of the church. Lay members of the Annual Conference are electors only in, or for, the particular conference session or sessions in which they serve. This latter fact, however, makes it possible for the lay membership of the church to influence, if not direct, the lay vote when a constitutional change has been proposed or where some momentous matter is made an issue in the church. For in such an event it is possible for lay people in the local congregations,

[6] *Opinions and Decisions*, Judicial Council of The Methodist Church (Beginning April 26, 1940), pp. 104, 125-33.

through their Quarterly Conference, to elect as their representatives men or women who will be in accord with their wishes upon such an issue or issues. To this extent the lay people of The Methodist Church can influence, or may even endeavor to direct, lay votes in the Annual, Jurisdictional, and perhaps General Conferences.

In practice, however, such an influence is rarely to be expected and is hardly ever exercised. This is chiefly because there has never been, and can scarcely be, a cleavage between clerical and lay people in Methodism, as these are all of a piece. Issues great enough to divide Methodism have usually divided both clerical and lay members proportionately, never clerical from lay. Furthermore, lay representatives are elected to the Annual Conference well in advance of any possible division over a specific issue. They are usually elected not because of some one attitude but by reason of general effectiveness and reputation. Even were there pending a possible alteration of the church's basic structure, the likelihood is that the local churches would feel that a tried-and-true lay representative would be able to protect all necessary interests as fairly and faithfully as would some new person who had become a protagonist of one or the other side. Lay desires and influence are usually and wisely registered not by isolated efforts to elect some man pledged to this or that course of conduct, but by putting in both the Annual and General Conferences upstanding laymen who thus actively and effectively exercise and take care of laity rights through and in both the bodies.

It should be emphasized again that when a constitutional change is proposed and voted upon, the members of the Annual Conferences vote as representatives of the whole church and not of the particular conference in which each happens to hold membership. The total vote of all conference members for, and the total vote against, a measure is the deciding factor, not the action or attitude of any number of conferences. Each Annual Conference acts in such cases simply as a polling place for the church's constitutional electors, not as a unit which must be "carried" in the voting.

This sovereign right—of acting as electors—exercised by Annual Conference members has, from the date of the Christmas Conference, been a distinguishing feature and privilege of American Methodist conference membership. In or with these members, therefore, resides the sovereignty of the church. For while the General Conference may take many actions of high moment, and while its action is necessary also to constitutional change, the real power to make or refuse to make such change resides where it always has—within the combined Annual Conference membership. As we have shown, in the early days that membership was entirely ministerial; then in part it became lay; and now in The Methodist Church it is almost equally divided between clerical and lay, since for every pastoral charge in the church there is also one lay member.

In actual fact, however, the Annual Conferences, because of their superannuated preachers and ministerial members in nonpastoral service, usually have more clerical than lay members on their rolls, and this in spite of the fact that many charges are served by "supplies" who are not members of the conference at all. Conference statistics, however, make plain the fact that a larger percentage of clerical than lay members attend the sessions of the Annual Conference.

The method of carrying out the principle of lay representation in the Annual Conferences of The Methodist Church was much discussed previous to arranging the Plan of Union. There were in effect three different systems in the three uniting churches, but that of the Methodist Protestant Church, of allowing each pastoral charge to have one lay representative in each Annual Conference, was finally adopted and written into the constitution of The Methodist Church. In the former Methodist Episcopal Church the lay conference, consisting of lay representatives from each charge, was not at all equivalent to the Annual Conference of ministers. The two conferences met at the same time and engaged in certain actions together; but the lay conference was not co-ordinate in power and authority with the Annual Conference. In fact, the laymen usually made a practice of taking one day during the conference session as their day, and were present in numbers on that day only.

Likewise in the Methodist Episcopal Church, South, while laymen were in actual fact members of the Annual Conference and did not sit as a separate group as the lay conference did in the Methodist Episcopal Church, they were elected on the basis of church membership in the separate presiding elders' districts, and not by pastoral charges. Southern Methodist laymen were elected to the Annual Conference not by their local congregations but by the District Conference, and under regulations which specifically limited the number of such laymen. For many years in the Methodist Episcopal Church, South, each presiding elder's district was allowed to elect eight laymen to membership in the Annual Conference, "one of whom may be a local preacher." In 1926 this was altered so as to allow one lay representative for each "800 church members or major fraction thereof in each presiding elder's district." [7] This gave the larger and more populous districts a greater representation, and in-

[7] *Journal*, 1926, p. 253.

deed increased the percentage of lay representatives in almost all the conferences of the Methodist Episcopal Church, South. In 1938, with the Plan of Union already influencing that church's action, the General Conference of the Methodist Episcopal Church, South, adopted the plan which was to be that of the united church—one layman from each pastoral charge. So it now stands in The Methodist Church and there is no more lay conference, as in the former Methodist Episcopal days.

This plan has the advantage of making each charge feel that it is a participant, through an elected representative, in all the actions of the Annual Conference. It does not, however, allow for any numerical difference between the large church and the small. The great city churches have only one lay representative, just as have the rural and smaller charges. Thus it happens that representatives of the larger churches find themselves seated in a conference where they, representing many times as many people as do the laymen from the small charges, are themselves greatly outnumbered by these laymen, since there are many more small charges than large.

It has been pointed out also that laymen in the Annual Conference, unless a constitutional change is pending or some very debatable issue is to the fore, have neither the opportunity nor the interest to take anything like a leading part. The Annual Conference, from its time-honored and necessary pattern of doing business, must perforce be concerned chiefly with ministerial actions, reports, and appointments. It is in essence a preachers' conference. It was created to be such and must necessarily remain so because of its specialized work. Its general committees, promotional plans, and work are, of course, important, and in these the laymen may, and should, find a great opportunity to serve. But conference journals and records make it clear that the routine business and important questions asked by the presiding bishop all have to do with the roster of ministers, the admission of ministers, the ordination of ministers, the reports of ministers, and the stationing of the ministers. Such actions necessarily give a character to the Annual Conference which no amount of lay interest can quite take over. Laymen elected as conference members often perceive this situation without clearly understanding it, and, after hopefully attending a few sessions, or the opening address of an Annual Conference session, and finding little to do, grow weary and often cease to attend. When, however, a change in their own local pulpit impends, a much more important matter to them seems to summon them, and then they feel that it is well to be on hand at conference for whatever may transpire.

However, the assumption often held by laymen that it is necessary for a local church to have a representative in the Annual Conference in order to manage properly the matter of pulpit supply, is not too well-founded. Appointments are made usually in advance of the conference session, and are not subject to review by any conference member as such. One layman or one hundred laymen, in or out of the conference, may approach and petition the appointive power, and the actual conference membership of one particular layman does not as a rule influence to any extent the stationing of that man's minister. It is true, of course, that a regular representative can keep a watch on all proceedings and may thus be able to take appropriate action, if and when the traditional "last minute change" in the appointments seems to be impending.

The unwieldiness of present Annual Conferences in The Methodist Church has been much complained of. This is, of course, due to the doubling of conference membership in those conferences largely made up of former Methodist Episcopal or/and Methodist Episcopal Church, South, units. The admission of one layman for every pastoral charge had the effect of doubling such bodies, and at once presented conference entertainment committees, and those in charge of the conference program, with a problem in housing, feeding, and organizing such largely increased bodies. The expense of entertaining each Annual Conference leaped accordingly, and as a consequence there has been a tendency to cut to a minimum the actual time of holding such conferences. The program has been speeded up, with necessary activities given priority, and extraneous matters pushed to the side or allotted scant attention in the effort to complete the work of the annual session on a fast time schedule. This haste has been somewhat complained of by those who were used to a more leisurely type of conference session, but it seems to be the best that can be done in view of present circumstances.

SPECIAL FEATURES AND REGULATIONS

The Annual Conference is a geographic entity as well as an organizational one. The *Discipline* carefully prescribes the boundaries of each Annual Conference,[8] and no Annual Conference (of persons) may serve or man any of the charges which are within another conference (geographic area). Changes in Annual Conference boundaries, formerly made by the General Conference, are now to be made, if in the United States,

[8] 1944, ¶ 1712-1887.

by the Jurisdictional Conferences, if outside the United States, by the Central Conferences.[9]

The geographic outline of a conference area is determinative with respect to the conference membership of the ministers who serve charges within such area. No minister may be appointed as pastor of a charge within one conference and hold his membership in another conference, unless in rare and temporary cases where a superannuated or supernumerary member of one conference (who has thereby been released from travel) is used as a "supply" within the territory of another conference.[10] When a minister is to be placed in charge of a church within another conference area than the one in which he has been serving, his conference membership must be in the conference whose charge he is to serve. He thus becomes a "transfer," his membership in the new conference dating "from the date of his transfer, unless it be especially provided otherwise by the bishop by whom the transfer is made." [11]

Ministerial members of an Annual Conference who are elected or appointed to general church or connectional work as editors, executive secretaries, teachers in schools of theology, conference executives, and the like, may keep their conference membership within the conference from which they were elected or appointed.

All ministerial members of an Annual Conference are expected and directed to be present at its annual session with their reports,[12] and so are all regularly elected lay delegates. Where the latter cannot attend, duly elected alternates are expected to take their places. The probationers and "accepted supplies" are especially directed by the Discipline to be present at the "sessions" of their conference.[13] In case a conference member or a probationer or "supply" cannot possibly attend, he is expected to report that fact, so that the secretary of the conference may have his message as a matter of record. When the conference is in session and it is necessary for a conference member to absent himself from further sessions, he must get permission from the body for such absence ("unless hindered by sickness or otherwise" is the General Conference rule for its own delegates in treating of this matter). In large conferences requests for leave of absence can best be handled through the secretary who, to save time, may present in writing all requests of this nature at once

[9] Constitution, Div. II, Sec. VIII, Art. IV.
[10] R. J. Cooke, Judicial Decisions (1918), p. 458.
[11] Osmon C. Baker, A Guidebook in the Administration of the Discipline (1873), p. 49.
[12] Discipline, 1944, ¶ 636.
[13] Ibid.

A bishop presides over each Annual Conference, but if no bishop be present, the conference "shall by ballot, without nomination or debate, elect a president from among the traveling elders. The president thus elected shall discharge all the duties of a bishop except ordination." [14] Formerly, when a bishop could not be present to preside over an Annual Conference, he was directed to appoint a "Presiding Elder . . . by letter or otherwise" who should preside.[15] The Methodist Episcopal Church changed "presiding elder" in 1864 to "a member of the Conference appointed by the bishop." The Southern church called for a ballot to select the conference president "from among the traveling elders."

It is evident from the present legislation and the past history of this provision, that it is not the intent of the present church for the bishop in charge of a conference to select for that conference its president unless such president be another bishop. Bishops, however, when holding a conference, and compelled to be absent temporarily from certain of its sessions, frequently ask some respected conference member to "take the chair" for the time being, and preside.

During the sessions of the Annual Conference all clerical conference members, including the retired ministers and supernumeraries, are considered active. Retired men may speak, take part in all deliberations, be elected to committees or to the General Conference itself, if the conference so please.[16] An Annual Conference takes special action before each session closes with reference to every ministerial member on its roll. The character of each one must be passed and every one given an assignment. Those who are to be retired, or continued on the retired list, are so reported, and the conference by definite action places or replaces them in the retired or supernumerary relationship. For all others, Bishop Baker quotes the law which yet holds: "Every preacher belonging to the traveling connection, unless he sustains a superannuated relation or is under arrest of character, must receive an appointment." [17]

Previous to 1836 preachers were sometimes returned on the minutes as being "left without an appointment at their own request." The General Conference, however, at that date forbade this practice, except in the case of supernumerary preachers.

The conference year commences when the appointments are announced at the Annual Conference and continues until the announcing

[14] Ibid., ¶ 628.
[15] Discipline, 1804, p. 19.
[16] Baker, op. cit., p. 47.
[17] Ibid., p. 48.

of the appointments at the next Annual Conference. So held Bishop Waugh long ago and his judgment in this respect has become authoritative.[18]

An Annual Conference has no quorum. The persons who are ministerial members and regularly elected lay members present at the time and place announced, duly called to order by the bishop, and otherwise fulfilling orderly requirements, become the conference in session. Conferences have sometimes been attended by only a small portion of their actual membership, and at any session only a small number of members may actually be present and voting. However, no matter how few these may be, if a regular session of the conference is being held, and the officers of that body are duly present, it carries on legally its appointed work. When a two-thirds vote or a fractional vote of any sort is called for, this is understood to mean two thirds (or the required fraction) of those "present and voting." There is no such thing as voting by proxy, or absentee voting, in the Annual Conference—or in any Methodist conference. A decision of the General Conference of the former Methodist Episcopal Church was very definite on this.[19]

An Annual Conference is a continuous entity,[20] but whether it is a legal entity or not was much discussed previous to union. Methodist Episcopal authorities held that it was. However, at union this matter was treated permissively: "Annual Conferences may become severally bodies corporate, wherever practicable, under the law of the countries, states, and territories within whose bounds they are located." [21] This if done creates a legal entity of such bodies and enables them to hold property, buy and sell, sue and be sued, as any corporation. If, and when, an Annual Conference becomes incorporated it is probable that the matter of a quorum, which, as above stated, is not mentioned in Methodist law, would be regulated by whatever provisions the incorporating state demands of its legal corporations. This would no doubt have to do especially with reference to legal acts affecting property rights and the like.

May one session of an Annual Conference bind subsequent sessions to a specified course of conduct? Bishop Cooke, treating of this matter in connection with the General Conference, observes: "It is one of the unwritten laws of Methodism that one General Conference cannot bind

[18] Ibid., p. 43.
[19] Journal, 1916, pp. 423, 485-86.
[20] Cooke, op. cit., p. 117.
[21] Discipline, 1944, ¶ 625.

another; a popular notion which is subject like many other notions to modification." [22]

It would appear from the study of Methodist authorities that while no general rule can be adduced outlining how or in what respect an Annual Conference (or General Conference, for that matter) may consider itself free from, or bound by, its own past procedures, or able to bind its future sessions in the same way, the following holds in a general way: Where legal precedents or Methodist common law has been established by past action or pronouncement, such law or pronouncement may be relied upon as fixed and binding unless, and until, some very definite reason shall arise to discount them; and where the action or custom of a conference in its regular or announced course of procedure is relied upon by outside parties, so that these parties have rights and equities involved, a conference should feel itself morally, if not legally, bound to make no move which will injure such rights or break its own intrinsic integrity. Where the rights of others are not involved, a conference, like a person, may reverse itself, determine upon one course of conduct at one time and another at another, as people frequently do.

Any discussion of a Methodist Annual Conference as a structural and constitutional entity will necessarily fail to make clear the dynamic spiritual and moral power of the conference itself. Conferences are never disembodied organisms existing according to patterns on paper; rather they are assemblies of persons who are leaders in Christian and social life, united together for a high and holy purpose. So conference meetings, programs, and formal actions have great effect upon Methodist people over a wide area, and indeed over the whole region served by a conference. Its program of promotional, educational, social, civic, and spiritual plans and activities is always watched by thousands, with even the secular press keeping advised upon its moves and intent.

The Annual Conference of The Methodist Church is thus basic in its several capacities. It is composed of the sovereign electors of the church; it controls—its ministerial members do—admission to the traveling ministry and to ministerial orders. Above all, it has reserved to it by constitutional enactment all powers not given to the General Conference, except the power to change its own boundaries, which is a jurisdictional matter. Its nucleus is a permanent group of Methodist ministers who spend their lives together in manning its pulpits and serving a definite geographical area. The Annual Conference is in fact the most solid, irreducible unit of a solid, irreducible church.

[22] *Op. cit.*, p. 28.

XII

THE DISTRICT CONFERENCE

There may be organized in an Annual Conference, District Conferences.

—Constitution, Div. II, Sec. IX, Art. I

THE NAME "DISTRICT CONFERENCE" HAS APPEARED IN METHODIST records at three different times, each time referring to a different institution. In the earliest days, that is, from 1786 to 1796, the District Conferences, as referred to by Bishop Asbury, were simply the conferences of preachers held within a "district" or large indefinite geographical area, as "The Baltimore District," "The New York District," and so forth. Bishop Collins Denny asserts that there were "no Annual Conferences till 1796. Prior to that date the Conferences were called 'District Conferences,' which were held annually at a date fixed by the bishop." They were to consist of "not fewer than three, nor more than twelve" circuits.[1] As the annual meetings of the District Conferences proceeded, however, the word "annual" supplanted the word "district" and the Annual Conference became the prime organization of Methodism. The name "District Conference" was dropped.

But in 1820, after the presiding elders' districts had come to be a unit in each Annual Conference, it was decided to organize in each of these a District Conference to consist of local preachers only. These local preachers were to meet once a year, organize, and elect their own chairman, and then were to survey and plan their own district-wide work. Such District Conferences were doomed to failure from the start, for all district leadership and overall planning was of necessity in the hands of the presiding elder and traveling ministers. Distances were great, travel difficult, and what could the local preachers do when and if they did organize? It was an unworkable scheme, "never popular nor useful," Bishop Holland McTyeire observed, and in 1836 the legislation calling for this particular organization was done away.

But in 1870 in the Methodist Episcopal Church, South, and in 1872 in the Methodist Episcopal Church, District Conferences, after the pattern of those now in The Methodist Church, were first created. Such

[1] *A Manual of the Discipline* (1931), p. 39.

conferences were to consist of all the traveling preachers as well as local preachers in a given district; they were to be presided over by the presiding elder, or the bishop, if he should be present; and lay church officers and representatives of the various charges were also admitted. The District Conference, as thus created, provided an opportunity for each district to plan its work as a unit; heavy emphasis was put upon evangelistic and missionary activities with special reference to any "unchurched" area; and great importance was given to the devotional regimen at these conferences, with preaching playing the dominant part.

As stated, the two Methodist Episcopal churches established the "modern" District Conference at about the same time. But there was a great difference in the way each connection acted on this, for the District Conference was made mandatory by the Methodist Episcopal Church, South, but only permissive by the Methodist Episcopal Church. In the latter the establishment of each District Conference was made to depend upon the desire of a majority of the Quarterly Conferences in any district where it was proposed to establish such a conference; and it was also provided that a District Conference could be dissolved or done away by a majority of the Quarterly Conferences whenever these should so decide. With these provisos the legislation passed the Methodist Episcopal General Conference of 1872. District Conferences were to be held once or twice a year as might be determined.[2]

In the Methodist Episcopal Church, South, however, the District Conference was made a fixed part of its temporal economy by the General Conference of 1870, which ordered such a conference to be held in each presiding elder's district annually. Against the expressed fears of a strong minority in the General Conference of 1870, who endeavored to write the word "may" in place of "shall" ("There shall be held in each Presiding Elder's District"), the measure carried. District Conferences thereafter were held regularly in every district of Southern Methodism, as they are to this day. By 1886 the Southern bishops could say that they had found the District Conference to be "an increasingly efficient part of our system." [3]

Then in 1894 the Methodist Episcopal Church, South, went further and took from its Quarterly Conferences the right to license local preachers and to oversee their work, and lodged this power entirely in the District Conference. At the same time it transferred from the Quarterly Conference to the District Conference the right to recommend proper

[2] *Journal*, 1872, p. 410.
[3] H. M. Du Bose, *History of Methodism* (1916), p. 48.

persons for admission to the Annual Conferences and for ordination. This move was bitterly fought in a minority report brought before the General Conference of 1894. It was asserted that it was dangerous to give the District Conferences "executive and judicial prerogatives," and that if the proposed action should be taken, the Quarterly Conferences would be "much minified, impoverished, and reduced." Nevertheless, take it the General Conference of 1894 did, and the minority report lost by 155 to 132.[4] This action firmly put the District Conference of the Methodist Episcopal Church, South, into the key position it has since occupied in the economy of the Southern connection.

Under the permissive action granted by the General Conference of the Methodist Episcopal Church, District Conferences were never held with anything like regularity in that connection. The Quarterly Conferences were apparently well content to manage their own affairs efficiently, with no need to rely very greatly upon a district-wide organization. These Quarterly Conferences, of course, continued to license local preachers, to oversee their work, and to recommend "proper persons" to the Annual Conference for membership and for orders. There never was a serious move in the Methodist Episcopal Church looking to the transfer of these rights to the District Conference, which indeed was usually nonexistent. Many district superintendents did recognize the value of District Conferences, and took the lead in securing Quarterly Conference endorsement and so established their conferences. But there was no uniformity in this, though certain Annual Conferences throughout the Methodist Episcopal Church came to use the district organization on a wide scale. Others did not. The type of territory covered by an Annual Conference was an important factor here, as there would be a difference between the rural and urban areas in this respect. A rural situation in which the churches stood apart from each other with no great feeling of solidarity would present a somewhat different problem from that of a highly integrated city area where the district superintendent had all his churches and their Quarterly Conferences close at hand. The fact that the District Conference in the Methodist Episcopal Church was never more than a promotional agency, and that its spiritual and inspirational values might be expressed just as ably in the well-functioning Quarterly Conferences, also had a bearing on the result. As it was, there were not many of such conferences held in that connection at the time of union in 1939, though as statistics regarding such confer-

---

[4] *Journal*, 1894, pp. 147-48.

ences were not reported to the Annual Conferences, it is difficult to get accurate judgment on this matter.

When the Plan of Union was under discussion by the Joint Commission appointed for that purpose, the problem of the District Conference was studied carefully. The Methodist Protestant Church was not involved, as there were no presiding elders' districts and no District Conferences. But how to continue the mandatory, well-integrated District Conference of the South, which exercised very important powers of licensing and recommending preachers, and at the same time to protect the Quarterly Conferences of the North in their age-long right to continue licensing and recommending—this posed a special problem. The situation was resolved by writing the permissive District Conference into the constitution of the united Church, and so making this a part of the Plan of Union. But the article empowering such action provided that the General Conference should have the right to determine the composition and to fix the powers of such District Conferences: "There may be organized in an Annual Conference, District Conferences composed of such persons and invested with such powers as the General Conference may determine." [5]

Under this constitutional warrant the Uniting Conference and subse-quent General Conferences have allowed each Annual Conference to determine for itself whether or not there shall be District Conferences within its bounds.[6] Where such District Conferences are held, however, the General Conference prescribes their composition and duties. Thus uniformity is obtained. The preachers—traveling, local, superannuate, and supernumerary—all are members of such conferences, together with the exhorters, district officials, and lay representatives from the several charges; and such other persons as are prescribed.[7] The preachers make up the nucleus of these conferences, but are not usually a majority since the lay representatives and district officials compose the greater part of the membership.

In The Methodist Church the District Conference, where and when properly established, until quite recently had the right to license persons to preach and to renew such licenses; it could also recommend proper persons to the Annual Conference for admission on trial or for elder's or deacon's orders. But in 1952 the General Conference put the power to license persons to preach and to recommend persons to the Annual

[5] Constitution, Div. II, Sec. IX, Art. I.
[6] Discipline, 1952, ¶ 666.
[7] Ibid., ¶ 667.

Conference in the hands of a District Committee on Ministerial Qualifications. This committee, it should be noted, is to be elected by the Annual Conference on the nomination of the district superintendent. It is not to be created by the District Conference, for there are sections of the church where there are no District Conferences. But it is provided that where there is a District Conference, it must take "final action" upon the license of any person to whom the District Committee on Ministerial Qualifications has first granted a license to preach.

Where an Annual Conference determines that there shall be District Conferences within its borders, such determination on the part of the Annual Conference not only creates District Conferences but transfers to them the important right of setting the final seal upon the license of each one inducted into the preaching ministry. Where an Annual Conference does not call for or create District Conferences, there must, nevertheless, be a District Committee on Ministerial Qualifications; and this committee, rather than the Quarterly Conference as was formerly the case (where there were no District Conferences), is in the future empowered to license men.

In practice the District Conference system has been continued in all those Annual Conferences formerly connected with the Methodist Episcopal Church, South, and its very real value, when properly created and directed, has made for its increasing appearance in the conferences of the former Methodist Episcopal connection, and indeed over the whole church.

Of recent years, however, the District Conference, even in the Southern conferences, where it was traditionally strongly entrenched, has lost something of its former pristine power due to several intangible factors. One is the faster tempo of modern life which makes it more difficult to assemble ministers and laymen for sufficient periods of fellowship, prayer, and preaching, after the pattern of an older day. Feeding and housing present-day delegates is difficult, and with the usual modern district well knit by telephonic and automobile communication, and with the district superintendent able to call together his preachers or laymen for any special emergency, the need for the District Conference organization is not what it was in former days. Furthermore, the custom and practice put into effect within recent years by bishops, district superintendents, and church-wide agencies, whereby district-wide meetings of preachers and laymen were often called in order to hear of or promote some special activity of the church, has had a tendency to relegate the formal District

146

Conference itself somewhat to the background, and to make its annual meeting less significant.

But withal, the church needs this specific organization where the laity of the various charges can be integrated with the larger church life of which they are a part; and where the district superintendent, upon whom so much depends, can frankly and officially assume the leadership of his district, present his program, and act as the spiritual and temporal superintendent of all the work of the church thus entrusted to him.

The District Conference gives promise, as these lines are written, of becoming an increasingly useful agency in the larger organization of The Methodist Church.

XIII

THE QUARTERLY CONFERENCE

There shall be organized in each pastoral charge a Quarterly Conference composed of such persons and invested with such powers as the General Conference shall provide.
—Constitution, Div. II, Sec. X, Art. I

THE QUARTERLY CONFERENCE IS THE TRADITIONAL BUSINESS AND governing body of the local charge or station. It is so at present, though it may now abrogate its rights in certain important particulars to an Official Board should it decide to do so. The ultimate sovereignty of the local church, however, always remains in its hands and it is, in the language of the present *Discipline*, "the basic body of control." [1]

The constitution of The Methodist Church makes it mandatory that there shall be organized in every pastoral charge a Quarterly Conference; and statutory directions of the present provide that there must be held at least two meetings of each such Quarterly Conference during the year, a first and fourth. The second and third meetings of this organization may be held at the discretion of the district superintendent.

The Quarterly Conference is composed of all the traveling, supernumerary, and retired preachers residing within the circuit or charge,[2] and to these are added the local preachers, exhorters, deaconesses, and so forth. But making up the vast majority of members of this body are the local church lay officials—stewards, trustees, financial secretaries, treasurers, church-school superintendents, and other ex officio members. The Quarterly Conference thus tends to become a roster of the lay leadership of any local church, and under present disciplinary provisions every important interest of the local church has its representative upon its roll.

By law the district superintendent is the president of the Quarterly Conference.[3] In presiding he has no vote, not even to resolve a tie, since he is not a member of the conference itself.[4] In the absence of the district superintendent, "the elder designated by him" shall preside. In the ab-

---

[1] *Discipline*, 1952, ¶ 137.
[2] *Ibid.*, ¶ 138.
[3] *Ibid.*, ¶ 139.
[4] Collins Denny, *A Manual of the Discipline* (1931), p. 69.

148

sence of the district superintendent or the designated elder, the pastor shall preside, and as he is a member of the body may "vote on a ballot or on a call of the yeas and nays, or give the casting vote." [5] It is important to note that there is no quorum required for a Quarterly Conference, as "the members present at the time and place regularly appointed for a Quarterly Conference constitute a quorum." [6] However, there was a regulation in the former Methodist Episcopal Church, South, that no Quarterly Conference could purchase, sell, create a lien upon, or otherwise dispose of church property unless at least ten days notice had been given regarding the meeting of such conference, and unless there were at least five members of the conference itself present when such action was taken.[7] This, of course, was to prevent hasty action by a minority of church officials who might dispose of the property entrusted to all. In matters affecting property, however, there has always been the safeguard that such property is usually held by trustees, who, while under the direction of the Quarterly Conference, have a certain independent standing of their own since they have been recognized by the courts; and state and civil regulations always prescribe the methods by which property is to be sold, mortgaged, or purchased. These regulations naturally supersede church regulations where there is any conflict between the two.

The functions of the Quarterly Conference may be studied most conveniently under its electoral powers, its supervisory powers, and its property holding ability.

ELECTORAL POWERS

The Quarterly Conference has the right to elect its own members with the exception of the clerical—the ministerial members—who belong to the Annual Conference. Local preachers, although no longer licensed by it, become members of the Quarterly Conference by virtue of their office. Deaconesses, if any, and the president of the Woman's Society of Christian Service, are also members of the Quarterly Conference by virtue of their respective offices and not by action of the Quarterly Conference itself. There may be also certain minor church officials whose election to an office which entitles them to membership in the Quarterly Conference may not be subject to confirmation by that body; but the vast majority of lay members composing the Quarterly Conference—and the usual Quarterly Conference is over-

[5] *Ibid.*
[6] *Ibid.*
[7] *Ibid.*

whelmingly lay—are the stewards, trustees, church-school officials, and the like, who are elected to their respective positions by the Quarterly Conference itself.

To be sure, the Quarterly Conference has the right to provide for the election of these officials by a formal church conference if it shall so decide; but the primary right to elect the majority of its own members still inheres in the Quarterly Conference, as it has almost from the beginning of American Methodism.

In early days and up to recent times the Quarterly Conference consisted solely of the local and resident preachers, with stewards and trustees. Within recent years, however, other persons have been admitted ex officio to this membership, until now the Quarterly Conference is representative of every organized interest of the local church.

The preacher in charge had the right, for long years in episcopal Methodism, to nominate the lay officials of the church; and since these lay officials usually made up, as they do now, the majority of the Quarterly Conference, to that extent the pastor exercised a potential control of that body. This right of the pastor to nominate his stewards, Sunday-school superintendents, and, in many instances, trustees of church property, followed directly the pristine polity of early Methodism. There the preacher himself *named* and *appointed* all officials directly. In their notes appended to the 1798 *Discipline*, Bishops Asbury and Coke explain:

In every large society there are usually two or four stewards. . . . These are appointed, as well as the circuit stewards, by the preacher who has the charge of the circuit. He is himself to have as little as possible to do with temporal affairs, but has the appointment of the officers of the society invested in him, as being likely to be the best judge of the society at large, and of each member in particular. Nevertheless, he is to advise with the quarterly meeting on the appointment of *circuit stewards*, and with the leaders of each society respectively on the appointment of *society stewards*.

This practice on the part of the early church in giving this power to the preacher was objected to by protagonists of lay rights in the days before the organization of the Methodist Protestant Church. Later on both episcopal Methodisms made the office of steward depend on the *election* of the Quarterly Conference, not upon its "advice," as was the case in the Asburian *Discipline*. However, the right to nominate the persons to be stewards, and so forth, was retained by the pastor in the Methodist Episcopal Church, South, up to the time of union in 1939, and in the Methodist Episcopal Church until the matter of election was otherwise or alternately provided for in later years.

Inasmuch as the Quarterly Conference is largely composed of stewards and trustees, who were elected to their respective positions on nomination of the pastor, and are today in many instances elected on nomination of a committee of which he is chairman, it may be well to state the opposing views over this prerogative of the preacher in charge.

The fact that the minister has the power to control the membership of the group which, in episcopal Methodist polity, governed the church was, as has been said, bitterly opposed by the advocates of lay rights. The Methodist Protestant Church, which was organized to fulfill the demand for those rights, resolved the matter after its organization by creating a church conference in which all the membership of the church functioned directly in electing necessary church officials.[8] But in episcopal Methodism the right of the minister to appoint, and later to nominate, the stewards, was defended on the following grounds: The stewards and trustees of a charge in effect make up the pastor's cabinet, and as his success depends upon the effectiveness with which these officials support him in his plans and church-wide undertakings, any pastor will be hindered, perhaps blocked, if not allowed the right to say who should and who should not constitute the "official board." Furthermore, the old argument of Asbury, that the pastor is apt to be the best judge of the qualifications of those who should occupy this place, was not forgotten. Advocates of the pastoral nomination also usually called attention to the fact that the Quarterly Conference itself did the electing, and could refuse to elect a pastoral nominee at any time for any cause.

Practically, the power of the pastor to nominate the stewards—and other church officers—did not, and his present chairmanship of the committee on nominations does not, impress The Methodist Church as being any more dangerous than to allow such persons to be nominated "from the floor" or by others. There have been instances where pastors, following personal differences, have "left off the board" officials whom the local church felt should be kept on it; there have been many instances where men have been placed upon the board at the nomination of the pastor, and this induction later proved to be a manifest mistake. But such mistakes might have happened under any other system of nomination. In practice and in the usual charge, with some exceptions, of course, the men who should be stewards and officials, and upon whom the church can depend, have generally been appointed to these respective

[8] *Discipline*, Methodist Protestant Church, 1876, ¶ 29; Constitution, Methodist Protestant Church, Art. XI.

official positions. A minister ran, and today may run, a great risk whenever he refuses to renominate for the position of steward or trustee one who has been serving in that capacity, and who perhaps has friends and followers who feel that he is being unfairly treated by action of the pastor. Even where there are bitter differences between the pastor and certain of his officials, the usual minister is liberal enough to appreciate the different viewpoint of his official opponents; and where he is not, he often is wise enough to see that he may injure himself as well as the charge more by leaving off a worrisome opponent than by keeping him on.

The relationship of the pastor to this electoral power of the Quarterly Conference has been treated rather fully at this point because the pastor-Quarterly Conference relation presents a focal point of prime importance in the Methodist economy. In response to the argument of those who felt that the local church government should not be too much under the control of the pastor, since he was not himself a permanent part of the local church, the Methodist Episcopal Church later provided an alternate method of electing stewards and trustees. This was to be done by an "annual church meeting" which was to be held in connection with the "Quarterly Conference next preceding the Annual Conference." [9] This meeting was to be composed of all members of the church of "not less than twenty-one years of age," and there were adequate provisions for announcement and notice of such meeting. The district superintendent, or an elder appointed by him, or, in their absence, the pastor, was to preside. The vote for trustees was to be by ballot; and the vote for both stewards and trustees was to be "upon nomination of the Nominating Committee." No directions, however, were given concerning the appointment or composition of such committee.[10]

This plan in the Methodist Episcopal Church was, however, dependent upon Quarterly Conference action for its inception, but it seems to have been widely adopted. The Methodist Episcopal Church, South, continued to elect its local church officials by the Quarterly Conference upon direct nomination of the pastor alone, until 1939, when The Methodist Church provided the present alternate system.

At Methodist union in 1939 both the above plans were continued in effect, with the Quarterly Conference making the decision as to whether it would itself elect "church officials" directly or provide that this be done by an "Annual Church Conference." In the latter case, the Annual

[9] *Discipline*, 1936, ¶ 923 (1).
[10] *Ibid.* Also ¶ 1012.

Church Conference is to be held in connection with the last Quarterly
Conference (the fourth) and the district superintendent shall preside,
or, in his absence, the pastor. The *Discipline* does not make it clear
whether or not there is to be a nominating committee at such Annual
Church Conference. It merely provides that such conference may "elect
such officers of the charge as would otherwise be elected by the Quarterly Conference (¶¶ 32, 143-45)." [11] Paragraph 143, however, refers to
the officials and committees which are to be elected by the Quarterly
Conference, and provides that it "shall elect . . . on nomination of the
Committee on Nominations, or . . . the pastor if there is no such committee." It is thus clear that if the Quarterly Conference wishes to retain
its electoral power with relation to its own important members—trustees,
stewards, church-school superintendents, district steward, reserve district
steward, communion steward, financial secretary, treasurer or treasurers
of local church, member and reserve lay member of the Annual Conference (a most important election), members of the District Conference where there are such conferences, director of Christian education,
and the like—it must elect them "on nomination of the Committee on
Nominations, or . . . the pastor if there is no such committee."

In general it may be said that since union the respective local churches
have continued to use the system of election to which they had become
accustomed under their former polity. The Quarterly Conference over
the territory formerly covered by the Methodist Episcopal Church, South,
continues to elect by Quarterly Conference action and on nomination of
the pastor, although many Southern charges under the new legislation
have created nominating committees under the chairmanship of the
pastor. Through charges of the former Methodist Episcopal Church
and Methodist Protestant Church, the Annual Church Conference, acting as electoral body for the charge, seems to be popular and continues
to function.

As has been indicated, it devolves upon the Quarterly Conference to
elect also the layman who will represent the local church in the Annual
Conference, and to elect the delegates to the District Conference when
there is a District Conference. In electing the member and reserve lay
member of the Annual Conference, such election may be either for a
four-year term or for a single year as the Annual Conference to which the
charge belongs shall direct. If an Annual Conference decides to require
the Quarterly Conferences within its bounds to elect lay delegates for a

[11] *Discipline*, 1952, ¶ 198.

four-year term, such election is usually held at the beginning of each General Conference quadrennium.

In respect to the delegates who may be elected to the District Conference (where such District Conference has been established) the number to be elected from each charge is at the determination of the Annual Conference. An Annual Conference may allow a fixed number of lay delegates from each charge irrespective of the size of the charge, or may provide for proportional representation. However, since recent legislation has made a large number of persons in each charge members of the District Conference by virtue of their offices, it is not likely that the respective Annual Conferences will provide for many additional ones.

A traditional and important function of the Quarterly Conference was until 1952 the licensing of persons to become local preachers and the recommending of such local preachers, or other proper persons, to the Annual Conference for the traveling ministry; that is, for admission into the Annual Conference. A person's local church was—and is now—held to be better qualified than any other body to pass upon his ministerial and preaching powers. But the General Conference of 1952 took away from the Quarterly Conference the right to license local preachers and put this in the hands of a District Committee on Ministerial Qualifications. The Quarterly Conference, however, must still *recommend* to that committee any person from its local charge who seeks a license to preach. Likewise, where a woman belonging to the local charge desires to become a deaconess, the Quarterly Conference must recommend and send to the Annual Conference Deaconess Board the credentials of such person.

Thus the pristine right of the Quarterly Conference to "license and recommend" was done away in 1952. Up to that time the District Conference, if one existed, took over these powers from the Quarterly Conference in those Annual Conferences where District Conferences were called for. In 1952, at the recommendation of a commission which had been created to study and make recommendations regarding the structure of the local church, the General Conference adopted new legislation in regard to the licensing authority. It created in each district a District Committee on Ministerial Qualifications, and this committee was empowered to do all that the Quarterly Conference or District Conference had hitherto done in licensing and recommending.

The Quarterly Conference, however, still retains the power to license exhorters and to "certify" lay speakers. It is also directed to inquire annually into the work and character of these minor church officials. Where

154

a District Conference exists, that conference must review the action of the District Committee in each instance, and "final action" on the licensing of each local preacher must be taken by the District Conference.

In spite of this action in 1952, by virtue of its inaugural position in the recommending of persons for license to preach, the Quarterly Conference in every case still controls the entrance to the Methodist preaching ministry.

SUPERVISORY POWERS

Beside its electoral powers, the Quarterly Conference has an important supervisory authority over the local church and all its agencies. There are a number of committees which the Quarterly Conference is obliged to create in conformity to the action of the General Conference; and there are other committees which are optional or suggested for creation by the Quarterly Conference. These committees, when mandatory, tie in with the general program of the whole church and help to implement that program in the local congregations. The other committees suggested by the *Discipline* are to be appointed when deemed advisable by the Quarterly Conference. Naturally each Quarterly Conference may also create its own special committees from time to time as may seem needed.

Under the supervisory powers of the Quarterly Conference comes its duty to represent the church when there is any change or contemplated change of pastor. Formerly such representation, or the wishes of the charge, were sometimes expressed by petitions properly passed by the Quarterly Conference and put before the bishop or presiding elder or district superintendent, especially when there was any impending or rumored change. Quarterly Conferences were allowed to have the right, as they do yet, to request a change or request the return of the pastor. In cases where a definite opening had occurred and there was a consequent need for filling the pulpit, Quarterly Conferences sometimes petitioned for a certain man to be sent to the church as pastor. This, under former regulations and Methodist custom, sometimes proved awkward, though from 1928 on in the Methodist Episcopal Church there was a pulpit supply committee very like the present one. Since union in 1939, such matters, especially for those of the Methodist Episcopal Church, South, connection, have been better provided for by frank disciplinary directions. One of the mandatory committees of each present Quarterly Conference is The Committee on Pastoral Relations, which must provide for the temporary supply of the pulpit during a pastoral absence; and must co-operate with the district superintendent and bishop and consult with the pastor when a definite change in pastoral relations "is contemplated." This committee, however, is itself amenable to the Quarterly Conference, and cannot therefore act independently of the wishes or instructions of that body, certainly not when these have been definitely expressed.

A most important function of the Quarterly Conference since earliest days has been its control over all financial matters having to do with the local church or charge. The support of the preacher has always devolved directly upon the Quarterly Conference, as it does today, though the conference is now expressly directed to put this responsibility directly upon the Official Board as its administrative agent. Formerly the money that was raised for the support of the district superintendent or presiding elder was also a direct charge upon the Quarterly Conference, and it was the well-known minute question, "What has been raised for the support of the ministry and how has it been applied?" which provided the real reason for the holding of the Quarterly Conference in many past situations.

The Quarterly Conference today is still directly responsible for ministerial support and is required to agree upon the minimum salary for the preacher in charge for any one year previous to the holding of the Annual Conference for that year. This advance certification by the Quarterly Conference as to what salary shall be provided during the coming year, gives the appointive power necessary information in the making of the appointments. It also prevents the first Quarterly Conference of a new year from fixing a salary below what was promised previous to holding the Annual Conference.

In addition to providing oversight of the financial matters of the charge through its Official Board, the Quarterly Conference is vested with authority and power in matters relating to the real and personal property of the local church. This has always been a pristine duty of the Quarterly Conference in Methodism. And in order to fulfill this particular duty more effectively, the General Conference of 1952 provided that there shall be a Quarterly Conference organized in every church upon a circuit. This Church Quarterly Conference, and not the Charge Quarterly Conference, is now given the authority and power in matters relating to the real and personal property of the local church. Thus while there is a Charge Quarterly Conference to deal with general church matters, there is also a Church Quarterly Conference established in every circuit church, and this must deal specifically with the property of the local church. This puts an end to the former difficulties often found in administering the property of a local church through a Quarterly Conference composed of members of other churches.

THE OFFICIAL BOARD

The development of the Official Board and the frank recognition of that organization in The Methodist Church as a supplementary and, in some cases, a substitute power for the Quarterly Conference, must now be treated. As has been noted, the Quarterly Conference has always been largely composed of the trustees and stewards of each local church. With the development and increasing appearance of "station appointments" in cities and towns over the country, it became increasingly awkward to attempt to keep the local church's financial system on a quarterly, that is, a three-month basis. Practically all other persons and organizations had adopted the month as the financial unit, and bills and financial obligations were expected to be met on a monthly basis in ordinary American life. This put the local church, which was compelled to wait for the Quarterly Conference, at a disadvantage, and soon the custom grew of having a finance committee, or the stewards themselves, meet monthly to clear finances, and take other needed action as might seem wise. The Quarterly Conference, when it met, was expected to approve such actions, and as the stewards themselves comprised the majority of its members, there was no trouble in having their usual moves properly authenticated and approved.

As the urbanization of the nation progressed and large and ever larger churches grew with their consequent well-articulated organization, it was almost inevitable that the stewards and trustees should consider a monthly meeting of their board essential, as indeed it was. These board meetings were tacitly understood to have the power to supervise all executive matters connected with the charge, and as a well-organized local church and ably presented reports were always a joy at Quarterly Conference time, the district superintendent, pastor, and all others rejoiced in each efficient board. In time, however, the great official board with its recurrent monthly meeting and its life and thought entirely within its own local church tended to supplant the less frequent and more connectional Quarterly Conference. The board could, of course, work through the Quarterly Conference easier than the Quarterly Conference could work through the board.

The Methodist Episcopal Church, having this situation brought acutely to its attention, took frank cognizance of the rise of the Official Board, and in disciplinary directions a long while previous to church union provided that the Quarterly Conference might organize and "continue during its pleasure an Official Board to have supervision of the several activities of the charge." [17] What these "several activities" were was not closely specified. Those who were to compose the Official Board were, however, carefully prescribed and it was directed that the pastor should "preside over its deliberations." This in effect made of the board a permanent committee to which the Quarterly Conference might entrust much of its work, as indeed it did. The dependence of the Official Board in the Methodist Episcopal Church upon the Quarterly Conference is further shown by the requirement that all minutes and actions of the board were to be presented formally to the Quarterly Conference for keeping with its records.

In the Methodist Episcopal Church, South, Official Boards (composed almost entirely of stewards) met and conducted the affairs of their respective local charges in much the same way as described above, but such boards were never given formal recognition in the *Discipline* of the Southern church as was the Official Board in the Methodist Episcopal Church.

There was a curious distinction between stewards and trustees noted at the time of church union with reference to the way the respective Methodist Episcopal churches used and depended upon these two classes of church officials. In the Methodist Episcopal Church, South, the stewards were the Official Board, and while the trustees of church property were quite often stewards—and even when not, were tacitly assumed to belong to the Board—yet in the polity of the Methodist Episcopal Church, South, "the Official Board" always meant the Board of Stewards. But in the Methodist Episcopal Church the "Official Board" as a rule consisted both of trustees and stewards with the resident ministry also as members. Furthermore, in Methodist Episcopal polity, trustees were usually thought of as taking precedence over stewards. It was always "trustees and stewards" in the *Discipline* of the Methodist Episcopal Church. It was always "stewards and trustees" in the South.

The Board of Stewards in the Methodist Episcopal Church, South, always elected its own chairman and it was rare indeed for the pastor to preside over it. The pastor met with the board and, after the manner of an executive secretary reporting to the organization which employs

[17] *Discipline*, 1908, ¶ 103.

him, or like a college president reporting to his trustees, took his place at the monthly meeting and stood ready to recommend or suggest whatever action seemed wise.

The minutes and reports of the Official Board in the former Methodist Episcopal Church, South, were not as a rule called for by the Quarterly Conference, nor were such reports usually presented to that body, as was the case with the Official Board of the Methodist Episcopal Church.

At union in 1939 the regulation of the Methodist Episcopal Church establishing an "executive body" to be known as the Official Board, but doing this through the Quarterly Conference, was adopted by the Uniting Conference. But the interrelationship of these two bodies still proved troublesome and contradictory. To resolve this matter, as well as other organizational problems, a commission was created by the General Conference of 1944 to study the structure of the local church. This commission presented to the General Conference in 1952 a complete plan of reorganization for all local church agencies. Its report was heard with great attention and was adopted by the conference with minor changes.

The legislation as adopted recognized and continued the Quarterly Conference in its time-honored position as the sovereign body of the local church, but ordered that there should be in every church of every pastoral charge an Official Board. This was declared to be "an administrative body . . . responsible to the Quarterly Conference." [18] Carefully drawn regulations prescribe the membership of the Official Board. The pastor, or pastors, are definitely put upon it, as are deaconesses, if any, and, of course, stewards and trustees. Trustees who are not members of The Methodist Church are not, however, to be members of the Official Board. A distinction is made between elective stewards, those who are elected such by the Quarterly Conference, and ex officio stewards, or persons who are such by virtue of the office they hold in the local church. The church-school superintendent, president of the Woman's Society of Christian Service, and the president of Methodist Men, for instance, are ex officio stewards. As such they have all the rights and privileges of elective stewards, and there is no distinction between them in the board itself.

The Official Board as thus constituted must meet monthly, must elect its own officers annually, and "as the administrative agency of the Quarterly Conference" must promote and have "general . . . oversight

[18] *Discipline*, 1952, ¶ 206.

of the work of the local church, both spiritual and temporal, under the direction of the pastor." [19]

The methods and committees to be used by the board in carrying out its work are carefully outlined. Provision is made for additional committees, or for such special agencies as the board itself may deem necessary. The board has the duty of recommending to the Quarterly Conference the salary to be paid for ministerial support. Its recommendation must be presented to the session of the Quarterly Conference next preceding the Annual Conference. It can only be made after consultation with the pastor. As the duties of the board are largely financial, the provisions having to do with the proper carrying out of such duties are described in some detail.

It is clear that the General Conference intended to correlate the work of the Quarterly Conference and Official Board more intimately, still keeping the Quarterly Conference as the sovereign body. The Official Board fundamentally remains as the administrative committee of the Quarterly Conference. But today, as in the past, there is happily no practical difficulty in the parallel working of these two agencies, since they are composed of the same persons. All possibility of conflict or misunderstanding between these two organizations is minimized, if not obviated, by the fact that every member of the Official Board is also a member of the Quarterly Conference. That is to say, the officials of a local church may function either as the Official Board or as the Quarterly Conference, or as both, as occasion demands.

[19] *Discipline*, 1952, ¶ 215.

XIV

THE CHURCH CONFERENCE

There may be a Church Conference in each church, having
such powers and duties as the General Conference may prescribe.

—Constitution, Div. II, Sec. XI

THE CHURCH CONFERENCE, IN THE TECHNICAL MEANING OF THAT
term, was an organization peculiar to the polity of the Methodist Episcopal Church, South, at the time of union. Though there was also a disciplinary "Monthly Meeting" comparable to it in the Methodist Episcopal Church, this was rarely called, and is not to be confused with the
"Annual Meeting" at which gathering of the congregation, elections of
trustees and stewards were held as, and when, the Quarterly Conference
so directed. The Church Conference of the Methodist Episcopal Church,
South, originated in 1866 when that church practically reorganized following the Civil War.

The Church Conference was created in order to allow the lay people
of the Methodist Episcopal Church, South, to have a greater voice in controlling their own affairs. Specifically this conference was given the right
to say how or in what way the money for ministerial support—fixed by
the stewards—should be raised, and how the assessment levied by the
Annual Conference upon the local charge should be met. Stewards were
allowed to adopt the plan of "assessment with consent" only when a
Church Conference had "declined or failed to adopt that or some other
method," explained Bishop Collins Denny. "In no event can stewards
or Annual Conferences invade this primal right of the Church." [1]

All members of the local church regardless of age were members of the
Church Conference of the Methodist Episcopal Church, South, as were
the "resident ministers." The pastor was the president of such conference
but it elected its own secretary. Its records were to be furnished to the
Quarterly Conference at stated intervals.

For long years there was a disciplinary regulation calling for the Church
Conference to be held monthly in every charge, but this proved impracticable, and the 1934 General Conference of the Methodist Episcopal

[1] A Manual of the Discipline (1931), p. 75.

161

Church, South, ordered these conferences held "as often as necessary." Such necessity as a practical matter came to depend on the fact that the Church Conference was the only power in the Methodist Episcopal Church, South, which had the right to drop from the church roll the name of any member who had "been lost sight of" for twelve months.[2]

A pastor who wished to "clear the roll" was thus compelled to call a Church Conference and have the names of those whose whereabouts were uncertain removed by regular vote of the conference. For this purpose a Church Conference was held from time to time in each local church. Its original power over the financial system of the local church was seldom formally exercised. Many pastors also found that a Church Conference, especially if held at the end of a particular year, gave a splendid opportunity for receiving formal reports from the various local church organizations and officers in a public, official way. This proved an excellent promotional and inspirational plan when well managed and was often eagerly participated in by the representatives of all groups.

At church union, Church Conferences were provided for by permissive constitutional direction, but the powers and duties of such conferences were put specifically under the control of the General Conference. That body, in subsequent legislation concerning the powers of the Church Conference, made the authorization for each such conference to depend upon the Quarterly Conference of the respective charges.[3] It also fixed an age limit, eighteen years and over, for all church members who may belong to such a conference. The pastor is to preside and may call the Church Conference. In his absence a chairman may be elected from the members. No mention of any right to strike a name from the church roll is found in the present legislation of The Methodist Church, nor is there any mention of a plan regarding finances. The present Church Conference is expected to be almost entirely a promotional agency.

An "Annual Church Conference"—not a regular "Church Conference"—may also be constituted and provided for by the Quarterly Conference, and this body, meeting at the time of the last Quarterly Conference, has the right to review the work of the year, to hear reports, and to elect officers for the church, as has been said elsewhere. The authorization to elect officials for the local church, however, depends on the formal grant of such power to the Annual Church Conference by the Quarterly Conference.[4]

[2] *Discipline*, 1938, ¶ 113.
[3] *Discipline*, 1944, ¶ 161.
[4] *Ibid.*, ¶¶ 162-64.

It is clear that under present practice the Church Conference, as the Methodist Episcopal Church, South, had developed it, has largely been discontinued; but it is also clear that the powers of promotion held by this organization, as well as many of the powers of the congregational meeting of the Methodist Protestant Church, can be conserved by and expressed through an Annual Church Conference. This body can hear reports, make plans, and elect officials when the local church, through its Quarterly Conference, so desires. Coming at the end of a church year, the Annual Church Conference is thus in a key position to enlist the interest and exercise the power of the whole charge in a unique way. Pastors who are good executives make full use of its powers.

It is clear that the executive power of the local church is vested in the Quarterly Conference. It exercises sovereignty for the local charge in every particular, under the framework of the legislation enacted for its governance by the General Conference under the constitution. Also, the general church reserves the right to name the preacher in charge, following the age-old pattern of the Methodist itineracy. But in everything else—and for all practical purposes, in that also—the Quarterly Conference is the controlling body of the local charge.

General Conclusions

Such is the conference system of The Methodist Church as outlined in its constitution and *Discipline*. Each Conference has certain rights and powers vested in it, and each is to a great degree dependent upon the others. The General Conference depends for its personnel upon the Annual Conferences and their elections, and so does the Jurisdictional Conference. The Annual Conference depends for its clerical personnel upon the original action of a Quarterly Conference and upon a District Committee licensing and recommending its clerical members. For its lay members the Annual Conference depends directly upon the Quarterly Conference of each individual charge. District Conferences depend almost entirely upon Quarterly Conference action for personnel. The Church Conference can exercise immediate powers of great importance if directed to do so by the Quarterly Conferences.

A system of record-keeping and checking also ties the conferences together. The General church records are compiled and kept by order of the General Conference, which provides for the compilation of these in the *General Minutes*. Annual Conferences, in some areas, check the records of their District Conferences, and "the committee to report on

Quarterly Conference records" has long been a feature of the District Conference in those areas where it has been held.

In comparison with the episcopacy, the conference system of Methodism has grown stronger rather than weaker through the years. However, this strength does not now inhere to such a great degree in the General Conference alone, as was formerly the case. That conference does indeed possess vast powers, though these are not so great as it possessed in the Methodist Episcopal Church or even in the Methodist Episcopal Church, South, previous to union. But the conference system—the General, Jurisdictional, Central, Annual, District, and Quarterly Conferences, as a catena of powerful parliamentary organizations—together form the spirit and manage the work of The Methodist Church to a greater degree than ever before. It is true that the Judicial Council, representing a new feature in Methodist polity, and taking, as a co-ordinate part of the church's life, part of the former power vested in the General Conference or in the bishops, has subtracted somewhat both from General Conference and episcopal power. But with all that, the conferences of Methodism are, as they of right ought to be, the governing authority of the church, and through them, all theory to the contrary notwithstanding, Methodist people get their will expressed and carried out as surely and swiftly as in any other church of the present day.

PART THREE

The Jurisdictional Division

XV

THE JURISDICTIONAL PLAN

There shall be Jurisdictional Conferences for the Church in the United States of America, with such powers, duties, and privileges as are hereinafter set worth.

—Constitution, Div. II (2)

A MOST DISTINCTIVE AND RADICAL ALTERATION IN THE FUNDAMENTAL pattern of American Methodism came about when, under the Plan of Union, The Methodist Church in the United States was organized in six jurisdictions. These jurisdictions, five by geographic boundaries and one by racial collocation, were created and established by constitutional process at the adoption of the Plan of Union. In that plan it is declared:

Article I.—The Methodist Church in the United States of America shall have Jurisdictional Conferences made up as follows:

Northeastern—Maine, New Hampshire, Vermont, Massachusetts, Rhode Island, New York, Connecticut, Pennsylvania, New Jersey, Maryland, West Virginia, Delaware, District of Columbia, Puerto Rico.

Southeastern—Virginia, North Carolina, South Carolina, Georgia, Florida, Alabama, Tennessee, Kentucky, Mississippi, Cuba.

Central—The Negro Annual Conferences, the Negro Mission Conferences and Missions in the United States of America.

North Central—Ohio, Indiana, Illinois, Michigan, Wisconsin, Minnesota, Iowa, North Dakota, South Dakota.

South Central—Missouri, Arkansas, Louisiana, Nebraska, Kansas, Oklahoma, Texas, New Mexico.

Western—Washington, Idaho, Oregon, California, Nevada, Utah, Arizona, Montana, Wyoming, Colorado, Alaska, Hawaiian Islands.[1]

The powers and prerogatives of the six Jurisdictional Conferences as such will be hereafter discussed. Before going farther, however, it will be necessary to trace briefly the history of the jurisdictional idea as it finally became embodied in the constitution of The Methodist Church.

No feature of the Plan of Union was more debated before the adoption of that plan than was the jurisdictional or regional division, and since the organization of The Methodist Church none has been more

[1] Constitution, Div. II, Sec. VIII, Art. I.

167

carefully scrutinized and energetically discussed as life and time make their pragmatic tests.

Bishop John M. Moore, in his book *The Long Road to Methodist Union*, outlines the growth and the final adoption of the jurisdictional pattern as it became the basis for union, especially as between the former Methodist Episcopal Church and Methodist Episcopal Church, South. Into the long, involved, and tortuous record of the negotiations which finally resulted in union it will not be necessary to go, except to say that every commission which studied the possibility of such union had before it a jurisdictional plan in some form. No formal recommendations for union were ever made, nor does it seem any could have been made with any degree of success, without the inclusion of this plan.

As early as 1846, when the Methodist Episcopal Church, South, was in process of organization, the Southern convention closed its corporate declaration with the express desire "to entertain, and duly and carefully consider, any proposition or plan having for its object the union of two great bodies, in the North and South, whether such proposed union is jurisdictional or connectional." [2] Bishop Moore calls special attention to the word "jurisdictional" as used at that early date. Subsequently, during the latter half of the nineteenth century several tentative but fruitless plans were put forth suggesting union on the basis of the jurisdictional concept.

But not until the joint commissions of the two Methodist Episcopal churches and the Methodist Protestant Church met in 1911 could the full import of the regional plan and its importance especially to the Southern Church, be seen in full perspective. At that time, a subcommittee of nine, with three members from each of the three participating churches, was appointed to explore the possibilities in "any plan" for organic union. This subcommittee in turn broke into its three church groups, and each of these eventually presented a plan. That of the Methodist Episcopal Church, with Bishop Earl Cranston at the head, suggested that there be five ecclesiastical jurisdictions with the Negro membership of the church in one of these; that each jurisdiction be allowed to nominate (not elect) its pro rata representation in the Board of Bishops; that it should suggest legislative action, and manage its own affairs in all matters not entrusted to the General Conference. The General Conference, keeping its supremacy, was to manage all matters for the Jurisdictional Conferences, and bishops were to be bishops of, and for, the entire connection. Significantly enough, it was also recommended that there "shall

[2] John M. Moore, *The Long Road to Methodist Union* (1943), p. 76.

be a Judicial Council elected from the jurisdictions and having all appellate power." The proposed council could, however, be reversed by a two-thirds vote of the Annual Conferences.

Bishop E. E. Hoss, representing the Southern group of the subcommittee of nine, asked for an organization "under the jurisdiction of a General Conference meeting every five years, and four quadrennial conferences." The General Conference was to have all connectional powers, legislative and administrative; the quadrennial conferences were to "name their Bishops and other officers and be vested with all powers not expressly granted to the General Conference." No judicial council was called for by name, but it was suggested that there be "lodged somewhere outside the General and Quadrennial Conferences the power to arrest unconstitutional legislation."

The Methodist Protestant group, with Dr. T. H. Lewis at its head, was concerned with the name of the proposed united church. The Methodist Protestants were naturally not fond of the word "episcopal." They also were anxious to write into the fundamental constitution of the new church well-defined provisions for safeguarding lay rights. Especially were lay rights demanded for, and in, the Annual Conferences. "I think it is safe to say," declared Dr. Lewis, "that the laymen generally feel more concerned with the action of an Annual than a General Conference." His group also suggested that the Annual Conferences might well have the right to elect their presiding elders.

The upshot of all this was the final recommendation by the joint commission of a plan of union with "one General Conference" and "three or four quadrennial conferences." The General Conference was to be in two houses, lay and clerical; there was to be lay representation in the Annual Conferences. The quadrennial conferences were to "name the Bishops from their several jurisdictions," and these bishops were in turn to be confirmed by the "first house" [clerical] of the General Conference.

As it turned out this plan was debated with great vigor and cogency by the joint commission. Able speakers explored with great thoroughness all the possibilities inherent in it, and no feature caused greater discussion than that of the quadrennial conferences. "We never would consider four General Conferences," said Bishop Cranston. "We never can think of four Methodisms in place of what we now have. That would not be unification but quadrification. . . . What are these Quadrennial Conferences? We might say, in justification of what we were willing to agree to tentatively as a basis, that those will be simple matters, having only local bearing, which will be administered under the powers given to the Quadrennial Conferences. . . . From our standpoint the discretionary power should be in the General Conference and the restrictions should be laid upon the Quadrennial Conferences instead of the reverse."

But this entire plan, after receiving general approval, was nullified by a last minute vote of the commission to the effect that all was simply "tentative" and "in no sense are these suggestions a plan." Bishop Collins Denny, of the Methodist Episcopal Church, South, who announced that he had voted against all the items of the report, offered the resolution embodying the tentative affirmation, and his resolution was adopted. The participating churches, therefore, were in doubt when their General Conferences met as to whether they had anything properly before them from the 1911 meetings. These proceedings are mentioned in order to show the weight and influence of the jurisdictional pattern at that date.

The joint commissions of 1916 and 1920 are given credit by Bishop John M. Moore for producing the Plan of Union which finally, twenty years later, actually brought union. The same authority states flatly that "the jurisdictional or regional idea, which is central in the plan, had long existed in some form." [3] Just how much the growth of that idea was to affect the final details of the Plan of Union itself, Bishop Moore is at pains to make clear, and a complete study of the moves that led to church union corroborates his argument in this respect.

Dr. Edgar Blake, secretary of the Sunday School Board of the Methodist Episcopal Church, and later a bishop, is given credit by Bishop Moore for being "the most creative, inventive, resourceful, and efficient member of the Commission in devising, formulating, perfecting, and adopting the provisions of the Plan of Union." Wrote Bishop Moore: "He early saw that union could not be achieved except by the distribution of ecclesiastical power through the Jurisdictional Conference and Judicial Council." [4]

The jurisdictional idea, as the previous paragraphs make clear, and as Bishop Moore admits, was a Southern concept, and while there were many in the North who also recognized its value—as the entire church was formally to do after a time—yet its chief protagonists were in the Methodist Episcopal Church, South. The General Conference of that church in 1914 formally approved the "tentative" plan of 1911, and the Southern commission subsequently stated: "We, therefore, are com-

[3] *Ibid.*, p. 125.
[4] *Ibid.*, p. 168.

pelled to regard the Regional Conference as a basic principle of genuine unification of our Methodist Bodies."[5] Bishop Moore, who was himself a prime believer in the jurisdictional pattern, affirmed: "No Commission of the Church, South, and no member of any Commission of that Church, ever departed from that basic principle. No Union would come and no union would successfully remain without the complete and constant recognition of that basic principle." [6]

So it came about that the plan formulated by the joint commissions meeting in 1918 again embodied this same principle. In the plan of 1920, which the commission meeting first in 1918 produced, seven regional conferences were called for. Six of these were to be geographic, one to consist of the "Annual Conferences, Mission Conferences, and Missions embracing the work among colored people in the United States." The Plan of 1920 also called for a judicial council and was in every respect the structural pattern which was adopted for The Methodist Church almost twenty years later. The 1920 plan, however, did not receive formal approval from the General Conference of the Methodist Episcopal Church, though it was not definitely rejected. The commission of that church was continued, as were the commissions of the other two churches, with the advice that negotiations be continued.

The next plan, that of the early twenties, called for two jurisdictions, these jurisdictions to consist almost en bloc of the two big episcopal Methodist churches. This plan likewise failed of adoption, as it did not receive the necessary three-fourths vote of the Southern conferences. The two jurisdictions called for by the plan of 1924-26 were not quite like those of the plan of 1918 except in broad principle.

The historic record of events has been followed thus far in the endeavor to trace carefully the history of the jurisdictional idea and to indicate the prime part it played in the mind of one section of the church previous to union.

The final plan of 1936-38, which became the constitution of The Methodist Church, is a matter of record and need not be studied minutely here. As this chapter indicates, the plan embodied finally and completely the regional pattern along the lines agreed upon by the joint commissions of 1918-20.

While the Plan of Union was pending, and being presented to the three participating churches, all its provisions were scrutinized with great care. None of its provisions caused more questioning or elicited more debate

[5] *Ibid.*, p. 134.
[6] *Ibid.*, p. 134.

than the jurisdictional pattern. The church press was alive with articles expressing favor or disfavor, and such debate as occurred in the General Conference of the Methodist Episcopal Church dealt almost entirely with this feature.

Lending great weight to the argument for jurisdictions was the undeniable fact that a church as large as united Methodism promised to be, would have difficulty in operating and efficiently administering its vast work through one enormous General Conference. Such a representative body, it was admitted, could and should make laws as the sovereign power in all church-wide matters. But for administrative work, in electing bishops, providing for purely regional work, promotional activity, and the like, something more flexible was called for. The jurisdictional plan seemed to provide the answer. Bishop John M. Walden said in 1911 regarding the plan of that date: "I did not believe that it would be possible for me ever to consent to a united Methodism divided into four districts. But when I heard the brethren in the subcommittee I thought I saw some justification for it. When the question of majorities and minorities was presented, and I am American enough to know that constitutions are made to protect minorities, I was then willing to make the concession that has been made in the report now before us." [7]

The fact that the Methodist Episcopal Church already had Central Conferences, with great inherent powers, local sovereignty, and with the right to elect bishops, was also of great weight with the members and commissioners of that church.[8] But there were equally powerful arguments against the whole proposal. It was felt that strong Jurisdictional Conferences would make for several separate churches, not one church, and that the itinerant general superintendency would be destroyed at once by jurisdictional fission. It was also pointed out that neither bishops nor connectional officers might have sufficient church-wide standing unless, and until, a General Conference could elect and commission them for the whole church.

All sorts of suggestions were put forth in the effort to keep the General Conference as the final authority in electing such men. One proposal was that these general church officers be "nominated" by jurisdictions but elected by the General Conference; another was that they be elected by jurisdictions subject to the General Conference approval; still another that they be elected by jurisdictions but "consecrated" or inducted into office by the succeeding General Conference. The deep-set previous

---

[7] *Ibid.*, p. 102.

[8] *Proceedings of the Joint Commission on Unification*, II, 558-59.

process of all three Methodisms in relying on the General Conference for such elections was hard to overcome and supplant.

More important than any outwardly expressed agreement was an intangible but very real difference in fundamental attitudes on the part of the Methodist Episcopal and Methodist Episcopal Church, South, toward what may be called "regional consciousness." Such a consciousness is and has been for a long while a very real part of Southern life. No such marked regional consciousness is met with in the states of the North, though the West knows it to a certain degree. This feeling of regional distinctiveness is impossible of explanation to those who are not aware of it. It is something which may be allowed as a concept but not felt at all as a reality. Bishop John M. Moore, in emphasizing the Southern attitude with reference to jurisdictionalizing the church says:

The North thought in terms of centralized authority with centralized agencies. The South thought of sufficient sectional control and agencies to ensure its protection against a dominant majority and to give latitude for its own expression. . . . There is still a North and a South in this country, and there is an East and a West, and they are not merely geographical. They are social, economic, ethnic, cultural, civilizational, ideological. To be sure, they are not so extremely so as to be divisional, but they are sufficiently distinct to create varied human characteristics and values.[9]

Bishop Moore is, of course, here expressing the viewpoint of one who stood strongly for the jurisdictional plan. The opposing side was put forward by Bishop John W. Hamilton in the discussion of the plan of union of 1918:

I would like to see no more solid North, no more solid South, but unification in which your bishops shall preside over our territory and ours over yours and we sit in one common conference of bishops. Then all these geographic matters and local matters that come up, occasioned either by prejudice or by actual conditions, could be readily adjusted.[10]

Bishop William F. McDowell joined in even more strongly:

It is possible for us to make a reorganized Church which shall not be a unified Church. . . . We can make a series of Jurisdictional Conferences which might prodigiously minister to local efficiency, which might greatly satisfy local sentiment and the desire for local autonomy. . . . We can do it in such fashion as to cut the strong off from the weak, the weak from the

[9] Op. cit., pp. 189, 226.
[10] Proceedings of the Joint Commission on Unification, I, 73.

strong. . . . Now, brothers, I am not anxious for a union that is simply going to make a new barrier between Minnesota and Virginia. . . . In facing this question of Jurisdictional Conferences we have to have regard, not simply for local autonomy, not simply for the following of natural lines locally defined. We have to have regard for that unity of co-operation and self-consciousness that will enable us to throw the whole weight of our Church wherever Christ's kingdom demands it.[11]

A somewhat different point of view was stated by Dr. C. M. Bishop, of the Southern commission of 1918:

We do not conceive . . . that these separate jurisdictional lines will at all interfere with the oneness of the Church, with the unity that shall prevail across all these invisible lines. . . . We do not propose to constitute a lot of little churches. We propose to unify Methodism in America, so reorganized as to give it larger efficiency and appeal both to the local loyalties and to the widespread general interests of every earnest Methodist in the world.[12]

The fact that the Negro conferences of the united church were to be comprehended in one jurisdiction made for much more debate and intensified the differences over the jurisdictional pattern. The hated word "segregation" was mentioned more than once, and it was argued that this was being written into the fundamental law of the church. But the administrative argument had tremendous weight in offsetting this, as there were no biracial conferences, and the Negro membership was already organized into Annual Conferences, North as well as South. In a long-remembered speech which Dr. Edgar Blake made to the joint commission this fact was pointed out with force and effectiveness:

We have preached the doctrine of racial equality and then turned around and denied it in our practice. We have done a magnificent work for the Negro, and, brethren of the South, I make no apology for what we have done for the Negro in the Southland. I thank God for it, and I look upon it as the finest home missionary contribution that the Methodist Episcopal Church has made in America. We have done magnificent work for the Negro, but it has been a work away from home. We have drawn the color line. We have our separate congregations and our separate Annual Conferences. We have separation all the way up to our General Conference. We have no mixed congregations in the North, except occasionally we find two or three persons of color in our congregations.[13]

[11] *Ibid.*, I, 105-6.
[12] *Ibid.*, I, 115-16.
[13] *Ibid.*, II, 349.

These separately organized Annual Conferences serving the Negro membership in the Methodist Episcopal Church made it almost inevitable, as Dr. Blake pointed out, that there be a jurisdictional grouping of such conferences if the jurisdictional plan were to be adopted at all. Otherwise the Negro conferences would be so scattered and divided as to represent a minority group in each jurisdiction; or, if the jurisdictional pattern were not adopted, and all Methodism were managed as one administrative unit, the Negro conferences would be an even smaller minority in the united church than they were in the Methodist Episcopal. In either case, whether in jurisdictions or in the whole church, a separate action would have to be taken, or at least arranged for, by consent whenever the Negro membership should need to have a bishop or general officer elected or a general board member appointed. The former Methodist Episcopal Church felt obliged to do it that way when it called for election of Negro bishops in 1920 by special resolution. The jurisdictional plan, so its proponents held, seemed to promise a greater degree of autonomy for the Negro conferences than they had exercised before, or than they could be expected to exercise under an integrally united Methodist church. Proponents of the jurisdictional idea, not liking to be charged with supporting a discriminatory plan, pointed out that neither in the General Conference nor in any of the boards or general church agencies, not even in the most intimate committees or agencies of the church, was there any disposition to keep the Negro conferences from having their proportionate representation. On the contrary, it was insisted that each jurisdiction should be equally represented in all these. Only in the jurisdictions themselves, created for executive and administrative purposes, did the separate Negro conferences seem to need joint collocation in order to be an autonomous executive group.

Enough has been said in the preceding pages to indicate that the jurisdictional pattern was not arrived at or accepted by a swiftly executed move by the last commission on church union. It was the general plan about which all moves for union sooner or later came to revolve as the years passed. The plan was bitterly opposed and powerfully championed. But when the Uniting Conference at Kansas City closed on a note of triumph in 1939, that pattern and that plan had become the fundamental law of The Methodist Church. Be it said to the credit of those who opposed, as well of those who supported this plan, that since that date every effort has been made to accept and use the jurisdictional pattern in all promising ways.

XVI

THE JURISDICTIONAL CONFERENCES

THE JURISDICTIONS, AS PROVIDED BY THE PLAN OF UNION, FUNCTION—
or to date have functioned—chiefly in and through the respective Jurisdictional Conferences. As now existing, these Jurisdictional Conferences
have constitutional powers as follows: Each Jurisdictional Conference is
on a parity with the other Jurisdictional Conferences[1] with relation to its
"privileges of action"; and in regard to "ratio of representation of the
Annual Conferences in the General Conference." In other words, the
Annual Conferences of one jurisdiction may not be given a greater or
less representation in the General Conference than those of another
jurisdiction.

Each Jurisdictional Conference must be composed of an equal number
of lay delegates and clerical delegates, each "order" to be elected by the
persons in the Annual Conferences representing that order.

Each Jurisdictional Conference is compelled to meet within the twelve
months succeeding the meeting of the General Conference. Time and
place of such meeting must be decided by the former Jurisdictional Conference or by a committee appointed by it.[2] This provision effectively
prohibits a Jurisdictional Conference from meeting previous to the General Conference, as was proposed many times during the discussion on
the plan of church union.

Protagonists of this idea wished to have bishops elected by the Jurisdictional Conferences so that these, with other general church officers,
might later be confirmed, consecrated, or commissioned at the ensuing
General Conference. It was felt that this would give such bishops and
officers better church-wide standing; it would also give Jurisdictional
Conferences the opportunity to sift memorials, formulate plans, and
propose legislation for the General Conference about to meet.

Against this view, however, it was argued that the Jurisdictional Conference would be no more than a nominating convention or regional
caucus if its elections must be confirmed and sealed by later General
Conference action; and that pre–General Conference debate on proposed

[1] Constitution, Div. II, Sec. IV, Art. II.
[2] *Ibid.*, Art. IV.

176

legislation would waste time and tend to create "bloc" voting by juris-dictions in the General Conference itself. The prevailing view was that the Jurisdictional Conferences should be the promotional and adminis-trative agencies of the church, "stepping down" the actions and legisla-tion of the General Conference and so giving them better effect in each area—and that view finally prevailed. The General Conference–Jurisdic-tional Conference sequence was made fundamental. The General Con-ference must be followed—not preceded by—the Jurisdictional Confer-ences. That provision is constitutional.

Under the constitution also the Jurisdictional Conference has the following powers and duties:

1. To promote the evangelistic, educational, missionary, and benevolent interests of the church, and to provide for interests and institutions within their boundaries.
2. To elect bishops and to co-operate in carrying out such plans for their support as may be determined by the General Conference.
3. To establish and constitute Jurisdictional Conference boards as aux-iliary to the general boards of the church as the need may appear, and to choose their representatives in such manner as the General Conference may determine.
4. To determine the boundaries of their Annual Conferences, provided that there shall be no Annual Conference with a membership of fewer than fifty members in full connection, except by the consent of the General Con-ference.
5. To make rules and regulations for the administration of the work of the church within the jurisdiction, subject to such powers as have been or shall be vested in the General Conference.
6. To appoint a Committee on Appeals to hear and determine the appeal of a traveling preacher of that jurisdiction from the decision of a trial com-mittee.[3]

Other powers and duties may be conferred upon the Jurisdictional Conference by the General Conference, provided that such a grant or commission on the part of the General Conference does not infringe any other part of the constitution.

There is no definitive provision as to the number of representatives each Annual Conference may have in the Jurisdictional Conference. This is put at the direction of the General Conference. The General Conference can therefore make the number large or small but must provide "a uniform basis," to apply everywhere. It must, of course, keep

[3] *Ibid.*, Art. V.

the ministerial and lay representatives equal in number, and it may not give to one conference or one jurisdiction more representatives than it gives to another. Statutory legislation in any General Conference, however, could reduce or enlarge Annual Conference representation in the Jurisdictional Conferences. At present, by action of the General Conference of 1940, one ministerial representative is allowed for each thirty ministerial members, and an equal number of lay representatives from each Annual Conference.

"The bishops of the several Jurisdictional Conferences shall preside in the sessions of their respective Jurisdictional Conferences." [4] This is constitutional. The bishops of any jurisdiction, at their Jurisdictional Conferences, arrange the order of their presidency among them, though they may request that a committee of the conference act or advise on this matter.

Each Jurisdictional Conference adopts its own rules of order though it is customary—practically Methodist common law—for Methodist conferences of all sorts to adopt the "rules of order of the last General Conference" for parliamentary order and governance "insofar as these apply."

The Jurisdictional Conference has the constitutional right to alter the bounds of Annual Conferences which are included within its area, but it may not allow an Annual Conference to exist with a membership of less than fifty ministers in full connection, unless the General Conference shall consent to such conference existing or continuing to exist.[5]

Jurisdictional Conferences have no power to change or alter their own boundaries even by mutual agreement. The General Conference, however, has the power "to change the number and the boundaries of Jurisdictional Conferences upon the consent of a majority of the Annual Conferences in each Jurisdictional Conference involved." [6] As the jurisdictions were carefully drawn and defined in the Plan of Union, the General Conference is given by this provision the constitutional right to alter the constitution in other than the usual way. To be sure, a majority of the conferences in the jurisdictions involved must support any such proposal, but they act here as conferences, not as is the case in amending the constitution in the regular way, as conference members.

[4] Constitution, Div. III, Art. VIII.
[5] *Ibid.*, Art. V (4).
[6] Constitution, Div. II, Sec. I, Art. IV (12).

SINCE UNION

As was to be expected, the jurisdictional system has been under scrutiny more than any other feature of the Plan of Union. The first Jurisdictional Conferences met in 1940, following the meeting of the first General Conference. At that time the delegates from the General Conference proceeded to their respective jurisdictional meetings within a few weeks, and were joined there by the additional jurisdictional delegates allowed to each of the respective Annual Conferences. But in 1940 no bishops were elected in four of the six jurisdictions, and as there was no possibility of passing legislation, the selection of representatives on the various general boards turned out to be a somewhat perfunctory matter. These first Jurisdictional Conferences, following as they did the colorful Uniting Conference and the first General Conference of The Methodist Church, seemed somewhat lackadaisical and insipid.

During the first quadrennium an unenthusiastic impression regarding the Jurisdictional Conferences seemed to be held rather generally. Those who had never believed in the value of this special organization were not slow to point out its apparent lack of vitality. Articles appeared in the church press with reference to this matter, and one written by Dr. Paul Quillian, of Texas, renewed the old suggestion that the Jurisdictional Conference should be made to precede the General Conference. Bishop John M. Moore brought out *The Long Road to Methodist Union* in part, at least, to call attention to the need of developing to the full the inherent resources of the jurisdictional plan.

At the beginning of the second quadrennium, however, a better opportunity was presented to the jurisdictional bodies. Practically all jurisdictions were called upon to elect bishops, and the interest in this proceeding, always immensely strong in Methodist bodies, served to enhance interest in the Jurisdictional Conferences to a far greater degree than had been the case in 1940.

In addition to this, the two Southern Jurisdictions, the Southeastern and South Central, anxious to develop to the full the inherent powers residing in the jurisdictional organization, formulated and put into effect programs of jurisdictional work designed to administer the work in their respective areas in accordance with the peculiar needs of such work. The Southeastern Jurisdiction set up a well-wrought plan, not only calling for jurisdictional boards but creating a Jurisdictional Council and electing an executive secretary to oversee a general program throughout the jurisdiction. The South Central Jurisdiction likewise created special jurisdictional agencies, though perhaps not to the extent that the Southeastern did. Other jurisdictions named to a greater degree supplementary boards and agencies designed to co-operate with the general boards or to project regional work as need might demand. The result of all this, coupled with the very real value of the jurisdictional representatives as electors of bishops and board members for or from the respective areas, all somewhat strengthened the jurisdictional plan as it moved through its second quadrennium.

The question of the Central Jurisdiction has continued to be fraught with deep import. Wrote Dr. Frederick B. Newell, of the New York East Conference:

The place of the Negro in The Methodist Church is perhaps the most serious question which united Methodism faces. . . . The question lies at the heart of Methodism's approach to the racial tensions of America and must be faced. First of all it is self-evident that, as of the present, jurisdictionalism cannot be dissolved without friction and possible disunity. Even an effort to this end might prove disastrous to our new church at this hour. This does not mean that jurisdictionalism is socially just or racially righteous. It simply means that jurisdictionalism has in it certain practical values for the governing of 8,500,000 people and to liquidate it suddenly would be impracticable.[7]

Members of the Central Jurisdiction, while they deplore the situation which resulted in a jurisdictional division along racial lines, are inclined to accept this as "the best the church could do in 1939." Dr. Matthew W. Clair, Jr., a distinguished member of the Central Jurisdiction, has published certain replies to a questionnaire with which he queried those whom he terms "leaders in the Central Jurisdiction." These replies naturally vary, but their common resultant seems to be an acceptance of the situation as it is, coupled with a decided antipathy toward its permanent continuance. One of these replies stated:

While the Central Jurisdictional set-up is not and never has been an ideal situation in The Methodist Church, yet with the background of separation of the races both among Negroes and white people, it seems to me to be the best practical solution of the present problem. No matter what offers are made to Negroes by white churches, for several generations yet Negroes will prefer their own local church organization, and of course the administration of such churches can be done better by men of the Negro group. Personally I hope the day will come when America can become Christ-minded enough for The Methodist Church to become one integrated organization without any racial lines whatever.

[7] *The Drew Gateway,* XVIII, No. 2, Winter, 1947.

Another said:

The jurisdictional arrangement in The Methodist Church, and especially
the Central Jurisdiction, was the best that the church could do in 1939. The
paganistic influences would at that time make no greater concessions—it was
all that the traffic would bear. It was a move in the right direction. It was not
more than a step. It reveals, rather than covers, our sins. If Methodism is to
continue to be an outstanding Christian movement, it must scrap its Central
Jurisdiction.

A third replied:

I do think that the Negro has prospered in the Central Jurisdiction set-up.
He has had a chance to demonstrate beyond a doubt that he is working
better under his own leadership. I don't think that the Central Jurisdiction
should be continued forever, but that the Negroes should be integrated into
the general church on a democratic and Christian basis.[8]

Dr. Newell, in the article previously quoted, offers the constructive
suggestion that this whole question "be approached from long range to
see if the polity cannot be so adjusted within the Jurisdictional system as
to alleviate the social injustice which it promotes and at the same time
retain the freedom of self-government and the eligibility of office which
the present system affords."

A real obstacle to a complete and far-reaching utilization of the jurisdictional organization is that any program put on by a jurisdiction must
be supported by funds raised by that jurisdiction, and since both the
Annual Conferences and the General Conference have their own assessments and levy on the churches to support these, a further assessment
to take care of a jurisdictional program is not easily secured. In addition
to this fact there is a strong tendency in The Methodist Church to
look to the great boards of the church and the General Conference
agencies to do what work is needed rather than taking measures to do
such work through more local agencies. This is, of course, but a reflection
within the church of what appears at present to be a drift toward centralization everywhere in government. Whether this should be the case
or not, is not a subject for debate in these pages. It is simply recorded
here as a fact. And this universal drift toward centralization is making it
more difficult for those who call, and with some justice, for more regional, state, or local government. But that the drift in Methodism,
highly centralized as episcopal Methodism has always been, is away from

[8] W. K. Anderson, ed., *Methodism* (1947), pp. 247-48.

the regional administration to vast overreaching general administration cannot be denied. The years are yet to say how far that drift shall modify the basic patterns of the present church.

Meanwhile members of other churches are watching with interest the jurisdictional plan as it functions in the largest Protestant denomination. A distinguished ecclesiastic of another denomination, in discussing the coming world church, said that he thought there might well be an ecumenical organization for the world on the order of "Methodism's regional plan." That plan, now subjected to the test of experience and life, will survive if it is useful, and disappear if it is not. No argument will save it if it manifests itself in time as cumbersome and useless; and no argument will destroy it if it fulfills a useful function in the life of a growing vital church. Time, which tests all things, will bring the answer.

XVII

THE CENTRAL CONFERENCES

There shall be Central Conferences for the work of the church outside the United States of America.

—Constitution, Div. II, Sec. V, Art. I

THE METHODIST CHURCH IS A WORLD CHURCH AND AS SUCH MUST PROvide for its work and administration in every land. As long as the church in the United States was sending out missionaries and providing for their support, it made laws and regulations for its mission work exactly as it did for its home conferences. But with the rapid development, especially during recent years, of the autonomous churches in many lands, an entirely different situation from that of the church's "Colonial era" was presented. In certain lands—notably Mexico, Brazil, and Korea—autonomous Methodist churches were set off by united Methodist action early in 1930. In other lands the growth of the work and the consequent call for more autonomy and better correlation in facing material problems brought about regional conferences composed of missions and mission Annual Conferences. India provided the first organized move of this sort on a large scale. As early as 1879 the North India Conference and South India Conference proposed and effected in 1881 a "Delegated Conference," as it was called. Pursuant to its meeting, and following memorials presented by its Annual Conferences, the Methodist Episcopal General Conference of 1884 enacted legislation which permitted the organization of Central Mission Conferences "when in any of our foreign fields there is more than one Annual Conference or Mission, or more than one form of Methodism." [1] The name "Central Conference" rather than "Delegated Conference" was then given in recognition of the central nature of these conferences in each area where one should be held.

Legislation concerning Central Conferences continued to appear in Methodist Episcopal *Disciplines* from that time on, and in 1900 such conferences were definitely written into the constitution of the church. These conferences were to be composed of "Annual Conferences, Mission Conferences, and Missions" in such numbers as the General Conference by a two-thirds vote might determine. The powers delegated to,

[1] Marvin Henry Harper, *The Methodist Episcopal Church in India* (1936), p. 41.

183

or outlined for, such Central Conferences were also to be decided by a two-thirds vote of the General Conference. Under this provision and statutory legislation of the General Conference pursuant thereto, Central Conferences in connection with the Methodist Episcopal Church were at the time of union functioning in Eastern Asia (China), Southern Asia (India), Latin America (South America with the exception of Brazil), and Germany. These conferences had the right to manage the work within their own areas under the regulations passed by the General Conference, and could elect bishops if and when a specific authorization to do so was passed by the General Conference. Such bishops, however, could exercise episcopal functions only in the area of the Central Conference electing them, and the Central Conference also was expected to provide largely for their support.

The Methodist Episcopal Church, South, had no planetary organizations in its mission areas comparable to the Central Conferences of the Methodist Episcopal Church, nor did the Methodist Protestants. Annual and Mission Conferences attached to the Methodist Episcopal Church, South, which might have developed into regional conferences comparable to the Central Conferences, became organized into regular indigenous Methodist churches in Mexico, Brazil, and Korea before a local organization comparable to the Central Conference was organized in these regions.

At union in 1939 the provision for Central Conferences was written into the constitution of The Methodist Church and in much the same language as the like provision had been phrased in the Methodist Episcopal *Discipline*. Such conferences were to be "in such numbers and with such boundaries as the Uniting Conference might determine"; and it was provided that subsequently the General Conference should have the right to alter the number and boundaries of such conferences. The powers of Central Conferences were constitutionally outlined in a definite way, though the General Conference was given the right to "confer" such other powers as might be necessary. These powers were as follows:

1. To promote evangelistic, educational, missionary, and benevolent interests and institutions of the church within their own boundaries.

2. To elect the bishops for the respective Central Conferences in number as may be determined from time to time, upon a basis fixed by the General Conference, and to co-operate in carrying out such plans for the support of their bishops as may be determined by the General Conference.

3. To establish and constitute such Central Conference boards as may be required and to elect their administrative officers.

4. To determine the boundaries of the Annual Conferences within their respective areas.

5. To make such rules and regulations for the administration of the work within their boundaries as the conditions in the respective areas may require, subject to the powers that have been or shall be vested in the General Conference.

6. To appoint a Committee on Appeals to hear and determine the appeal of a traveling preacher of that Central Conference from the decisions of a Committee on Trial.[2]

It is to be noted that bishops are to be elected by Central Conferences upon "a basis fixed by the General Conference." That basis to date requires specific action by the General Conference authorizing each such election, just as was the case in the Methodist Episcopal Church. It is worthy of note that some Central Conferences have adopted "term episcopacy," electing their bishops for a stated term rather than for life, as is the case in The Methodist Church. A bishop elected by, and consecrated for, one Central Conference may not exercise episcopal functions within another such conference unless, and until, invited to do so by the conference in question. Central Conference bishops are received as bishops within the territory of the entire Methodist Church and accorded all the honors commensurate with that office, except actual superintendency outside their areas. They sit with the Council of Bishops as members of that body and have a voice but no vote, except when the matter at issue touches their own particular Central Conference area.

It will be clear that the Central Conference, like the Jurisdictional Conference which it resembles—or which resembles it, to keep chronology straight—has very great and definite powers within its own area touching administrative matters. Its elections are in its own hands and it has a very large measure of autonomy in speaking for and to its own area.

[2] Constitution, Div. II, Sec. V, Art. IV.

PART FOUR

Methodist Law

and

the Judicial Council

XVIII

ADMINISTRATIVE AND TRIAL LAW

The right to organize voluntary religious associations ... and to create tribunals for the decision of controverted questions of faith within the association, and for the ecclesiastical government of all the individual members, congregations, and officers ... is unquestioned.

—United States Supreme Court (13 Wallace 679)

THE CREATION OF THE JUDICIAL COUNCIL AND ITS INCLUSION IN THE constitutional structure of The Methodist Church was a feature of the Plan of Union which has received universal acclaim. This council provides a tribunal for the church which can act independently of bishops, boards and conferences, and can interpret for all the fundamental law. It also provides a less spectacular, but more often used, appellate court, which can and does settle certain matters of appeal finally referred to it.

The Methodist Church has formulated in a unique way its own law and developed its peculiar legal processes as need called for these during the years. Ecclesiastical law, as that was known and administered in England, was not bequeathed to American Methodism. Indeed few of the canons or rubrics of the Church of England were incorporated into the Methodist Episcopal Church in the United States, and none of these as such, with the exception of certain rubrics of the ritual. To be sure, Christian conduct and canonical law coalesced in many instances, and the prevailing customs and usages of Christian conduct were binding upon early Methodists, perhaps more so than they were upon all Christians. But it may truly be said that in its evolution from a loose connection of societies to the present church, Methodism has made its own law, its own discipline. It is significant that its book of law is known as *The Discipline.*

In the early days the societies settled matters affecting the character of members and censured, reprimanded, or expelled members in as summary a way as the usual family sifts a situation within a home. But as the societies grew, especially when conferences of preachers came into being, and the Methodists on this side of the ocean became a church, something more of due legal process was called for. Thus in time, and little

189

by little, there evolved rules for the proper "discipline" of the body, and eventually regulations for the trial of members, of deaconesses, of local preachers, of traveling preachers, and of bishops—the five classes of persons for whom trials are at present outlined in the *Discipline*. There also grew a large body of church law having to do with the technical organization of the Methodist Church itself.

These two kinds of law, trial law or the application of discipline to Methodist ministers and members; and organic, administrative law, or that having to do with the technical processes and procedures of the Methodist organization, grew and developed together. For purposes of this study it will be convenient to examine each of these separately, taking up first the growth and interrelation of Methodist administrative law in its larger nonpersonal aspects; and then turning to the immediate application of the law itself to individuals and cases.

ADMINISTRATIVE LAW

In the study of the episcopacy it has been made clear by what process the bishops, serving as conference presidents, are entrusted with the power to interpret Methodist law. The bishop was from the beginning given this power, but not until 1840 was it made a matter of formal record in the *Discipline*. At that date it was stated that one of the duties of a bishop was: "To decide all questions of law in an annual conference, subject to an appeal to the General Conference; but in all cases the application of the law shall be with the conference."

This regulation, with a slight change in wording ("questions of law involved in proceedings pending")[1] and ("questions of law coming before him in the regular business of an Annual Conference")[2] remained in episcopal Methodist *Disciplines* until union and is now in the *Discipline* of the united church. But as has been elsewhere indicated, the ruling of a bishop upon a law question in episcopal Methodism had to be reported and confirmed by another body before it could be taken as definitive Methodist law—to the General Conference of the Methodist Episcopal Church; or to the College of Bishops of the Methodist Episcopal Church, South. When, or if, these bodies, acting as a bench of delegates, or a bench of bishops, as the case might be, had approved an individual bishop's ruling, it became and was published as authoritative law.

But the ruling of the bishop on a question of law was—as experience and General Conference enactment soon made clear—not to be given

[1] *Discipline*, Methodist Episcopal Church, 1872.
[2] *Discipline*, Methodist Episcopal Church, South, 1854.

casually or irrelevantly. While regulations differed in their language some-what in the *Disciplines* of the two episcopal Methodisms, both these churches made it plain that a bishop could not rule upon a matter which was not actually pending or that was not related to the immediate business of the conference. No hypothetical questions could be brought before a bishop, nor could any private opinion given outside of a formal conference session be of any value. Neither could a single individual or minority group obtain a ruling unless by formal request duly entered on the conference minutes. The bishop's ruling in every instance must also be formally made a matter of record. All this indicates the care with which the churches felt a bishop's power to interpret the law should be guarded.

In the present Methodist Church, to bring this matter up to date, the old regulations are continued or enforced in even stronger language. The bishop now must rule upon a legal question when presiding over a Dis-trict, Annual, or Jurisdictional Conference (not a General Conference, be it noted),[3] providing that this comes before him in the regular business of the session, and that the questions be presented in writing. His ruling, of course, must be made a part of the conference record. No decision is authoritative, except for the case pending, until it has been again passed on by the Judicial Council. Each bishop must report all his rulings to that council "in writing annually," and the council may then "affirm, modify, or reverse" such rulings. Its action is final.[4]

Thus the present church interprets its own law as that law is met with or affects conference action. The enactment of law, not its interpretation, remains, of course, the province of the General Conference.

METHODIST TRIAL LAW

In the United States there have never been church courts after the English pattern, and with our theory of "a free church in a free land" there cannot be. But all denominational groups of any size do have their own courts or judicial processes whereby they administer discipline among their members, as well as pronounce upon their own intrinsic questions of polity or law. The Methodist Church, as has been sug-gested, has a vast body of such law. Its provisions as found in the present *Discipline* cover many pages, and give all manner of directions concern-ing trials and appeals.

In the United States no church court has any civil power over its

[3] Constitution, Div. III, Art. VII.
[4] *Ibid.*

members, nor any right to affect them in any other way than in their relationship to it—the church. No church court can fine a man or send him to prison. But it can censure, it can reprimand, it can suspend, and it can, as a last resort, expel. The power to do this, if properly carried out, is not called in question by the civil courts or by any other authority. "In the United States," observed Judge Henry Wade Rogers, "all questions relating to faith, practice, discipline of the Church and of its members belong not to the civil courts but to the ecclesiastical tribunals to which the members of the Church are subject, and the decisions of those tribunals are final." [5] The civil courts do not take any jurisdiction except in cases in which temporal rights are involved, and they will not review the decisions of church courts in matters which are properly within the province of such tribunals. If a competent church authority expels a member or minister, and the person expelled wishes to sue the church body for defamation of character or for injuring his public standing, the civil court will not take jurisdiction. It takes the position that a competent church authority has acted, and that the person became subject to this special discipline when he joined that particular organization. A great many cases in the civil courts have made plain the above-mentioned statement. It must be evident, however, that the church court in question carried out faithfully its own legal processes.

Church courts themselves usually conduct their trials under processes which are heavily influenced by English common law. Especially in Methodist courts and by trial committees is this fact manifest. The right to be represented by counsel, to be faced by one's accuser, to be tried by a jury—that is, a committee of one's peers—all this is deeply written into church law. Certainly it is so in Methodist law. Grand jury action—that is, investigation into the need for a formal trial—is always put into effect by the church through a "committee of investigation," which itself must follow definite rules in sifting allegations and preparing its bill of specific charges.

There is, however, a profound difference in the spirit that pervades church law and that underlying civil law. In civil law, no penalty or blame can attach to one who is not proved guilty of an overt act. A man may intend to steal and plan to commit murder, but unless he does these things or threatens in a tangible way to commit such actual breach of peace, civil courts can take no notice. The law cannot deal with intent, unless intent is made clear by an outward act. But the church, in administering its discipline, is vastly concerned with intent, for intent is part

[5] Arthur Benton Sanford, *Reports of the Committee on Judiciary* (1924), p. vii.

and parcel of a person's own spiritual attitudes. "The church," as a minister once observed, "is trying to prove or disprove the existence of sin, and not some one special outward expression of it."

Church trial committees have sometimes overlooked this fact. A person, for instance, who has been tried for immorality but against whom an outward case could not be proved, but who has nevertheless given clear evidence of an intent to act immorally, has sometimes been let off by a church court with a warning or by a reprimand. This nullifies discipline by that much. It is quite true that church courts face as great a difficulty as do those of the state when they attempt to enter into the realm of intent to find out what a person wills to do. But church courts will fail to do their ideal duty if they proceed entirely by the hard inflexible system which English common law, or even courts of equity, have worked out through the years and in which outward acts are the only criterion.

Expulsion, which is the greatest penalty the church can inflict upon its members, does not usually worry to any extent a lay member who is expelled, unless such expulsion shall reflect greatly upon his public character. Even then he has no redress if the church court proceeded correctly and according to its own law. Thousands of lay members, who could and would be tried and put out of a church should a formal trial be held, resign of their own accord before being brought to trial. Others never bother to answer the summons which a church court may issue. Some become very angry and "demand their letter" or ask that their names be struck from the roll when their pastor calls their conduct, or rumors regarding it, to their attention. This saves ministers and church officials from having to conduct many an unlovely church trial which neighborhood feelings and newspaper coverage might make embarrassing and difficult.

When a church member is accused of a crime by the civil authorities, or is under trial for some misdemeanor which would also be an offense to the church, ministers and church courts always wait until the civil courts have acted before they take any steps to apply discipline. If a prominent steward should be accused of embezzlement and is under indictment for the same, and his church should appoint a trial committee to investigate this matter, it is perfectly evident that the church court could not possibly have the facilities to try this case as ably as the civil authority. If that authority clears the man, he is considered clear by the church—at least for that particular accusation. If it convicts him, he is convicted and there is no need for a church trial.

But where a minister—not a layman—is accused of an offense and is to be tried by a church court, a far different situation prevails from that which affects lay members. Expulsion from the church, or even censure passed upon a minister by his brethren, vastly affects his life and fortune. Expulsion indeed may mean a minister's ruin, especially if coupled with it there are charges which affect his character, for other Christian denominations scarcely welcome a minister who has been publicly convicted of immoral action. The man thus loses his reputation, his profession, and even his livelihood as the result of a church trial. For this reason the trials of ministers are attended with a dread and solemnity almost impossible to describe. They are usually accompanied also with a bitterness which leaves deep marks upon all who have become involved in them. When there is a conviction and there is any possibility at all of appealing the case to a higher authority, such appeal is always made. This explains the number and the intensity of such appeals in Methodist judicial history.

The right of a trial and of an appeal was considered so fundamental in early Methodism that by the time 1808 had come, and the General Conference was set up as the governing body of the church, a Restrictive Rule was written to prevent any General Conference from encroaching upon such right. It is not clear that any General Conference might have been tempted to encroach upon it, but the fathers of 1808, under the influence of the long struggle of Englishmen to get these rights firmly established, decided to write trial and appeal into their fundamental law. There they remain to this day, as far beyond the reach of the present General Conference, or of any other group, as they ever have been.

As has been stated, there is a distinction made among five classes of persons in The Methodist Church with respect to trials and conducting trials. These five classes are: (1) lay members; (2) deaconesses; (3) local preachers and accepted supply preachers; (4) traveling preachers; (5) bishops. Appropriate processes for preliminary investigation and trial in each case are carefully outlined in the *Discipline*, and all trials are conducted in accordance with such provisions.[6]

The trial of church members is today rather rare, as the usual member, if a trial is really warranted, prefers to withdraw and surrender membership before a formal public hearing takes place. Methodist authorities formerly took the position that if the accused absented himself from a trial after sufficient notice had been given, and no person had been asked to appear in his behalf, the trial should nevertheless go on. So held

[6] *Discipline*, 1944, ¶¶ 921-77.

Bishop Collins Denny, who quotes with approval Bishop Osmon C. Baker upon this matter.[7] However, although ministers are expected to maintain discipline and to see that persons guilty of improper actions are strictly dealt with by remonstrance and warning on the part of the minister, and, if necessary, by a formal trial, it is undeniable that through the years there has come to be some looseness in this regard. Heinous offenses or public actions which bring evil notoriety upon the person or the church of which he is a member are indeed sometimes dealt with; but many infractions of discipline, which would have meant trial and expulsion in Methodist societies a hundred years ago, are ignored today.

With the ministry, however, a different situation prevails. Local preachers, to be sure, have come to be regarded more as laymen who preach occasionally than as preachers who make their living in some lay activity. Consequently there is not quite as strict a discipline administered with reference to them as was formerly the case. Where there are charges or doubts affecting the character of a local minister, this matter comes to the fore when he requests, if he does request, a continuation of his license, and it is sometimes settled by refusal on the part of a Quarterly or District Conference to renew such license. No formal trial takes place in such instance; the license is simply not renewed and the man is no longer a local preacher.

With the traveling ministry, however, and with bishops, there is great sensitivity upon this whole matter of actionable offenses. The people themselves will not have a minister against whom there is any allegation affecting such a man's character or conduct. The district superintendent is expected to see that any specific charges, or even rumors, reflecting upon the character of any minister in his district shall be sifted at once if need requires, and the fact that every minister's character must be examined at each Annual Conference forces the district superintendent either to "pass" or to "arrest" the character of every man who is under his supervision.

It will not be necessary to examine deeply into the rules and regulations which The Methodist Church at present keeps for the guidance of those who are called upon to conduct church trials or who must participate in them. The present *Discipline* elaborates in great detail the necessary procedures having to do with this whole matter. Those who are called upon to be responsible for the application of discipline or to represent either the church or the accused at a church trial do well to study carefully every word in the disciplinary paragraphs bearing upon such particu-

[7] *A Manual of the Discipline* (1931), p. 157.

lars. Even then, because the church is not fundamentally the creator of a code of laws but has developed its judicial processes and punitive powers against its own will, as it were, great ambiguity is often discovered within church law today. With all the provisions of the *Discipline* treating of this matter, there is often opportunity for variant interpretations, for differences over matters of procedure, for appeal to a higher court, and nearly always for recrimination and bitterness, in the usual church trial. Ministers themselves, as a rule, make poor judges, their very profession demanding of them that they be pleaders, advocates, and evangels rather than cool, judicially-minded jurists. But discipline must be had and by so much as a wrongdoer is allowed to continue wrongdoing in the church of God, by that much is the entire church hurt and weakened, and the way made easier for others to do evil also.

XIX

APPEALS

As was previously indicated, the great number of appeals in Methodist organizational life comes about by virtue of the fact that in a church as large as The Methodist Church all manner of trials, as all manner of rulings by presiding officers, actions of conferences, bishops, and the like, are open to question. In the early days an appeal was just that. A person told his story to the Annual Conference brotherhood and asked redress. In many instances his plea did not involve any question of moral wrongdoing but was simply some situation in which the appellant wanted sympathy or relief. The Methodist Protestants, it may be remembered, desired—and arranged within their own connection—for an appeal to the Annual Conference on the part of any minister when a pending appointment was considered onerous or unfair.

The Rev. Thomas Owens, a quaint character of the Southwest in the very early days, was once censured by his brethren because he indulged in humor in the pulpit and "made the people laugh." His apparently artless "appeal" to the conference to bear with him in this regard was couched so as to draw uncontrolled laughter from the censuring brethren themselves.

But appeals after a time grew weightier as the church increased, and conference and ministerial responsibilities were enhanced. A crucial one had to do with the right of an Annual Conference to "locate," that is, put out of the traveling ministry, an individual member of the conference itself. A minister could, of course, always ask for location and be located by formal conference action, if the conference so agreed. But could a preacher be located without his own consent? As early as 1820 a General Conference "committee on rights and privileges" had looked into this matter on instructions of the General Conference itself.[1] Nothing, however, was done about this until 1836, when the General Conference, accepting the report of its Judiciary Committee, decided that an Annual Conference did have the right to locate a man without his consent.[2] The man was allowed to appeal to the conference—or rather, to be heard by the conference—if he should so desire, or to have one represent

[1] *Journals*, I, 189.
[2] *Journals*, I, 492-93.

him and plead that he be not located. He was also to be allowed the right of a formal appeal to the next General Conference, so Nathan Bangs, who reported on this matter, stated.[3] But it was then established clearly, and has never since been called in question, that an Annual Conference can locate one of its members for "unacceptability in the traveling connection."

This is a tremendous power which any conference exercises over its individual members. It has sometimes been used as a disciplinary move, and indeed the fathers of 1836, in their report, suggested that "habitual neglect of duty" might give a conference reason to locate a man. But Methodist authorities deprecate the idea of using location as a penalty, or causing it to be regarded as a punishment. "This," said Bishop Collins Denny, "would be a grave reflection upon our local ministers who occupy a status which is of the highest repute in the Church." [4] Location against a man's consent simply means that in the judgment of his brethren he is not a satisfactory worker in the traveling ministry and should not be kept upon the roll for a pastoral appointment. Just as all good men are not meant to be preachers, so some good preachers are not meant to be preachers-in-charge of regular appointments.

At an early date the General Conference became the court of appeals for those who felt aggrieved by action of their Annual Conference. Ultimate appellate power thus in a very few years headed up in the General Conference itself. That body, having but a brief time to sit, and having all manner of weighty matters before it—legislation, committee work and reports, elections, important decisions—soon had recourse to special committees created to hear appeals and recommend needed action upon them. The growth of these committees of appeal, with their establishment in time as a well-nigh permanent committee, was almost inevitable.

Up to and including the General Conference of 1844 there were succeeding committees on appeal appointed by each General Conference. This committee was three times during these earlier years known as the "Committee on Judiciary," and under this name the Methodist Episcopal Church finally established a distinct committee for its own connection, though it gave this committee somewhat wider powers than is here shown.

The Methodist Episcopal Church, South, also in time constituted a committee on appeals with one delegate from each Annual Conference, with a bishop and one or more secretaries of the General Conference

[3] History of the Methodist Episcopal Church, IV, 241.
[4] A Manual of the Discipline (1931), p. 143.

present. In the Southern church this was always known as the "Committee on Appeals."

Explained Bishop Collins Denny, of the Methodist Episcopal Church, South, to the Joint Commission on Unification of 1918:

We generally try only by committee. A matter rarely goes before the entire Conference. I have never known it to go before the entire Conference unless the Conference was very small, and then it goes before a Committee on Appeals which consists of seven, I believe, with a bishop who presides, but who cannot vote. He presides simply as moderator of the body. That committee gives a man a hearing, but it may take a year—I have known cases to occur in our own Church where two years elapsed before a man got a hearing by the Committee on Appeals, but he has had his hearing before the committee of his brethren, and all the Committee on Appeals can do is to take the written record and decide upon it.[5]

It has already been pointed out that the General Conference of the Methodist Episcopal Church was the final and sole interpreter of its own law, and that in the Methodist Episcopal Church, South, the episcopal decisions of the College of Bishops were also final. That either plan was open to objection was a well-recognized fact among Methodists, South as well as North. "For nearly seventy-five years," wrote Judge Henry Wade Rogers, chairman of the Committee on Judiciary of the Methodist Episcopal Church from 1908 to 1920, "thoughtful leaders in the Church have been more or less dissatisfied with the exercise of judicial power by the General Conference." [6]

This same authority outlined the many years of effort which had been made up to that date to solve this problem by the establishment of a tribunal of high moment. As early as 1848, just after the separation with, or of, the Methodist Episcopal Church, South, when the question of General Conference vs. episcopacy had been to the fore, the bishops of the Methodist Episcopal Church recommended to their General Conference that

steps should be taken toward the organization of a delegated Annual Conference, to consist of one delegate from each Annual Conference to receive and try appeals from the members of the Annual Conferences, and to review the acts of the General Conference, and suspend the operations of such of its enactments as are decided to be unconstitutional, until the next succeed-

---

[5] *Proceedings of the Joint Commission on Unification*, II, 97.

[6] *Reports of the Committee on Judiciary* (1924), p. xv.

ing General Conference, or such other constitutional tribunal, with appellate jurisdiction, as they may judge proper.[7]

This recommendation was passed on to the next session of the General Conference in 1852, which heard a lengthy report but laid the report on the table late in the session. This report is of interest in its statement of underlying conviction:

We could not consent to give the contemplated power [to hear appeals and pass upon constitutionality] to the Episcopacy, and thereby form a bench of Bishops, with supreme judicial power; . . . to refer the right to the several Annual Conferences, to pronounce on the constitutionality of the acts and doings of the General Conference, which, in the opinion of your Committee, would produce confusion and cause divisions.[8]

So the final recommendation of this committee was that there should be a "Conference of Appeals" which should have strictly "appellate," and not "original" powers.

As has been said, this report was tabled. In 1856 the Methodist Episcopal bishops again brought up this subject but no final action was taken. However, in 1860 progress was made and definite action was taken organizing a Court of Appeals. Each Annual Conference was allowed to put one member on this court, which became, in reality, a standing committee of the General Conference, created to save the conference itself from the necessity of trying appeals.

At the General Conference of 1868 the Committee on Appeals— rather than Court of Appeals, as it had first been called—was made a standing committee, and it was provided that this committee should be divided into two sections so that it could handle appeal cases the more readily. One half of the appeal cases would be referred to one section, one half to the other.[9]

In 1876 the General Conference, upon formal motion, appointed a committee of twelve to be known as the Judiciary Committee, and to this committee "all questions of law contained in the records and documents submitted to it by Judicial Conferences," as well as all questions of appeal were to be submitted. So under this name finally came into being the powerful committee which in the Methodist Episcopal Church continued up to the time of union as the arbiter of Methodist law. Its reports, as we have elsewhere indicated, were subject to action of the

[7] Ibid.
[8] Ibid., pp. xvii-xviii.
[9] Journal, 1868, p. 154.

General Conference, but these reports were almost always adopted as the committee brought them in.

Meanwhile attempts were made from time to time to establish a final court of appeals which might serve between sessions of the General Conference. In 1912 a well-wrought document calling for such a court was put before the General Conference, but it does not appear to have come to a vote. The call for such a court appears to have proceeded from the realization that as the Committee on Judiciary was a creature of the General Conference, it might be reversed by that body at any time, and that there should be a "supreme court" somewhere which might be able to speak with finality.

At the 1912 General Conference Dr. A. B. Leonard, who then was the corresponding secretary of the Board of Foreign Missions, introduced a resolution which would have continued the Committee on Judiciary during the ensuing quadrennium, and would have given to it the power "to hear and decide questions of law . . . that would properly come before the General Conference on appeal." The resolution provided also that the decisions of the committee should be reported to the next General Conference and be subject to its approval. Dr. Edgar Blake, later bishop, moved to insert an amendment giving power to the Judiciary Committee as thus continued to pass upon the constitutionality of the acts of the General Conference. Dr. Leonard accepted the Blake amendment, but William F. McDowell, moved that the whole thing be laid on the table. This was done.[10]

The Methodist Episcopal Church simplified its "lower court" processes by creating in 1872 a statutory body of men known as "triers of appeals." Each Annual Conference was directed to select seven men from among its elders—"men of experience and sound judgment in the affairs of the Church"—who should be known as triers of appeals. When any appeal was pending the president of the conference in which the appellant resided was empowered to call together the triers of appeals of three conferences "near that from which the appeal is taken." [11] These men together then constituted a "Judicial Conference" empowered to hear and decide the appeals which came before them, but subject to an appeal to the General Conference. Judicial Conferences and their reports figure very largely in later Methodist Episcopal history.

It has already been explained how in the Methodist Episcopal Church, South, the judicial processes of that organization, soon after 1844,

[10] Journal, 1912, p. 488.
[11] Discipline, 1876, ¶ 235.

headed up in the episcopacy. This was by the 1854 enactment—really a reinsertion of the old 1840 provision—that the bishop should decide all questions of law arising before him, and the new unprecedented action of that same year giving the bishops the power to arrest legislation of the General Conference when such legislation was considered unconstitutional.

But this regulation itself appeared to many to be unconstitutional, as it was clearly "constitutional matter," and had been adopted by a simple majority of the General Conference which enacted it. It was therefore continually called in question for some years in the Southern church. Not until 1870, when an extremely able paper read to the General Conference by Dr. Leroy Lee challenged directly the constitutionality of this measure and pointed the way out, was needed action taken. Then the General Conference, convinced of the value of the "episcopal check," passed the necessary provision on down to the Annual Conferences by the necessary majority, and upon their concurrent action the measure was written into the fundamental law of the Southern church. There it remained until 1934, when a Judicial Council was created by the Methodist Episcopal Church, South, and the council then took over the power which previously had belonged to the bishops. Southern bishops, however, only twice availed themselves of the privilege of "checking" what they considered unconstitutional actions of the General Conference.

The Methodist Protestant Church, smaller than the larger episcopal Methodist bodies, kept its appellate system much after the fashion of the early Methodist Church. It had a well-wrought procedure for the trial of members and ministers, and the right of appeal to the Annual Conferences was, of course, fundamental in the case of a minister. But the Committee on Appeals of the Methodist Protestant Church was historically connected with the idea of a minister appealing against an appointment to which he was to be assigned. Preachers always had this right in the Methodist Protestant Church, but they seldom exercised it, as an appeal against one proposed appointment meant, in effect, an appeal against all other appointments, since many were often conditioned on the one. So appeals rarely got far and were not often undertaken as there was a well-weighted feeling against such an appellant.

The presidents of the Methodist Protestant Annual Conferences were expected to rule on questions of law as these arose in the administration of the conferences. They must, however, report their rulings to the ensuing General Conference of the church for such action as that body should take. When their rulings were approved they became tantamount to law.

With the creation of the powerful Executive Committee in 1920, with which the Methodist Protestants obtained a far more centralized control than they had ever had before, all appellate power was lodged in this body. The Executive Committee, therefore, became, in effect, a high court of law for the denomination. Methodist Protestantism, however, was fortunate in having nothing like the great number of appeals and tangles in administrative law which were constantly requiring attention in episcopal Methodism.

At union in 1939, therefore, the three participating churches had in effect different methods for deciding constitutional questions and ruling upon ultimate points of law; but their appellate system, as that had to do with trial and appeal on the part of ministers and members, was very much alike in all three churches. It was therefore not difficult to arrange it at union so that this latter phase of the matter—appeals against the decisions of conferences or lower church courts—should be referred to a superior tribunal after the pattern of the old Committee on Appeals. It was decided to create a Committee on Appeals in each separate jurisdiction to attend to this matter. In the constitution of The Methodist Church the Jurisdictional Conferences are directed to create Committees on Appeals for each respective jurisdiction.[12] These committees are final in acting upon such appeals. Only in the case of a bishop, who may wish to appeal the action of a trial committee, may such appeal come before the Judicial Council acting as an appellate court.

In hearing all appeals, church courts, like civil appellate courts, do not try the case itself but study the manner in which the case has been tried. They therefore call for all documents—"the record"—having to do with such cases and carefully study these before giving their decision. They may reaffirm, reverse, or remand the case for a new trial as they may adjudge proper.

[12] Div. II, Sec. IV, Art. V (6).

XX

THE JUDICIAL COUNCIL

There shall be a Judicial Council.
—Constitution, Div. IV, Art. I

THE ACTUAL FORMULATION OF CONCRETE PROPOSALS LOOKING TOWARD the establishment of a supreme court of Methodist law was one which enlisted the keenest interest. It was one feature of the Plan of Union—of the many plans of union—which seemed to find unanimous consent from the very first. Especially were distinguished laymen—who were often lawyers—intrigued by the possibilities in the plan. It was recognized at an early date, and very definitely by the Joint Commission on Union in 1918, that neither the General Conference nor the episcopacy should act as the final arbiter on constitutional questions. The pattern set by the federal government, with its legislative, executive, and judicial departments, was in the minds of all when a new and united church was envisioned. And while constitutional questions do not often arise in the ongoing of the church, there are many lesser legal questions requiring decision from time to time, and a final arbiter is needed in many instances. Therefore, in creating the Judicial Council it was decided to give this body not only supreme authority in interpreting the constitution of the church, but final authority as a court of law and on certain types of appeal.

The vital debates and discussions over the Judicial Council took place in 1918-20 in that commission which Bishop John M. Moore says actually gave to the church the present Plan of Union. All commissioners agreed at once to the general idea of the Judicial Council, but the actual embodiment in concrete proposals having to do with the name, number of members, and how they should be elected, and so forth, posed questions.

The Judicial Council was, after much discussion, written into the Plan of Union of 1918-20; and again into the plan for a union under two jurisdictions, adopted by the Methodist Episcopal General Conference of 1924 (adopted also by a called General Conference of the Methodist Episcopal Church, South, but rejected by the Southern Annual Conferences). The idea of the Judicial Council, however, had so commended itself that in 1930, when a well-integrated and formally written constitution was put before the General Conference of the Methodist Episcopal Church, South, for adoption, a Judicial Council, very much like the one which had been in the then defunct Plan of Union, was part of the proposed constitution. The constitution itself failed of adoption by the General Conference of the Methodist Episcopal Church, South, but at its failure Dr. T. D. Ellis moved that the section of the proposed constitution ordering and constituting a Judicial Council should be adopted by the General Conference and sent down to the Annual Conferences for affirmative constitutional action. This was done, and the proposal passed the General Conferences and then the Annual Conferences of the Southern church by the necessary majorities. At the General Conference of 1934 the bishops of the Methodist Episcopal Church, South, declared that the measure calling for a Judicial Council had been adopted, and that such a council was thenceforth to be a part of the organic structure of the church. Thereupon the conference elected the requisite members of the Judicial Council, who at once organized and functioned as a council until five years later when the Methodist Episcopal Church, South, ended as a separate corporate structure.

In the Plan of Union adopted for The Methodist Church the present Judicial Council was called for and created. The constitutional provisions establishing this tribunal are as follows:

Article I.—There shall be a Judicial Council. The General Conference shall determine the number and qualifications of its members, their terms of office, and the method of election and the filling of vacancies.

Article II.—The Judicial Council shall have authority:

1. To determine the constitutionality of any act of the General Conference upon an appeal of a majority of the Council of Bishops, or one fifth of the members of the General Conference; and to determine the constitutionality of any act of a Jurisdictional or Central Conference upon an appeal of a majority of the bishops of that Jurisdictional or Central Conference or upon the appeal of one fifth of the members of that Jurisdictional or Central Conference.

2. To hear and determine any appeal from a bishop's decision on a question of law made in the Annual or District Conference when said appeal has been made by one fifth of that conference present and voting.

3. To pass upon decisions of law made by bishops in Annual or District Conferences.

4. To hear and determine the legality of any action taken therein by any General Conference board or Jurisdictional or Central Conference board or body, upon appeal of one third of the members thereof, or upon request of

the Council of Bishops or a majority of the bishops of a Jurisdictional or a Central Conference.

5. To have such other duties and powers as may be conferred upon it by the General Conference.

6. To provide its own methods of organization and procedure.

Article III.—All decisions of the Judicial Council shall be final. However, when the Judicial Council shall declare any act of the General Conference unconstitutional, that decision shall be reported back to that General Conference immediately.

Pursuant to the authority given the General Conference under the first paragraph above, the General Conference of 1940 made provision for the organization of a Judicial Council of nine members—five ministers and four laymen. All must be forty years of age or over and all members of The Methodist Church. It should be mentioned that there was an ad interim Judicial Council established by the Uniting Conference in 1939 while waiting for the first General Conference of 1940. The latter body, as stated above, established the statutory regulations for the permanent council.

The method of nominating members of the Judicial Council calls for the bishops to nominate four times as many proposed members, clerical and lay, as there may be positions to be filled. From the floor nominations may also be properly made at the time the bishops' nominations are announced. All nominations, with the conference affiliation publicly named in each instance, are to be published in two issues of the General Conference *Daily Advocate*. Then at a time fixed by order of the General Conference, balloting is had without discussion, until the requisite number of persons from each "class"—minsters and laymen—have received a majority of the votes cast and are declared elected. The term for which each member is elected is eight years, but it was provided at the first General Conference of the united church that four of the council should be elected at that time for four years, and five for eight; thus providing a tribunal all of whose members do not require re-election or replacement at any one General Conference.[1]

Likewise, alternates are to be elected by the General Conference from the names of those remaining in each "class," after the regular members of the Judicial Council have been elected. In case of a vacancy on the council between sessions of the General Conference, the vacancy is to be filled by the alternate or alternates of the same class, for the unexpired term of the member whose place is thus being filled. In case of the un-

[1] *Discipline*, 1944, ¶ 901.

avoidable absence of one or more members of the Judicial Council during a General Conference session, such vacancy shall be filled by the alternates in order, and from the respective class of the absentee. But the alternate may serve only for that session of the General Conference, or the remainder of its session. All terms of members of the council and of alternates expire at the adjournment of the General Conference session at which their successors are elected.[2]

The council provides its own method of organization. This has been to date by the election of a president, vice-president, and secretary, each chosen from among the members. It fixes its own times for meeting, except that it must meet at the time and place of the General Conference and must remain in session as long as that body does; and it must meet once a year to review bishops' decisions. A separate section of seats or desks for members of the Judicial Council is always provided in the hall or place of assembly where the General Conference is held. There the Judicial Council as such may sit with the General Conference in a position of honor as befits the dignity of the council. It meets, of course, privately for the transaction of its own business. It has a well-formulated system of rules and procedures which it has adopted for its own guidance in attending to its own duties. These rules were published in the *Discipline* of 1944 (¶ 2001.).

POWERS AND DUTIES

A study of the powers and duties of the Judicial Council indicates that these may be classified under four main divisions:

I. The council is the authoritative and final judge of constitutionality. The council is empowered and mandated to "determine the constitutionality of any act of the General Conference" when a majority of the Council of Bishops asks that this be done, or when "one fifth of the members of the General Conference" itself so request.[3] The *Discipline* terms such requests the "appeal" of a majority of the Council of Bishops, or of one fifth of the members of the General Conference. Presumably such an appeal is to be registered by official action on the part of the Council of Bishops, and by a formal public vote, in the case of the General Conference membership, duly made by that body in session and after a count indicates that one fifth or more of the body joins in making such an appeal. A private petition circulated off the floor and signed by individual members of the General Conference appealing for a certain

[2] *Ibid.*
[3] *Ibid.*, ¶ 43.

action could scarcely be taken by the Judicial Council as representing "one fifth of the members of the General Conference," as the presumption is that appeals should be properly made and forwarded by the respective episcopal majority in case of the bishops, and by the officers of the General Conference certifying the one-fifth fraction, in case of the General Conference, and from formal sessions of these bodies.

No limitation is fixed by the *Discipline* or by the rules of the procedure of the Judicial Council to the length of time which may elapse before an appeal for a ruling on the constitutionality of a General Conference action may be presented.

Since a majority of the Council of Bishops has the right to appeal to the Judicial Council for a ruling on the constitutionality of a General Conference action, it is possible that such an appeal from the bishops might not come until some time after a particular General Conference had adjourned, and the bishops have opportunity to question some particular measure more carefully than was possible when the General Conference enacted it. In practice, however, appeals for a ruling on the constitutionality of a General Conference action are usually made at once as soon as the General Conference enacts the measure whose constitutionality is to be appealed. The Judicial Council itself, however, must report immediately to the General Conference when it has decided that any action of that body is unconstitutional. This will allow the conference to decide whether it wishes to propose the measure as a constitutional enactment to be acted upon by the Annual Conferences or to drop the matter entirely.

The Judicial Council is empowered likewise to determine the constitutionality of any act of a Jurisdictional or Central Conference "upon an appeal of a majority of the bishops of that Jurisdictional or Central Conference or upon the appeal of one fifth of the members of that Jurisdictional or Central Conference." As Jurisdictional and Central Conferences are not in session at the time of the General Conference, when the Judicial Council always is, and as Jurisdictional Conferences do not usually meet simultaneously, it is evident that any ruling by the Judicial Council which declares unconstitutional an act of one of these conferences could scarcely be reported to such conference while it is in session. The Judicial Council in such instances would have to decide after the adjournment of the conference whose action is appealed.

II. The Judicial Council is empowered to "hear and determine" the legality of any action taken by "any General Conference board or Jurisdictional or Central Conference board or body." The words "or body" presumably are to be attached to the General Conference as well as to the Jurisdictional or Central Conferences. This means, in effect, that any and all agencies set up by the authority of any of the three types of conferences mentioned may be appealed against when the actions of such bodies are considered illegal.

Such appeals, however, can only come from "one third of the members thereof"—meaning one third of the "body" whose action is being appealed—or "upon request of the Council of Bishops"—meaning a formal appeal regarding legality by the Council of Bishops—or by "a majority of the bishops of the Jurisdictional or Central Conference"—that is, the bishops of the particular Jurisdictional or Central Conference whose "board" or "body" has been responsible for the action being appealed.[4]

Protection against illegal action on the part of any board, whether created by General Conference, Jurisdictional or Central Conferences, is further extended to Annual Conferences and to Provisional Annual Conferences. Whenever two thirds of the members of an Annual Conference or Provisional Annual Conference "present and voting" shall appeal the legality of any action of any General Conference board, or any Jurisdictional or Central Conference "board or body," the Judicial Council is empowered to hear and determine such an appeal. This provision, however, docs not give to Annual or Provisional Conferences the right to appeal against a law or action of the General Conference, or against an action of the Jurisdictional or Central Conference in whose territory the conference may be. Only against the action of a board or body which is created by such conferences is this appeal allowed and then by a two-thirds conference vote.[5]

III. The Judicial Council is empowered to hear and determine all appeals from episcopal decisions which may be given by a bishop on questions of law arising in Annual or District Conferences. Such appeals must be made by one fifth of the Annual or District Conference "present and voting," presumably at and when the appealed decision is made. Such appeals must be submitted in writing to the bishop and "reported in writing to the council with a syllabus of each case." The council may then "affirm, modify, or reverse them."[6]

For the purpose of hearing and clearing all decisions of law made by bishops in Annual or District Conferences, the Judicial Council must meet at least once each year. Each episcopal decision which has been

[4] *Ibid.*, ¶ 906.
[5] *Ibid.*, ¶ 907.
[6] *Ibid.*, ¶ 909.

rendered during the year is then reviewed by the council. None has any force or effect, except in the instance where it was given, until the Judicial Council has reviewed it. But when any such decision is affirmed by the council it becomes "the law of the church." [7]

The Judicial Council does not hear appeals on matters of trial by church courts for offenses against the doctrines or discipline of the church, except in one instance—that of bishops. When a bishop has been tried by the Trial Court and desires to appeal the ruling or judgment of such court, the Judicial Council is empowered "to hear and determine" his appeal. Presumably the council may follow the practice of other courts of appeal in such an instance, and affirm, modify, or reverse the finding of the trial court, or remand the case for another trial.

No person other than a bishop has the right to appeal to the Judicial Council over the findings of any Trial Court. The bishop alone, as a general church officer, has an appeal to this general church tribunal. The Committee on Appeals in and of each respective Jurisdictional or of each Central Conference area, is the final court of appeals for a minister who may seek redress from the action of a trial committee of his conference. Such committees in each jurisdiction are made mandatory by the constitution of the church.[8]

The interesting possibility of a conflict in the interpretation of law between the Committees on Appeals in two different jurisdictions is treated at some length in disciplinary provisions respecting the Judicial Council. That body is empowered to review the documents and findings of the respective Committees on Appeal when there is a difference in interpreting the law. Without passing on the individual cases as such, the council is empowered to decide the question of law involved. So possible conflict between the law in different areas or jurisdictions will be obviated.

It should be emphasized, before dismissing the appellate powers of the Judicial Council, that "appeals from individuals cannot be heard," as Bishop John M. Moore states.[9] Only appeals from conferences, boards, and bishops, and these under carefully prescribed conditions, can be heard. Individuals obtain redress through other agencies. It was provided, however, in 1944 that questions of law and the ruling on such questions may very properly be appealed, "step by step, to the Judicial Council." [10] This may open the door for an individual standing trial to appeal to the

[7] *Ibid.*

[8] Div. II, Sec. IV, Art. V (6).

[9] *The Long Road to Methodist Union* (1943), p. 224.

[10] *Discipline*, 1944, ¶ 1033.

Judicial Council, but only on the questions of law involved in his appeal.[11]

IV. At the 1944 General Conference a measure was passed giving to the Judicial Council the power to utter declaratory decisions:

When the General Conference shall have passed any act or legislation that appears to be subject to more than one interpretation, or when any paragraph or paragraphs of the *Discipline* seem to be of doubtful meaning or application, any authority in the Church affected thereby, that would have the right to appeal thereon to the Judicial Council under the law of the Church from any action of any Conference, ruling of a Bishop, or of any Board, Commission or body of the Church, may petition the Judicial Council for a ruling in the nature of a declaratory decision as to the meaning, application and effect of such act, legislation or paragraph, or paragraphs, of the *Discipline*, and the decision of the Judicial Council thereon shall be as binding and effectual as a decision on appeal under the law relating to appeals to the Judicial Council.

But only those who could appeal from an action under such act, legislation, or laws can ask for such declaratory decision by the Judicial Council. Moot and hypothetical questions will not be decided, but only those where some action is desired and some doubt or question as to the meaning or application of the act, legislation, action or ruling is apparent. The Judicial Council shall determine from the facts in connection with each such petition whether or not it has jurisdiction to hear and determine the same.

When a declaratory decision is sought all persons or bodies who have or claim any interest which would be affected by the declaration shall be parties to the proceeding, and the petition shall name such parties. If the Council determines that other parties not named by the petition would be affected by such a decision, such additional parties shall also be added; and the petitioner, or petitioners, shall then be required to serve all parties so joined with a copy of the petition within 15 days after the filing of the same with the Judicial Council. In like manner any interested party may on his, or its own motion intervene, and answer, plead, or interplead.[12]

The report of the Committee on Judiciary of the General Conference embodying this action was presented by Judge Leslie J. Lyons, of Kansas City, Missouri, chairman. It was, as Judge Lyons admitted, "new legislation," but was thought necessary because there seemed at times need for some definite interpretation of law before an action or law whose legality was in doubt had actually been effected. It had just happened that that very General Conference had found itself in doubt as to whether or not it had the right to elect missionary bishops. There was no

[11] *Ibid.*, ¶¶ 1034-35.
[12] *Journal*, 1944, p. 610.

way to test its legal right to elect such bishops other than to vote to elect them, and then support an appeal to the Judicial Council to pass upon its right to do so. This was done, with Dr. L. O. Hartman, later bishop, making the proposal that the conference should order the election of missionary bishops and then appeal the legality of its action to the Judicial Council. This was done. An appeal was at once made, and the Judicial Council decided that the General Conference had no right to elect bishops at all.

This situation showed the need for a different method of ascertaining the legality of a proposed action, and for giving to the Judicial Council "declaratory" power. Had the Judicial Council had the power to issue declaratory decisions before the missionary bishops issue arose, it could have been appealed to directly by the General Conference for a ruling. Judge Lyons, in presenting the report of his committee calling for this new legislation, stated that his committee was calling for "declaratory decisions" not "declaratory judgments." The report as presented by his committee was adopted, and the legislation was forthwith put in the *Discipline*.[13]

The power thus granted in 1944 to utter declaratory decisions is a very great one indeed. Jurists have sometimes expressed fear of such power when given to civil courts, since courts possessing it may in effect make laws instead of interpreting them. But rightly used, the declaratory power can be of great help to the church at large.

As the names of other distinguished Methodist leaders have appeared in these pages, it is not out of place here to record the names of the nine men who composed the Judicial Council for the first years of its life and who, with one exception, were all elected in 1940: president, Francis R. Bayley, minister, Baltimore; vice-president, Martin E. Lawson, lawyer, Liberty, Missouri; secretary, Henry R. Van Deusen, lawyer, Scranton, Pennsylvania; Walter C. Buckner, minister, Los Angeles; Marvin A. Childers, lawyer, San Antonio, Texas; Vincent P. Clarke, lawyer, Boston; J. Stewart French, minister, Bristol, Virginia; George R. Brown, minister, Liberty, North Carolina; Waights G. Henry, minister, Anniston, Alabama.

The above were all elected first in 1939 to the ad interim Judicial Council, then re-elected in 1940. In 1944 Charles B. Ketcham, minister, Alliance, Ohio, was elected in place of George R. Brown.

As is true of any court or judge, a reputation for judicial ability and impartiality always waits upon time. The Supreme Court of the United

---

[13] 1944, ¶ 914.

States itself provides a case in point, for the court's historian, Carson, observes that "there is no institution of our nation that had a harder fight to establish itself than the Supreme Court of the United States; and there is none today which enjoys higher prestige." These words were written some years ago, before there was any suggestion that a court might be aligned with any particular party or philosophy of government. For if there be any one thing that all the history of judicial decision teaches unmistakably it is that a court, a judge, must proceed by laws that transcend any immediacy of interest if it, or he, is to be respected by men on earth. If the Supreme Court does "follow the election returns," the court loses by that much in the esteem of the people, who look for it to support not temporary party aims but eternal principles. The great judges have been those who gave their decisions in line with that higher equity which is the soul of their profession, and they let the chips of political expediency fall where they may.

The Judicial Council of The Methodist Church has already made a favorable impression by the decisions it has to date rendered, and even more by the way it has arrived at and rendered them. The council gives the impression that its whole duty and aim is to affirm the law of the church and to make clear the principles of church government and constitutional law which are to be maintained in each instance.

All believe that the Judicial Council will grow in eminence and prestige as the years go by, and that among our eminent Methodist lawyers and well-balanced ministers it will be considered a high honor to sit upon this truly powerful and able Christian court. It has grown enormously in stature already in Methodist life.

PART FIVE

The Executive Agencies

XXI

THE EXECUTIVE AGENCIES

The General Conference shall . . . initiate and direct all connectional enterprises of the Church . . . and provide boards for their promotion and administration.
—Constitution, Div. II, Sec. I, Art. IV, 8

THE METHODIST CHURCH FUNCTIONS NOT ONLY THROUGH CONSTITUtional establishments—as through an episcopacy, conferences, the Judicial Council—but in a direct and continuing way through corporate agencies known as boards. There are also commissions and committees created or continued from time to time as need may demand. These corporate organizations in turn elect officers and provide subsidiary agencies or salaried personnel to carry forward their own special work, and, in the case of the large boards, become representative of the entire church through both personnel and staff members.

These boards have no constitutional status but are creatures of the General Conference, or, if they are Jurisdictional or Annual Conference boards, they are under the control of these respective bodies. Theoretically any General Conference at any session could do away or disestablish any of the boards, even the largest; but practically this would be almost as unthinkable as to do away episcopacy or denature the Annual Conferences. The boards in fact have become integral parts of the church's basic structure, not because of some parchment or charter granted them, but because they fulfill and will continue to fulfill an absolutely vital role in the life of The Methodist Church. They came into being in answer to a need which in turn grew as Methodism increased in numbers and effectiveness; and they will remain as long as the same needs persist, that is, as long as the church shall fulfill its manifold duty as a great ecclesiasticism. Were there no boards it would be necessary to create some immediately, and while the names of such organizations may be altered, their nature can scarcely be, since this is functionally determined.

The general boards are large or small, specialized or all-embracing, as their nature may demand, but almost all are incorporated. Incorporation gives these agencies the power to transact business as legal entities,

217

receive bequests, hold property, sue and be sued, after the manner of any other such corporation.

Commissions as a rule differ from boards in lacking legal incorporation, and they usually do work which is more or less temporary or specialized. Certain commissions which are seen to be conducting a continuing work of importance are sometimes given the power to organize as a regular board, as was the case at the 1944 General Conference when the Commission on Evangelism (which was already incorporated under the laws of Tennessee) became the Board of Evangelism. There are indeed unincorporated commissions which are continued steadily, and whose agents and executives are a very real part of the economy of the church, such as the Commission on Public Relations and Methodist Information, the Curriculum Committee of the Board of Education, and the University Senate. But as a general thing it appears that incorporation is the determining mark of any board. All the boards hold annual meetings at which their business is clarified with respect to their ongoing program, and appropriate measures are taken to carry forward their work.

The boards are the continuing, permanent agencies of the church in putting into effect the church's program. Through their executives and employed personnel the boards are in continual session, as it were. Conferences adjourn, bishops scatter to superintend their respective areas, the Judicial Council is in session only at General Conference or at such times as there is appellate grist for its judicial mill. But the boards of the church, from their nature and duty, must continually function through their officials and elected agents—and they do it ceaselessly. When war broke out in 1941 neither General Conference nor Council of Bishops was in session, but the mission work of Methodism was imperiled and involved in many lands. The Board of Missions and Church Extension, from its headquarters in New York, was able through its executives to act instantly as it relayed orders and money to its missionaries over its far-flung mission work. The headquarters at 150 Fifth Avenue, New York, appeared to be practically a governmental foreign office for a time, as emergency messages were sent or received from various combatant areas and as missionaries were recalled or given needed instructions or supplies. The boards of the church mediate and make continually effective the power of the church as this is to be applied to local situations.

As will be understood, the effectiveness and operation of the boards depend greatly upon the personnel of board members, and also to an even greater degree upon that of the employed executives. At this point there comes into play a factor of great importance, namely, the continuation in office of those persons who are acceptably serving in such office. According to the custom which has become Methodist common law, church officials are usually re-elected from time to time to the position each one holds, unless either such a person withdraws or asks leave to withdraw, or unless there is active opposition to such a person's continuance. In the latter case, opposition, if it shall succeed, must be quite strong and based upon reasoning which shall greatly impress the electors. This is true even when the position to be filled is a nonsalaried one, such as a recording steward or a trustee of local church property. Where the position is salaried, as is the case with officers of the boards or general church executives, the matter goes even deeper. Indeed, with families, homes, and other factors involved, it is scarcely equitable to call for a casual change in personnel unless there are extremely good reasons for such change. The result is that there is usually a continuance in office of board members and elected executives over a considerable period. This in the long run is advantageous on account of the specialized work such executives and board members are expected to perform, and because of the time required to acquire efficiency and experience. It has the disadvantage, in the case of representation on the general boards, of causing these agencies to become more and more introverted and specialized as time goes by, and their executive and salaried staffs sometimes become isolated from the other general work of the church. The boards in fact may draw apart from each other as their executives have a tendency to emphasize to the fullest extent their own particular trust and program. Good sense and the real ability of the very able men who are generally put in charge of these executive agencies usually counteracts much of this; but not the least of the perils of ecclesiastical bureaucracy is its divisive power as each agency surveys and works in its own special field.

There is an executive committee called for in each of the major boards, though this executive committee is not always so named. The committee meets at stated intervals, usually quarterly, in the interim between annual meetings of the entire board, and transacts such business as it may profitably complete. In case some momentous matter is pending, the action of the executive committee must, of course, be subject to the approval of the entire board. The personnel of the respective executive committees are sometimes so chosen as to provide persons who by reason of residence near one another, or near board headquarters, are available for the meetings at regular intervals. However, the expressed desire of the General Conference of 1948, that every jurisdiction should

219

be represented upon every important committee as well as board, has changed this somewhat.

Before 1952 certain of the boards provided that no salaried officer of the board should be a member. The General Conference of 1952, following the report of the Survey Commission, made this mandatory upon all general church agencies. Executive officers of the various boards are expected to sit with such boards when these are in session, or to be members ex *officio*, and are accorded the rights of the floor, either by specific rule, or perhaps by the rule of executive courtesy. But such executives are not allowed to vote on any matters pending.

All the boards except the Board of Publication obtain their revenues from the general church funds or from private sources, in bequests, collections, and gifts which they are allowed to solicit. In general, however, their principal support comes from the general benevolences or "world service" of the church. Each board is expected to furnish its "askings" to the Council on World Service and Finance at stated intervals, and then must conform its program to the amount of revenue it receives from this or other sources. The Board of Publication, however, is self-supporting. It manages the Publishing House, and as that institution usually produces revenue, the Board of Publication is not dependent upon the general funds of the church. Instead it becomes a contributor to the general church inasmuch as it must turn its "produce" or net gain back to the church to be used for the benefit of Conference claimants.

There are several important executive agencies of The Methodist Church which are not incorporated as are the boards, but by virtue of the work they do and the function they perform, they have been continued by the church upon a firm and well-nigh permanent basis. The General Conference itself appoints, and will continue to appoint from time to time, special commissions or committees entrusted with some immediate interest or work. The tenure of office of such bodies is only temporary, that is, it lasts until the completion of the special mission. Such was the Commission to Revise the Hymnal.

At the union of the three Methodisms in 1939 the boards and agencies of the uniting churches were correlated in so far as was practicable by the Uniting Conference. The missionary work of the three churches was put under one Board of Missions, the educational under the Board of Education, publishing interests under a Board of Publication, and so on. In spite of enormous difficulties this huge undertaking was carried through in a surprisingly advantageous way. The General Conference of

1940 further completed the work of the Uniting Conference, and the church entered upon its larger task with a well-integrated system of boards, commissions, and committees. Each of these was charged with some important phase of the general work. But by the end of the church's second quadrennium, it was evident that there was much over-lapping of work on the part of various agencies. Especially was this manifest in the field of publication and in the abundance of printed materials put out by the boards for promotional purposes. The General Conference of 1948 thereupon decided to create a commission which should study the entire structure of the church, and ordered it to bring in its report and recommendations to the 1952 General Conference.

The "Survey Commission" thus created employed technical help to study the functioning of each of the agencies. Over three years were spent in gathering information. Many meetings and conferences were visited, and the Survey Commission was able to present to the 1952 General Conference a carefully drawn study of the organizational work of the church as it then was, together with a plan designed to reorganize the general agencies so as to improve the efficiency of the church.

The Survey Report was alternately praised and condemned previous to the 1952 General Conference. In general the boards and agencies opposed its findings. But the General Conference proved to be disposed to favor any changes that looked constructive. After some parliamentary jockeying a committee of six persons was appointed by the General Conference to work through the Survey Report during the conference session and bring in recommendations regarding it.

Eventually a series of reports were presented to the General Conference which were adopted with little debate. These cut down membership on the big boards of the church; provided that no person other than a bishop could serve on more than one agency, and no bishop on more than three; ordered that no person could remain on any one agency of the church for more than eight years; and created a Co-ordinating Committee empowered to harmonize any conflicts or overlapping between boards and agencies as these might arise. The Discipline of 1952 in its section on administrative agencies was much amended in order to carry out the legislation putting into effect these and other changes.

On the following pages the incorporated boards and those agencies whose support devolves upon the World Service Fund will be studied in their general outlines. Important changes called for by the Discipline of 1952 will be indicated where these have been put into effect.

1. BOARD OF MISSIONS

This great organization, because of its size, its representative personnel, and its world-wide jurisdiction, deserves to rank foremost among the boards of The Methodist Church. It is incorporated as a general board and it also functions through three administrative divisions, each of which is in turn incorporated. These are the Division of World Missions, the Division of National Missions, and the Woman's Division of Christian Service. There is also a Joint Section of Education and Cultivation composed of representatives from the other divisions and having general charge of the publication and promotional moves of the board. This Joint Section is not incorporated.

The missionary work of The Methodist Church is so vast, and its development has been such a large part of Methodist history, that it is impossible to do more in this chapter than refer to it in the broadest possible way. Missions and Methodism have been well-nigh synonymous in the Methodist mind, and every Methodist has in a vital sense been a missionary. Early American Methodist preachers went out to pioneer settlements, sometimes to the Indies or Canada, and then the church began to send men across the wide seas. The story of the implantation of the church has become legendary in many lands, combining as it did romance and adventure and often statesmanship of high import. A vast literature has been produced dealing with the growth of the Methodist churches over the world, and at the time of union there was a commonwealth of Methodist organizational life under or closely related to the separate Boards of Missions of the three participating and uniting churches. To gather all this under one control for the united church, so that local autonomy and national wishes might be respected, provided no small problem.

It was accomplished after a great amount of preliminary work by the Standing Committee on Missions of the Uniting Conference, whose report, presented by John R. Mott, chairman, proved to be a lengthy, statesmanlike document. The provisions of this report as adopted in 1939, and subsequently implemented and strengthened by succeeding General Conferences, created the Board of Missions and Church Extension of The Methodist Church. That board functioned ably for twelve years under the organizational pattern created for it by the Uniting Conference. But in 1952, on the recommendation of the Survey Commission, the General Conference reorganized this agency and changed its name from the long one under which it had been functioning to the apt and sufficient title, the Board of Missions.

The board thus reconstituted is set up under the control of a Board of Managers. This consists of eighteen effective bishops resident in the United States and six bishops serving overseas. These last, designated by the Council of Bishops, have the status of members of the board in meetings which they may be able to attend. In addition to these bishops the Jurisdictional Conferences are empowered to elect

one minister and three lay members, two of whom shall be women, from each jurisdiction for each 600,000 members, or major fraction thereof, in the jurisdiction, and in addition one youth under twenty-one years of age from each jurisdiction. . . . In nominating and electing such members, the Jurisdictional Conference shall have as a basis for choice the following: (a) one minister and one lay man designated by each Annual Conference of the jurisdiction, on nomination of its Conference Board of Missions; (b) six additional names nominated by the College of Bishops of the jurisdiction; (c) twice the necessary number of lay women, designated by the Jurisdiction Woman's Society of Christian Service from three members nominated by each Conference Woman's Society of the jurisdiction; (d) one youth nominated by the youth organization of each Annual Conference in the jurisdiction. Vacancies among these members shall be filled by the bishops of the jurisdiction in which the vacancies occur.[1]

In addition to those elected by the jurisdictions there are to be:

3. Twenty-seven lay men, at least four from each jurisdiction, elected quadrennially by the board on nomination of the Council of Bishops, to serve as members at large of the board, and to be assigned as nearly equally as possible to the Divisions of World Missions and of National Missions.

4. Twelve women, two from each jurisdiction, elected quadrennially by the board on nomination of the Woman's Division of Christian Service, to serve as members at large of the board and of this division.

5. The chairman of the Commission on Christian Outreach of the General Youth Section of the National Conference of Methodist Youth.[2]

By the provisions above which the church puts into effect on this board, and the large number of persons elected to its membership by other than Jurisdictional Conferences, the Board of Missions is less dependent on jurisdictional action than any other board of the church.

The Board of Missions meets an-

nually. It elects quadrennially a president and four vice-presidents. The vice-presidents are the presidents of the four different divisions, and each presides over his own respective division in all regular as well as special meetings. A recording secretary and such other officers as it may need are also elected by the board.

The board functions *ad interim* through a general executive committee of thirty-eight members. This committee, which meets in March and September, is composed of a carefully prescribed number of persons from the separate divisions of the board. The number of women members from each division is definitely stated. The president of the board is a member of the general executive committee and acts as its chairman.

The Board of Missions elects as executive officers, on nomination of the divisions, the executive officers of the respective divisions. There is no general executive for the entire board, though from time to time there have been demands for one administrative head over all divisions. The general executives serve through their respective divisions, and these divisions fix by nomination the number and duties of such officers as they wish the board to elect and commission. The minutes of the Board of Missions refer to the chief officers of the respective divisions as the "Executive Secretary of World Missions Division"; the "Executive Secretaries of National Missions Division"; the "Executive Secretaries of the Woman's Division"; and the "Executive Secretaries of the Joint Section of Education and Cultivation." These are elected directly by the board on nomination of the respective divisions. It should be noted that the Woman's

[1] *Discipline*, 1952, ¶ 1172.
[2] *Ibid.*

223

Division has no general secretary but that each department of the Woman's Division has its executive secretaries.

The Board of Missions, exclusive of the Woman's Division of Christian Service, obtains its funds from world service "apportionments, assessments, or asking distributed to jurisdictions, Annual Conferences, and pastoral charges . . . in such manner as the General Conference may prescribe." [3] It also has the right to receive from any source gifts, donations, freewill offerings, and so forth, in the time-honored way. The Woman's Division gets its funds from its own local organization—its local church and conference societies—by "annual pledges or dues, special memberships, devises, bequests, annuities, special offerings, gifts, and moneys raised by special projects or collected in meetings held in the interest of the work of the division." [4]

DIVISION OF WORLD MISSIONS

In the administration of the foreign work, the Division of World Missions is guided by certain legislation with regard to the different types of development found in the respective mission fields or areas. Proper cooperation with the work of Central Conferences in lands where these are organized is called for, and there are regulations having to do with Provisional Central Conferences, and with the work in those lands where there is no Annual Conference. This division has entrusted to its oversight all the work of missions "outside the United States and its dependencies." All missionary work belonging to The Methodist Church, except

that of the Foreign Department of the Woman's Division, is under the supervision of this division. Work in Alaska, Hawaii, Puerto Rico, and the Dominican Republic does not come under the supervision of the foreign division, but of the Division of National Missions.

In carrying out its duties the Division of World Missions, as an incorporated body, has the right "to recommend fields of labor; to accept, train, and maintain workers; to buy and sell property; to secure and administer funds for the support of all work under its charge; to solicit and accept contributions subject to annuity under the board's regulations; and to recommend to the board appropriations for its work." [5]

The division administers a farflung missionary empire upon which the sun never sets. The chief administration officer of the division is its executive secretary. The various areas of activity in different parts of the globe are administered by associate secretaries who are elected by the board upon nominations of the division and are appointed to have the care of definite areas.

DIVISION OF NATIONAL MISSIONS

The Division of National Missions is likewise an incorporated body acting as an administrative division of the General Board of Missions. Its membership is composed of a certain number of the members of the General Board as provided by the *Discipline* (¶1210). The Division of National Missions is empowered to buy and sell property, secure and administer funds, and accept, train, and maintain workers. It nominates its

[3] *Ibid.,* ¶ 1185.
[4] *Ibid.,* ¶ 1250.

[5] *Ibid.,* ¶ 1196.

own officers and executives subject to election by the board, determines the powers and duties of the employed staff, as well as recommends the remuneration of each officer and employee.

This division has "general supervision and administration of the work of missions and church extension in the United States of America (including Alaska, Hawaii, Puerto Rico) and the Dominican Republic; and administration of all donation aid, loan funds, and endowment contributed . . . for the work of church extension, except such as may be administered by the Jurisdictional and Annual Conferences." [6]

In administering its work the division divides its membership into two sections: National Missions and Church Extension. Each section is provided with one or more executive secretaries, who administer the work of the section in which they serve, under the direction of the general executive secretary of the division.

In the Section of National Missions there are six departments, each with its own special field: (1) Department of City Work; (2) Department of Town and Country Work; (3) Department of Goodwill Industries; (4) Department of Negro Work; (5) Department of Spanish-Speaking and Indian Work in the Southwest; and (6) Department of Research and Surveys. These departments function in co-operation, particularly in areas where their work overlaps.

A special feature of the work of the Section of National Missions is its responsibility for bilingual and minority groups as these are related to Methodist work in the United States.

[6] Ibid., ¶ 1213.

This work is administered through the English-speaking conferences, except where there are organized missions.

The Section of Church Extension has to do with the time-honored work of aiding in the erection of churches, parsonages, and mission buildings in those areas where pioneering endeavors are called for or where there is great need. Donation aid, loan funds, and endowments given for church extension are administered by this section. As is necessary with regard to a work of this importance, a number of well-wrought regulatory provisions outline the manner and method in which the funds entrusted to the section are to be administered. All applications for church extension aid must first be cleared through, and approved by, the applicant's Annual Conference Board of Missions or similar Jurisdictional Board.

There is under this section a Department of Finance and Field Service, which has the very practical duty of assisting local congregations in securing and raising funds for repairing churches, parsonages, liquidating debts, assisting local churches in planning and erecting new buildings, making surveys of new fields, and the like.

The Division of National Missions administers its work outside the continental United States through its two sections in the same manner as it does in the forty-eight states, except in the Dominican Republic, where it supports and co-operates with the Board for Christian Work in Santo Domingo.

WOMAN'S DIVISION

The Woman's Division of Christian Service is also a co-ordinate incorporated division of the Board of Missions. It took over at the organization of The Methodist Church practically all the work carried on at that time by the woman's home and foreign mission organizations of various names and types in the three component churches. All women members of the Board of Missions are placed in the Woman's Division of Christian Service, and to these are added six bishops, one from each jurisdiction, and also one third of the youth members of the general board. Certain additional members may be elected to this division by the board from the other two divisions after a carefully prescribed procedure.

The Woman's Division has great authority with reference to its own special work, as have all the divisions. It nominates for election by the board such executive officers as it may need, including a treasurer—not to be confused with the treasurer of the general board—and determines the powers and duties of such officers and recommends the salary status in each instance.

The division has a charter which is in effect a constitution of its own, and this is in substance published in the *Discipline* in constitutional form. It was first adopted by the Woman's Society of Christian Service and then adopted by the General Conference for inclusion in the regulations governing and outlining that division of the Board of Missions and Church Extension. In adopting this constitution the Woman's Society acted as an autonomous organization. It then furnished its constitution, as adopted, to be included in the disciplinary regulations outlining this special department of board—and church—work.

The division also adopted and saw

placed in the *Discipline* by General Conference action a "Constitution of the Conference Woman's Society of Christian Service" for the guidance and direction of this organization in each Annual Conference;[7] a "Constitution of the District Woman's Society of Christian Service" for guidance and direction in each District;[8] and a constitution for a Woman's Society of Christian Service in each local church.[9] Proposals to amend these—Annual Conference and District Conference—constitutions shall be sent in writing to the recording secretary of the Woman's Division "at least forty days before the last annual meeting of the division in the quadrennium."

The funds for the support of the work of the Woman's Division are to be derived from the Woman's Societies of Christian Service through "annual pledges or dues, special memberships, devises, bequests, annuities, special offerings, gifts, and moneys raised by special projects,"[10] and the like. It is specially stipulated that all funds, except those designated for local purposes, shall be channelled through the conference treasurers of the conference societies to the treasurer of the Woman's Division. Thus the Woman's Society of Christian Service raises its own funds through its own membership and regularly allowed processes. It has the right to administer these funds for the support of all work under its charge and can also recommend to the board appropriations for its own work.[11] The division does not partici-

[7] *Ibid.*, ¶ 1256.
[8] *Ibid.*, ¶ 1257.
[9] *Ibid.*, ¶ 253.
[10] *Ibid.*, ¶ 1250.
[11] *Ibid.*, ¶ 1241.

pate in the funds received from World Service.

The Woman's Division, besides functioning as it does through its various Jurisdictional Conferences and local societies, has three departments. These are the Department of Work in Foreign Fields, the Department of Work in Home Fields—the United States, Alaska, Hawaii, Puerto Rico, and the Dominican Republic; and the Department of Christian Social Relations and Local-Church Activities.[12] The first two of these departments correspond in effect to the foreign and home divisions of the board.

The Department of Christian Social Relations and Local-Church Activities, as its name indicates, promotes the work of the division "along the lines of community service and social relations."

The Woman's Division has always had great responsibility toward the deaconess work of the church. For in the Woman's Division there has been created a Commission on Deaconess Work which has been given charge of all deaconess work in the United States and its dependencies. Deaconess work outside the United States and its dependencies is supervised by the Central Conferences or the Provisional Central Conferences concerned, or the Annual Conferences where there is no Central Conference.

JOINT SECTION OF EDUCATION AND CULTIVATION

A further large and important component of the Board of Missions is the Joint Section of Education and Cultivation. This section has no adminis-

trative functions and is not incorporated. It has upon its membership "six bishops, one from each jurisdiction; six men and two women from the Division of World Missions, elected by that division; six men and two women from the Division of National Missions, elected by that division; eight women from the Woman's Division of Christian Service, . . . elected by that division." [13] The Joint Section has itself two sections: a Woman's Section and a General Section.

This joint section has charge of awakening of interest on the part of the church in all missionary work. It may publish, sell, and circulate books, literature, and periodicals for the work of the board. It institutes councils and conventions, sees that an Annual Week of Prayer is observed for the purpose of developing a missionary spirit, spreading missionary information, and "acquainting the church with the plans and policies of the board." [14]

As with the administrative divisions, the joint section chooses its own president, and nominates him for election as a vice-president of the general board; nominates its executives, determines the powers and duties of its official staff, and recommends remuneration for the employed officials.

In addition to these important divisions of the Board of Missions there are many committees appointed to carry on certain parts of the board's work. Some of these are in overlapping fields and include representatives who can represent one or the other of the various phases of the work. There are also joint commit-

---

[12] Ibid., ¶¶ 1245-48.

[13] Ibid., ¶ 1268.
[14] Ibid., ¶¶ 1270-77.

tees and committees on co-operation which work with other boards or with boards of other denominational agencies. The whole schedule of such committees and commissions, with the written stipulations regarding membership and with duties, and with the changes in personnel which frequently occur, would prove difficult to outline. Suffice it to say here that the whole of the work which may be classified as falling within the purview of this great board has been carefully catalogued and provision made to cover and supervise it in every way possible.

The most important of these co-ordinating committees within the board itself are the Interdivision Committee on Foreign Work, and the Interdivision Committee on Work in Home Fields. Each one is composed of an equal number of representatives from the general division and its corresponding department of the Woman's Division.

2. BOARD OF EDUCATION

This major board has "general oversight of the educational interests of the church in the United States." [15] It has a co-operative relationship with the Board of Missions affecting the advancement of Christian education in lands outside the United States. As a board it took over at the time of the Uniting Conference all the work formerly conducted by the educational agencies of the three uniting churches.

Methodism always has been educationally-minded. One of the first connectional enterprises carried on in the United States was the building of the ill-fated Cokesbury College at Abingdon, Maryland. This institution did not survive long, but other colleges and schools were in time built under the auspices of Methodist conferences or by philanthropists or trustees who were within the Methodist fold. At the same time, the Sunday-school system began to develop in the local churches, this movement itself being largely credited to the work and support of John Wesley for its incipient strength in the church. By mid-century the work of Methodism through its colleges and in the field of higher education was beginning to bear fruit and to lift the educational standards of the people. Wesley's injunction to "unite the two so long divided, knowledge and vital piety" seems to be put into effect.

As the then divided Methodist connections progressed, there occurred within each a desire to have closer oversight of the educational program other than that given by isolated boards of trustees or Annual Conference managers working independently of each other. So in due time the Boards of Education of the respective churches came into being. The General Conference of 1860 in the Methodist Episcopal Church appointed a commission to investigate the possibilities of creating a permanent Board of Education, but this committee was forced to report four years later that it could "get no practical plan." [16] However, in 1868 such a

[15] Discipline, 1952, ¶ 1325.

[16] George L. Curtis, Manual of Methodist Episcopal Church History (1892), p. 241.

228

board was authorized though it was not organized until 1872. In 1892 in the Methodist Episcopal Church there was a board of control for the Epworth Leagues instituted, and this eventually became the Board of Epworth Leagues in 1920. It was merged in the Board of Education in 1924.

The Sunday schools have long been a prime feature of Methodist life and organizational work. John Wesley himself is given credit for doing pioneering work in this field. But while undoubtedly early Methodist preachers and class leaders gave much time to work in the Sunday school, a corporate organization to supervise such work in the connection was slow in coming. The Sunday School Union of the Methodist Episcopal Church seems to have originated in 1827, though its first report was not formally given to the church until 1845. Eventually this union came to be closely integrated with the regular organizational work of the church, and long after, in 1908, the General Conference created a Board of Sunday Schools. This board in 1924 became part of the General Board of Education.

The Board of Education for Negroes, which is still in effect as an organization of The Methodist Church, was an outgrowth of the Freedman's Aid Society. This in 1888 became Freedman's Aid and Southern Education. In 1904 it was merged with the Board of Education of the Methodist Episcopal Church, but before much time had elapsed it was again set apart separately to be once more the Board of Education for Negroes. In 1924, at the merger of several boards, this board was once more put under the Board of Education of the Methodist Episcopal

Church. It survived the merger of the three uniting churches in 1939 and is today perpetuated by order of the General Conference of The Methodist Church, which directs the election of a board of trustees for the Board of Education for Negroes and specifies how the work of this corporation is to be carried on.[17]

In or under the Board of Education of the Methodist Episcopal Church, there were, it is evident, at the time of the merger, several boards or interests which had been united under that one board in 1924. Meanwhile a somewhat similar process had been taking place within the Methodist Episcopal Church, South. The Board of Education of that church was organized in 1894. The General Conference of 1890 ordered such a board organized, but almost immediately rescinded its action. In 1898 there was a Commission on Education appointed, entrusted with the duty of having general oversight of the higher educational enterprises of the church. The Epworth Leagues of the Southern church were organized in the early nineties and were at first put under the Sunday School Board. In 1894 the leagues were put in and under a single and separate connectional department. The term "Epworth League Board" came into use in the Southern Discipline later, but it appears that this board was not an incorporated organization but simply a connectional committee having in charge all the work of the Epworth Leagues, and general oversight of its publications. The Epworth League Board was merged into the General Board of Education of the Methodist Episcopal Church, South, in 1930.

The Sunday-school work of the

[17] Discipline, 1952, ¶ 1328 (4).

Methodist Episcopal Church, South, was carried on for some years after the organization of that church in 1844 by the old Sunday School Union scheme which had been in effect in the undivided church. But in 1850 a connectional Sunday School Union was called for. Eventually a Sunday School Board of six members, with the Sunday-school editor acting as chairman, was set up, and for some years carried on this responsibility for the church. There was, however, in 1914 a thorough reorganization of the Sunday School Department. The church had grown enormously in extent by that time and its Sunday-school literature and the manifold agencies connected with the Sunday schools were such that a better overhead organization and control was felt to be imperative. So there was a disciplinary enlargement of the Sunday School Board in 1914, with a consequently increased importance given to this work of the church. Up to 1922 the executive officer of the Sunday School Board was the editor of Sunday-school periodicals. The General Conference of that year created the office of General Secretary of the General Sunday School Board, leaving the editor responsible for the curriculum materials.

In 1930, following the plan of merging boards, which had been effected by the Methodist Episcopal Church in 1924, the Methodist Episcopal Church, South, united all its educational agencies in a General Board of Education. The Sunday School Board, the Epworth League Board, and the former Board of Education all were merged into the new general board. For such a move, largely led by Dr.—now bishop—Paul B. Kern, it was argued that such a merger would reduce overlapping agencies and that the educative process was not one to be conducted by different agencies—that from the "cradle roll" through church school, college, and university, and on through life, Christian education should be one ongoing process. The General Conference of 1930 therefore correlated its different agencies under one new board, with a Department of Schools and Colleges, a Department of the Local Church, and an Editorial Department having charge of publications. This pattern, adopted in 1930 by the Southern church—and very like the 1924 unified board of the Methodist Episcopal Church—was taken as the basic organizational structure for the Board of Education of The Methodist Church some few years later.

In the discussions preceding church union there was under consideration the matter of having one unified board, or of dividing the work along the lines of the old Sunday School Board, Epworth League Board, and so forth. It was finally decided to have one unified board and the plan presented to the Uniting Conference called for such an organization.

A unified Board of Education, created in 1939, managed the educational affairs of The Methodist Church until 1952. In that year the General Conference made sweeping changes in the Board of Education, as it did in nearly all the other agencies of the church. As called for by the conference of that year, the board is

composed of seventeen effective Bishops of The Methodist Church resident in the United States, selected by the Council of Bishops, together with additional members selected as follows: Upon the nomination of its Committee on Education, each Jurisdictional Conference shall elect to membership in the board one minister and one layman without regard to the number of members within the jurisdiction, and, for addition, one minister and one layman for each 400,000 members or major fraction thereof within the jurisdiction. Each Jurisdictional Conference shall also elect, upon nomination of the National Conference of Methodist Youth, one youth or student representative, twenty-one years of age or under at the time of his election; *provided* that if any youth or student representative shall attain his twenty-fourth birthday during the quadrennium, his period of service shall terminate at the close of the annual session of the board next following, and he shall be replaced by one within the youth age range.[18]

Careful regulations are drawn up as to how the nominations shall be made to the Jurisdictional Conferences, especially in the case of the youth membership.

In addition to the above named persons "the board shall also elect members at large, on nomination of the Council of Bishops, in sufficient number to bring the membership of the board to a total of ninety-one. Not more than three members of the board shall come from any one Annual Conference." [19]

At its organization the Board of Education must have a nominating committee which shall be composed of one member from each jurisdiction, chosen by the members, and one bishop chosen by the bishops who are members of the board. This nominating committee shall nominate all the members of the board to its three important divisions. These divisions are: the Division of Educational Institutions, the Division of the Local Church, and the Editorial Division. It is provided that in selecting the

members for these divisions, the Divisions of Educational Institutions and Local Church shall have members chosen in the ratio of five and five, while the Editorial Division receives two. Also the nominating committee shall nominate a president and a recording secretary. The membership of the divisions and the president and the recording secretary are elected for the quadrennium.

Each of the divisions of this great board must elect a chairman, and these chairmen shall be vice-presidents of the board. The executive secretaries of the Division of Educational Institutions and of the Division of the Local Church are elected for the quadrennium by the board from nominations made by their respective divisions. The executive secretary of the Editorial Division is elected in a different manner, as will be noticed in the description of the Board of Publication.

The executive committee of the board is composed of the president, the vice-president and recording secretary of the board, and the members of the advisory committees of the three divisions, chosen so that Educational Institutions gets seven, Local Church gets seven, and Editorial gets four. The president of the board is ex officio a member of each advisory committee.

The treasurer of the board is the custodian of all the funds of the board. He must pay out funds upon the order of the executive secretaries of the Division of Educational Institutions and of the Division of the Local Church. The executive secretary of the Editorial Division clears his budget through the Board of Publication.

The separate divisions of the Board

[18] *Ibid.*, ¶ 1326.
[19] *Ibid.*

of Education may now be outlined.

THE DIVISION OF EDUCATIONAL INSTITUTIONS

This division of the Board of Education "shall represent The Methodist Church in all activities connected with secondary, higher, theological, and ministerial education. I shall have an advisory relationship to all universities, colleges, schools, theological schools, and Wesley Foundations affiliated with The Methodist Church." [20] Institutions owned or supervised by other boards are excepted from this provision, but upon request the division may assist institutions owned by other agencies. This division has also the power to receive and disburse funds which may be committed to the board for the purposes of this division. Its duties are outlined in a definite way in the *Discipline*, and these duties are quite comprehensive in the whole relationship of the church to its educational institutions.[21]

The division functions through an executive secretary who is the executive and legal representative thereof. This officer of the board reports to the board and acts under its general control.

The Division of Educational Institutions looks after the following: Christian education among Negroes; co-operative projects in connection with the Board of Missions; educational societies or foundations; Methodist Student Day; Race Relations Day; Student Loan and Scholarship Fund; Wesley Foundations; theological schools; and ministerial education.

[20] *Ibid.*, ¶ 1351.
[21] *Ibid.*, ¶¶ 1351-70.

There is a Campus-Church Relations Committee and also an Interconference Commission on Student Religious Work.

This division works in close co-operation with the University Senate of The Methodist Church, though no member of the University Senate shall be a member of the Board of Education.

The 1952 General Conference placed the training and indoctrination of the young ministers of the church under the administrative oversight of the Division of Educational Institutions. The division is therefore now composed of two sections: a Section of Secondary and Higher Education and a Section of Ministerial Education.

The training of young ministers and their indoctrination in specific Methodist doctrine and discipline has been a duty felt keenly by the church from its earliest days. Especially did the older preachers—indeed every preacher in the traveling connection—feel very decidedly that there should be a regimen of study as well as of service, obligatory upon young men who joined the conference, seeking "full connection." Admission on trial has always preceded full admission to the conference, and part of every minister's novitiate has been the traditional conference "course of study." No matter what college training a man may have had, or what his talents or advantages, every preacher who has ever joined a Methodist conference since the earliest day has been compelled to undergo this special course of reading, followed by an examination.

At first the "conference course" was a series of books outlining fundamentals of Christian doctrine as well as of Methodist doctrine, polity, and so forth. As early as 1816 the *Discipline* said:

It shall be the duty of the bishops or of a committee which they may appoint at each Annual Conference, to point out a course of reading and study proper to be pursued by candidates for the ministry. . . . And before any such candidate is received into full connection, he shall give satisfactory evidence respecting his knowledge of these particular subjects which have been recommended to his consideration.[22]

Later, further reading was prescribed for ministers already "admitted on trial," and thus began the famous "four-year course." Regulations creating such a course are to be found in the *Disciplines* of the past. The bishops for long years acted as a committee to choose the books which were to be in the course of study; but the examination of the individual candidate was left to a committee of the Annual Conference itself.

These committees naturally varied greatly in different conferences, as did their methods of examining the candidates. Sometimes the committee was strict, sometimes lax, with an occasional scholarly martinet or an occasional saintly veteran who was much more anxious to "help the young brother through" than to find out what he knew of Wesley's sermons or the intricacies of the *Discipline*. To end this rather chaotic state of affairs and to get some uniformity in the way the different conferences handled the matter, the Methodist Episcopal churches finally created church-wide agencies to have charge of the whole regimen of ministerial training. The Commission on the Course of Study for the Methodist Episcopal Church was created in 1916,

and for the Methodist Episcopal Church, South, in 1934. The Methodist Protestant Church handled this matter through its General Conference, prescribing in the *Discipline* the exact course which must be followed. These respective commissions and agencies took over from the bishops the actual matter of selecting the course of study itself; and in due time recognized and accredited the theological schools of the church with respect to the helpful part they had begun to play in training ministers. Also the commissions, through the promotion of summer schools for pastors, and correspondence schools, were of great help in training men for a better ministry.

At Methodist Union the reorganized church created a Commission on Ministerial Training. This consisted of bishops, pastors, theological school representatives, with the book editor of the church, and the executive secretary of the Division of Educational Institutions. This commission, after functioning as an independent entity for twelve years—1940-1952—and doing unusually constructive work, was changed from an independent body and made a part of the Board of Education by the General Conference of 1952.

As now organized the Section of Ministerial Education of the Division of Educational Institutions has two parts: (1) a Department of Theological Education, and (2) a Department of In-Service Training. Both departments are separate world service agencies and are administered independently.

The section is composed of six bishops and six ministers selected from the personnel of the Board of Education. The same body of twelve

[22] ¶ 34.

men acts at one time as a Commission on Theological Education and at another as a Commission on In-Service Training, each governing its respective department. They keep separate minutes of their meetings as separate commissions. In addition they have the privilege of having six advisory members in each commission. The advisors in the Commission on In-Service Training are chosen from the faculties of the Methodist schools of theology so that they may assist in selecting the courses of study. In the Commission on Theological Education the advisory members are chosen from the presidents or deans of the Methodist schools of theology. These absent themselves when the commission considers the distribution of the world service funds allotted to theological schools.

The new affiliation of a Section of Ministerial Education selected from and by the Division of Educational Institutions, for the first time in the history of Methodism, divorces the Council of Bishops from its historic responsibility for either deciding on the courses of study or choosing the personnel of the body responsible for ministerial education.

Traditionally the Department of In-Service Training co-operates with the Annual Conference Boards of Ministerial Training and Qualifications and helps in organizing finances, and in conducting short-term schools for pastors, or pastors' schools.

The Section of Ministerial Education has a direct responsibility for studying the actual needs of the ministry and of co-operating with the theological schools and Conference Boards of Ministerial Training and Qualifications in the development of effective methods for selective recruiting for the ministry. The section is expected to work in close co-operation with the conference boards and with the theological schools in all matters relating to the selecting, training, teaching, and otherwise guiding those who are entering the ministry of the church or considering entering it; and it is always ready to help those ministers who may wish to engage in further training, or to prepare themselves better for their life's work.[23]

THE DIVISION OF THE LOCAL CHURCH

This division is responsible for developing a "comprehensive and unified program of Christian education which shall lead to a knowledge of the Holy Scriptures, the Christian religion, and the Christian Church." [24] All the work except editorial, which was managed by the old Sunday School Boards and Epworth League Boards of the uniting churches, naturally came under this division at the time of union.

The local church school, according to ¶ 228 of the *Discipline*, includes the

Sunday school; extended sessions for children; Sunday evening and weekday meetings of children, youth, and adults; nursery and home roll; nursery schools and kindergartens; children, youth, and adult home members; vacation church school; leadership education agencies; parent study groups; and the Methodist Sunday Evening Fellowship.

A wide and manifold area of activity and list of duties devolves upon this imporant division. The *Discipline* describes in detail these duties and also outlines and processes by which they ought to be performed.

[23] For complete regulations with reference to ministerial training see *Discipline*, 1952, ¶¶ 1373-80.

[24] *Discipline*, 1952, ¶ 1396.

The General Conference authorized the Division of the Local Church to prepare manuals on educational work dealing with the local church. These manuals provide guidance for pastors and Christian educational workers in the church at large.

As the work of this great division has grown within recent years, more and more emphasis has been placed on its formal assemblies and institutional gatherings. The Methodist Conference on Christian Education is held from time to time in co-operation with the Jurisdictional and Conference Boards of Education, and with other agencies of the church. The youth of The Methodist Church between the ages of twelve and twenty-three inclusive, including all organizational units, are known as The Methodist Youth Fellowship. When anyone becomes a member in the Youth Division in a local Methodist church, he automatically becomes a member of The Methodist Youth Fellowship.

The National Conference of Methodist Youth provides for the free expression of the voice of youth and for the fellowship of Methodist youth and students from over the entire church. At the same time this National Conference selects projects of particular interest to youth, and gives youth free opportunity to participate creatively in planning the church's program. This conference meets annually, elects officers, and reports upon its meetings and activities to the Board of Education.

There is also a National Methodist Youth Fellowship Commission for the purpose of fellowship, evaluation, and program planning in areas that relate to general youth work. The constitution of the agency is careful-ly outlined by the *Discipline*, and its activities are emphasized, particularly in the local church.

Also under this division is a National Methodist Student Commission for the purpose of fellowship, evaluation, and program planning in areas that relate to student work. It is the purpose of this organization to emphasize religious work among the colleges and universities. Each one of these commissions has power to make recommendations to all groups, agencies, and boards in the church which work with youth.

The Division of The Local Church has authority to make plans for church-school extension throughout the church and to contribute to the support of church schools which may require assistance in mission territory. The division is expected to enter into agreements with Jurisdictional Boards of Education, and also to work in conjunction with Annual Conference Boards of Education in order to further the joint efforts of religion in its particular field.

The executive director of the Division of the Local Church has general supervision of the affairs of the division. He is the administrative and legal executive of it. He reports annually to the Board of Education and in all official acts is subject to the board itself. Assisting him is a strong staff of co-workers, each of whom is given one of the specialized departments of this vastly important division.

EDITORIAL DIVISION

The Editorial Division of the Board of Education is entrusted with the duty of providing all curriculum materials which the Board of Education needs for carrying on its work.

It does this largely through its editor of church-school publications, who has the right to appoint his assistants and staff members.

There is a close correlation between the Board of Education and the Board of Publication (hereafter to be described) in relation to the Editorial Division of the Board of Education. The editor of church-school publications must be nominated by a joint committee representing these two boards, and upon this committee the respective board chairmen shall sit; his election is to be by the Board of Education but is subject to confirmation by the Board of Publication, which fixes and pays his salary. The Board of Publication also pays the salaries of all the assistants to the editor of church-school publications and of the staff members; and assumes full financial responsibility for the entire work of the Editorial Division of the Board of Education. In turn the publications of the Board of Education must be manufactured, promoted, and distributed by The Methodist Publishing House—which institution is, of course, the chief responsibility of the Board of Publication, and the source of its revenue.

The editor of church-school publications must make up a budget for his annual expenses and that of his division after consultation with the publishing agents. This budget must in turn be approved by the Board of Publication.

In preparing all curriculum materials for the work of the church school, the editor of church-school publications must work through and in a Curriculum Committee, which is composed of the executive secretaries of the three divisions of the Board of Education, the book editor of the church, the executive secretary of the Interboard Committee on Missionary Education; and the publishing agents. The executive committee of the Board of Education has the right to name other members to the Curriculum Committee so that the entire committee shall consist of not less than eleven nor more than seventeen members. In naming the additional members the nominating committee of the executive committee of the board must give consideration to the necessity for having on the committee "at least three workers in local churches," as well as those who may represent other agencies of the church which use teaching materials. Other persons may be invited to act as consulting members of the Curriculum Committee. The entire staff of the Board of Education in its three divisions are consulting members of the Curriculum Committee, but without vote.

This powerful committee prepares and plans for all church-school literature, and projects needed books in the field of leadership education or curriculum training. All its work and projected program is turned over to the editor of church-school publications who then must bring it before the Board of Education for final approval. In practice the various departments and staff members, who have their own definite area of interest or work, plan and project their respective materials, support the call for these before the Curriculum Committee itself and answer any questions or queries put by other members of that committee with reference to their plan or work. The Board of Education as a whole is usually content to adopt the plan and program of the Curriculum Committee with a minimum of debate, just as the General Conference is usually inclined to take the work of an important technical committee with no great debate or discussion.

The chairman of The Editorial Division and the editor of church-school publications have the right to sit with the Board of Publication when that board meets; and the publishing agents, representing that board, may also sit with the Board of Education when it meets. These respective officers have the privileges of the floor, though without vote, when matters of interest appertaining to their own work is to the fore.

3. UNIVERSITY SENATE

The University Senate originated in the Methodist Episcopal Church in 1892 in response to the need for an authoritative body to fix and evaluate the educational standards for the church. The great growth of church universities and colleges and the number of church-related institutions brought about late in the nineteenth century a situation in which there were many different educational standards between the different schools and colleges. There was need for an arbiter to evaluate for the church the worth and grade of those institutions and educational processes which were being patronized by Annual Conferences or other church-wide groups. So the University Senate came into being, the first standardizing agency of its type in the United States. It antedated by about three years the powerful North Central Association of Colleges and Secondary Schools.

As created in 1892 the senate was constituted of "practical educators," selected one from each General Conference district, and one at large. The distinguished William Fairfield Warren was its first president. The senate was directed to visit, if need be, or at any rate to have advisory care (from the church) over the educational institutions of the church. It could determine what educational requirements should be met in order for a college to be properly accredited by the church, and it had the right also to determine what institutions claiming relationship with the church should be properly accredited. The senate was ordered to report at least quadrennially to the Board of Education of the Methodist Episcopal Church. It was that board's function to determine finally what educational institutions should be recognized as having met to list them accordingly.[25]

From 1892 to 1939, the University Senate grew in prestige in the Methodist Episcopal Church. In order to give it more complete independence, the General Conference specified in 1926 that the members of the senate should not be members of the Board of Education. They were all, however, to be "practical educators" or employed in the field of education.[26] The executive secretary of the Department of Educational Institutions of the Board had before that time been made the executive secretary of the University Senate.

[25] *Discipline*, 1892, ¶ 323; *Discipline*, 1900, ¶ 336.
[26] *Discipline*, 1926, ¶ 1267.

The support of the University Senate devolved upon the Board of Education, except in those instances when the senate might be requested by some other board to visit or evaluate an educational institution suping board. In such instances expenses of the senate's visitation fell upon the board asking this favor.

The University Senate of the Methodist Episcopal Church was carried over into The Methodist Church to become one of its firm executive agencies. Its support is provided for by the present Board of Education,[27] and the executive secretary of the senate is the executive secretary of the Division of Educational Institutions of that board.[28] Nevertheless the University Senate is independent of the Board of Education in making its evaluations, in providing educational standards for the church, and in listing in accord therewith the schools, colleges, and universities of the church.

The senate is composed of twenty-one persons, not members of the Board of Education, all of whom must be "actively engaged in the work of education and are fitted by training and experience for the technical work of establishing standards and evaluating educational institutions in accordance with such standards." [29] Eleven of the members must be elected quadrennially by the Board of Education, and ten are to be appointed by the Council of Bishops. Due regard must be had for the principle of obtaining representation for the senate from different types of educational institutions which may be included in, or under supervision of,

the senate. The senate elects its own presiding officer. It meets annually at its own instance and special meetings may be called under proper provisions.[30]

The primary work of the senate consists of establishing and maintaining standards for the educational institutions related to The Methodist Church in the United States. It sustains also an advisory capacity to the Board of Education in all matters of educational policy. It must report to the board annually a proper classification of all educational institutions in the United States which are related to The Methodist Church.[31] The use of this list is mandatory for the board, as well as for Annual Conferences in dealing with candidates for the ministry.

The senate has the right to investigate the personnel, scholastic requirements, and so forth, of any designated educational institution claiming to be, or adjudged to be, related to The Methodist Church.[32] It acts as a consultant and counselor on all educational matters having to do with the educational institutions related to the church. It may recommend to such institutions methods of improvement in educational or religious services.[33] It has great powers in accrediting and evaluating all these and other institutions, and possesses huge influence in correlating the work of such institutions with the educational work of the church. The president or other administrative officer of each educational institution related to The Methodist Church must furnish statistics and other information to the

[27] *Discipline*, 1952, ¶ 1389.
[28] *Ibid.*, ¶ 1388.
[29] *Ibid.*, ¶ 1383.

[30] *Ibid.*, ¶ 1388.
[31] *Ibid.*, ¶ 1384.
[32] *Ibid.*, ¶ 1385.
[33] *Ibid.*, ¶ 1386.

Division of Educational Institutions and to the University Senate. When the senate has classified any institution in accordance with the scheme of classification which the *Discipline* orders it to follow, such institution may not announce a different classification without first securing the approval of the senate and of the Division of Educational Institutions of the Board of Education.[34]

The sweeping powers of the University Senate are made clear by the following provision:

No educational institution or foundation of The Methodist Church shall hereafter be established until its plans and organization shall have been approved by the University Senate and the Division of Educational Institutions; and no Annual or Provisional Annual Conference in the United States shall acquire, or affiliate with, through any board or society, a school, college, university, or other educational institution, unless the approval of the division and the senate shall have been previously obtained and unless, in the judgment of the division, there is reasonable assurance of financial support sufficient to equip and maintain the institution in the classification approved for it by the University Senate.[35]

4. BOARD OF PUBLICATION

This great board of the church is charged with the direction and control of The Methodist Publishing House. The Publishing House, as defined in the somewhat tautological language of the *Discipline*, "comprises the publishing interests of The Methodist Church." [36] As an organized entity within the church, the Book Concern, which was the predecessor of the present Publishing House, was the earliest organized agency of American Methodism.

In May, 1789, in a conference held in Wesley Chapel, in John Street Church, New York, The Methodist Book Concern was set up. John Dickins, the secretary of the conference and a scholar and booklover, was the one who made it possible. There is reason to believe that Asbury had groomed Dickins for leadership in this project, as this was very important to him. Asbury knew how much the Wesleyan connection in England depended on the sale of Wesley's books for its revenue. He was anxious

for similar success in America, though the problems were—and are to this day—different. When it appeared that the whole project would fail through lack of financial resources, Dickins made one of those brief but vital speeches which sometimes become historic in conference annals. "Brethren, be of good courage and go forward," he said in substance, "I have one hundred and twenty pounds sterling [$600] the savings of my life's labors. I will lend every shilling of it to The Methodist Book Concern until such time as it can be returned to me." The conference, of course, accepted his offer and Dickins became the first book steward. Asbury stationed him in Philadelphia that he might better supervise the new business.[37]

Subsequently in the *Discipline* of 1792, is found the following:

Quest. 1. Who is employed to manage the printing business?

[34] *Ibid.,* ¶ 1390.
[35] *Ibid.,* ¶ 1392.

[36] 1952, ¶ 1121.
[37] W. F. Whitlock, *The Story of the Book Concern* (1903), p. 20.

Ans. John Dickins.

Quest. 2. What allowance shall be paid him annually for his services?

Ans. 1. Two hundred dollars for a dwelling house and for a book room.

2. Eighty dollars for a boy.

3. Fifty-three dollars and one-third for firewood, and

4. Three hundred and thirty-four dollars to clothe and feed himself, his wife, and children. In all, six hundred and sixty-six dollars and one-third.

From this small beginning there came in a century and a half the great business which at last reporting indicated an annual gross income of almost fifteen million dollars. For as early Methodism spread so also its use of the printed word increased, and every circuit rider considered himself a colporteur for the sale and distribution of books, tracts, periodicals, and other helpful literature.

The fact that the first headquarters for the business was in St. George's Church, Philadelphia, made it convenient, if not inevitable, that the over-all control of the Methodist "printing business" should be by the ministers of that city. So the first "Book Committee" was formally named of Philadelphia preachers. Again quoting the 1792 Discipline:

Quest. 4. Who shall form the Book Committee?

Ans. John Dickins, Henry Willis, Thomas Haskins and the Preacher who is stationed in Philadelphia from time to time.[38]

The Book Committee in 1796 was again put under the appointment of the Philadelphia Conference, and that conference in 1800 was directed to examine the books of the publishing business "at the time of its sitting." Books published by the concern

[38] Thomas Haskins had "located" in 1786 and was then a lawyer, but remained one of Asbury's most trusted helpers.

were to be sold by the preachers on commission, and the Agents were to print "by the advice of the Bishop and Philadelphia Conference." [39]

The second book steward of the church was Ezekiel Cooper, who took charge of the business first when Dickins was stricken with yellow fever. Subsequently, upon the death of Dickins in 1798, Cooper was given full charge. The Book Concern became a burden to the Philadelphia preachers and there was especial criticism of the fact that Cooper did not have to "move" as did the other brethren since Asbury kept him at Philadelphia to look after the "printing business." The General Conference of 1804 decided to move the business from Philadelphia, and Baltimore and New York both bid for it. New York won by a majority of two votes and the Book Concern was thereupon moved to that city. There it remained. Asbury then sent Cooper to be one of the preachers stationed in New York and, of course, to continue in charge of the Book Concern. Cooper assumed the title of editor and book steward. At the same time the New York Conference was directed to appoint annually a Book Committee of five. The name "Book Concern" was given to the publishing business of the church because of the triple question in the minutes of an early conference: "What shall we do with our concern for souls, our concern for education and our Book Concern." [40]

In time the Book Concern was enlarged and the election of its members taken over directly by the General

[39] David Sherman, History of the Revisions of the Discipline (1874), p. 30.

[40] Jennings, The Methodist Book Concern (1924), p. 31.

Conference. As time went by more definite rules and regulations were made providing for the election of Book Committee members so that due regional representation might be had upon this body. At length laymen in equal numbers together with ministers became Book Committee members, and in this particular agency of the church laymen have always come into their own in a magnificent way. The laymen chosen were usually men endowed with business acumen as well as with devotion to their church. It was sometimes said of the Book Committee that this was one organization in the church where laymen were able to play a prime part and where their management acquitted itself and their church. The Book Committee—or a Book Committee— functioning under that rather quaint name, continued to manage the publishing interests in the respective Episcopal Methodist churches until union in 1939.

The name "book steward," or "general book steward" as it was in 1804, was dropped from Methodist records in 1820 and "book agents," as administrative officers in charge of the Book Concern, were named instead. Nathan Bangs and Thomas Mason were the first book agents elected in 1820, Mason being designated as "assistant." [41]

New York continued to be headquarters for the Book Concern, but a book agent, Martin Ruter, was elected in 1820 and appointed "to reside in Cincinnati and manage the Concern in the Western country." Then in 1836 the General Conference directed that there should be "an establishment of the Book Concern in the city of Cincinnati." This was in due time (1839) incorporated under the laws of Ohio as the Western Methodist Book Concern and became a co-ordinated agency of the Methodist Episcopal Church. Book Agents were elected by successive General Conferences to manage the affairs of the two book concerns. In 1872 the agents of the two concerns were made co-ordinate in rank, with two to be elected for New York and two for Cincinnati, but not until there had been a tense debate and something of a legal battle afterward. In 1892 the title "publishing agent" instead of "book agent" was adopted to denominate these executive officers. In 1912 the General Conference unified the two houses and elected four publishing agents, one of whom was designated as the General Publishing Agent. All this, however, brought up debate and tension and the office of general publishing agent was abolished in 1920. At the time of Methodist union in 1939 there were three publishing agents functioning as the executive officers of the two branches of the Book Concern, one of these residing in New York, one in Cincinnati, and one in Chicago, where in 1852 another house of the Book Concern had been established.

Following the division of The Methodist Episcopal Church in 1844, the Methodist Episcopal Church, South, thereafter organized, was given its proportionate share of money and other properties inherent in the old Book Concern. This followed a decision of the Supreme Court of the United States in 1854 affirming the validity of the Plan of Separation. The Southern church after some years established its publishing business in Nashville, and a charter was granted by the state of Tennessee to the

[41] *Ibid.*, p. 24.

"Book Agents of the Methodist Episcopal Church, South." Such agents thus became the incorporated executive officers and administrators of the Publishing House of their church.

There was, as has been indicated, a Book Committee in the Church, South, in every way similar to that of the Methodist Episcopal Church, and elected, of course, by the General Conference. Laymen were put upon this body in due time, as has been stated, and at the time of union and for many years previous to that, the Southern church made a practice of having one of its publishing agents a layman and one a minister.

The Methodist Protestant Church after its organization in 1828 made haste to create and sponsor publications of its own and succeeded admirably. Mention has already been made of the able editors who carried on the fight for laity rights for a time within the Methodist Episcopal Church, and who, after the organization of the Methodist Protestant Church, continued to publish for that connection their periodicals.

Mention has been made of the division within the ranks of the Methodist Protestants and how the western section of that church drew apart from the eastern or Maryland group. This division resulted in establishing two separate centers of publication. In 1854 at Zanesville, Ohio, the western Methodist Protestants elected an "editor and book agent," Ancel H. Bassett, who, two years later, began to publish the *Western Methodist Protestant* at Springfield, Ohio.[42]

In Baltimore, always a strong Meth-

odist Protestant center, the church had from the first a "Book Committee."[43] John J. Harrod, of Baltimore, it should be noted, was the first book agent of the Methodist Protestant Church. Under his direction the paper, *Mutual Rights and the Methodis Protestant,* as the name soon became, was continued.[44] The name of this was eventually shortened to *The Methodist Protestant.*

In 1877, when the two divisions of Methodist Protestantism united again, a publication called the *Methodist Recorder* was being published at Pittsburgh and the *Methodist Protestant* at Baltimore, and both publications were continued as official organs of the church.

In Baltimore the name "The Stockton Press" was adopted by the Methodist Protestant Publishing House as a trade name. This name honored the wealthy and influential Methodist Protestant layman who had founded the old *Wesleyan Repository and Religious Intelligencer* far back in the 1820's.

The Stockton Press published the necessary books, tracts, and periodicals which the Methodist Protestant Church called for. The controlling body within the ranks of Methodist Protestantism which had charge of the publishing program of the church became known in time as the "Board of Publication of the Methodist Protestant Church." Its headquarters were in Pittsburgh, where it was incorporated under the laws of Pennsylvania. Pittsburgh and Baltimore continued up to the time of union to be the two centers of Methodist Protestant publication.

---

[42] Ancel H. Bassett, *A Concise History of the Methodist Protestant Church* (1882), p. 496.

[43] Methodist Protestant *Discipline,* 1830, ¶ 112.

[44] *Ibid.,* ¶ 115.

There was no book editor in the Methodist Protestant Church, but there was an editor of the church's official organ who was elected by the General Conference. There were also editors and others appointed or elected to have charge of Sunday-school materials and other literature.

Thus at the time of Methodist union in 1939 there were functioning four separate corporations having charge of the publishing interests of the merging churches. These were The Methodist Book Concern, a corporation existing under the laws of New York; The Methodist Book Concern, a corporation under the laws of Ohio; The Board of Publication of the Methodist Protestant Church, existing under the laws of Pennsylvania; and the Book Agents of the Methodist Episcopal Church, South, incorporated under the laws of Tennessee. These corporate bodies had to be united under one control at the organization of The Methodist Church.[45] In order to preserve charter rights, entailed properties, bequests, contractual obligations, and so forth, help by these four corporations respectively, it was determined that they should not be dissolved as legal entities but put under one over-all control. This was done by creating a Board of Publication for The Methodist Church, which can act as a holding corporation for the four corporations above described. These corporations, with their subsidiary book stores, printing plants, sales organization, and the like, are known as The Methodist Publishing House.

The name "Book Committee" was considered archaic and the Methodist Protestant title "Board of Publication" was taken to describe the new board within The Methodist Church. This board meets formally and officially under its own name to give general direction to all the work of the Publishing House.

Since unification the Board of Publication meets under its own name and also under the names of and as the four corporations comprising the Publishing House. This it does at its annual meetings when, after adjourning as the Board of Publication, it becomes successively and formally The Methodist Book Concern, a New York corporation; The Methodist Book Concern, an Ohio corporation; the Book Agents of the Methodist Episcopal Church, South, a Tennessee corporation; and the Board of Publication of the Methodist Protestant Church, a Pennsylvania corporation. Each one of these corporations, though composed of the same persons, keeps separate minutes and opens and adjourns in regular form.

But this awkwardness of control— done to safeguard rights and property belonging to the separate bodies— caused the board itself to sponsor legislation looking toward one board only. The General Conference of 1952 thereupon "authorized, empowered, and directed" the Board of Publication "in its discretion to cause to be created and established a new corporation to bear the name and style of The Methodist Publishing House, under the charter of which the operations and functions of The Methodist Publishing House may be carried on and executed." [46] At the time of this writing it appears that the Board of Publication "in its discretion" is working definitely toward the establishment of the one corporation. Mean-

[45] *Discipline*, 1952, ¶¶ 1126-27.   [46] *Ibid.*, ¶ 1127 § 2.

while until that is formed, the four existing corporations are to be continued.

At first the Board of Publication alone of the great boards was constituted "by the jurisdictions" with no General Conference direction as to how members for this board were to be chosen. Other boards were told how they should get certain of their members, or how nominations were to be made to their membership. The jurisdictions of course were given the number of members they might elect to the Board of Publication in line with the constitutional proviso that proportionate representation must be had from each jurisdiction. On the Board of Publication this was to be on the basis of one member of the board for each 150,000 church members or major fraction thereof. It was also ordered that ministers and laymen should be elected in equal numbers, as nearly as possible. But the 1952 General Conference, in following the recommendation of the Survey Commission to reduce the number of members upon each board, directed that the Board of Publication should thereafter consist of forty-five members, two of whom should be bishops elected by the bishops; and that the Jurisdictional Conferences should be allowed to elect such number of other representatives as would be proportionate to their total church membership. Laymen and ministers must be elected in equal numbers, and the two bishops (each of whom may serve for one quadrennium only) are to be counted among the ministerial members from the jurisdictions to which they belong.

The Board of Publication meets annually, with special meetings held at such times as it may decide, or upon the call of its chairman. One third of the members may request the chairman to call such a meeting. A majority constitutes a quorum.

The executive committee consists of sixteen members, including the chairman of the board, who acts as chairman of this committee. It is provided that not more than four members of the executive committee shall be from any one of the six jurisdictions. The two publishing agents are ex officio members of the Board of Publication and of the executive committee but have no vote.

Elected by the Board of Publication for quadrennial terms are two publishing agents; the book editor of the church; the editor of the *Christian Advocate*; and the editor of such other editions of the *Advocate* as the board may establish. At present it has established the *Central Christian Advocate* to serve the Central Jurisdiction, and the editor of that *Advocate* is elected by the Board of Publication. The board also has joint responsibility with the Board of Education for the election of the editor of church-school publications.

The publishing agents are empowered under the supervision and direction of the board to be the administrative officers of The Methodist Publishing House. As such they are required to give bond for the faithful discharge of their duties. They must also qualify legally to act as administrative officers for each of the four corporations included in The Methodist Publishing House. They are expected to make quarterly reports to the executive committee of the board upon the state of the current business of the Publishing House; and must also make a formal and complete annual report to the board at the time of its regular meeting.

By the law of the church all the "produce," that is the net result of the Publishing House operations, must be given over for distribution among the conference claimants. Therefore each year, and usually upon the recommendation of the publishing agents, the Board of Publication sets aside the amount of money which it decides may be distributed to the several Annual Conferences for their worn-out preachers, their wives, widows, and children. This sum is distributed to the Annual Conferences in proportion to the total annuity years each conference may claim for its "claimants." The Board of Conference Claimants of each conference makes final division to the individual claimants upon a uniform basis.

The Board of Publication and the publishing agents, as managers of a large commercial undertaking, must and do determine all such matters as the upkeep of buildings and machinery, the opening of new stores or outlets for trade, the purchase or sale of real estate, and the multiform procedures having to do with a gigantic financial enterprise. There is nothing in the law of the church to prevent —indeed the Publishing House is expected—to set up necessary financial reserves and develop its business. In contradistinction to other boards, the Publishing House is expected to pull its own weight financially, relying not upon the general funds of the church for accomplishing its purposes but upon its own ability and success as a commercial agency. The Publishing House has not, however, been created to make money but exists for "the advancement of the cause of Christianity by disseminating religious knowledge and useful literary and scientific information in the form of books, tracts, and periodicals." [47] That the Publishing House does and can make money is gratifying to the church and vastly helpful to the superannuated ministers; but its prime purpose, as stated above by the *Discipline*, is never forgotten.

BOOK PUBLICATION AND THE BOOK EDITOR

The primary work of the Book Concern, as the very name indicates, was book publication. This followed Wesley's plan of abridging and reprinting the best type of helpful books at low cost, as well as his plan of publishing new material. Books rather than magazines or periodicals were the principal production of the Publishing House for many years.

It may be noted in passing that a rigid censorship was put upon early Methodist preachers with reference to their own private publications. "Print nothing without the approbation of one or other of the Superintendents," ran the direction of 1787.[48] Later "the Conference and one of the Bishops" became the licensing power. But such stipulations were unpopular and ineffective and in 1824 it was provided that if any preacher should publish a "work or book of his own," he should be responsible to his own Conference for any obnoxious matter or doctrine therein contained." [49]

All this, of course, had no reference to the books put out by the Book Concern itself but only to private publication. The regularly issued

[47] *Ibid.*, ¶ 1122.
[48] David Sherman, *History of the Revisions of the Discipline* (1874), p. 247.
[49] *Discipline*, 1824, ¶ 188.

books of the Book Concern were assumed to be the responsibility of the whole connection by the Conference of 1787:

As it has been frequently recommended by the Preachers and people that such books as are wanted be printed in this country, we therefore propose,

1. That the advice of the Conference shall be desired concerning any valuable impression, and their consent be obtained before any steps be taken for the printing thereof.[50]

Obviously such general editing would not be practical, nor was it. Book stewards for a time acted as editors (Ezekiel Cooper was referred to as "Editor and General Book Steward" in the *Discipline* of 1799), and secured other editors to serve under them in the production of books, tracts, and periodicals. But at length both Episcopal Methodisms found it advisable to create the office of book editor and to provide for his election by the Book Committee.

It appears that the office of "General Book Editor" was created as a separate institution first by the Methodist Episcopal Church, South. Into that position at 1850 (or perhaps in 1854 if a more authoritative action be relied upon for the date) came Dr. Thomas O. Summers, who held this office in the Church, South, until 1888. This remarkable man, born in England, exerted a tremendous influence over his whole connection as long as he lived. Bishop McTyeire said of him: "He was a vat into which all learning had been poured, and as incapable of originality as he was of sin"—an aphorism which Southern Methodists enjoyed repeating.

The Southern *Discipline* of 1858 required the approval of the book editor before the "General Book Agent" could publish any book; and "in case of a difference between the Book Editor and the Book Agent the matter shall be referred to the Book Committee." [51] In the Southern church the book editor was also made editor of the *Methodist Quarterly Review,* a journal devoted to a high and representative type of Christian thought.

In the Methodist Episcopal Church the office of book editor was created as a separate ecclesiastical office only a few years later than in the Methodist Episcopal Church, South. "Editors" or "Editors of Books" are mentioned during early years as those perhaps employed to supervise the actual mechanical production of books. The *Discipline* of 1876 refers to "Book Editors," but subsequently in 1904 one person in the Methodist Episcopal Church came to fill this office and to share with the book agents the responsibility for carrying out the book program of the church. To the book editor also the various conference secretaries were directed to send their reports in order that the general statistics of the church might be compiled, and the *General Minutes* published. Thus the "Statistical Office" originated under the book editor.

From 1940 to 1952 the Statistical Office of the church was under the control and general direction of the publishing agents and book editor. But as part of the reorganization affected by the Survey Commission, the general conference of 1952 put the Statistical Office under the Council on World Service and Finance. The expenses of the office are to be borne by the General Administration Fund

[50] *Discipline,* 1785, ¶ 43.

[51] *Discipline,* 1858, ¶ 293.

of the church, and the specialized service of the office is at the disposal of "any official agency of the church for the conduct of special surveys, researches, and studies as may be required in its work," [52] providing the council agrees. The chief responsibility of the Statistical Office remains, of course, the publication of the *General Minutes* and statistics of the church.

The Methodist Protestant Church had no book editor but the book agents of that church were expected to be responsible for the books which were called for, needed by, or produced in that connection.

In The Methodist Church the book editor is elected by the Board of Publication quadrennially. It is directed that he "shall edit all the books of our publication, except those issued by other agencies of the church for promotional purposes, and books approved by the Curriculum Committee to be edited by the editor of church-school publications." [53] In the preparation of general textbooks which may fall within the field of Christian education the book editor must consult and collaborate with the editor of church-school publications. He must perform such other duties as the Board of Publication may require of him, and has the responsibility with the publishing agents in "passing on all manuscripts considered for publication." [54]

The book editor is the editor of the *Discipline*, and the custodian of the Methodist Hymnal, the Ritual, and the official documents of the church. He is directed by the General Conference to act as editor of the

quarterly journal *Religion in Life*. This publication was begun in 1931 by Dr. John W. Langdale, the book editor of the Methodist Episcopal Church. It is interdenominational in its scope and circulation, and has taken the place in The Methodist Church of the former *Methodist Review*, and *Methodist Quarterly Review*, publications which served their respective Methodisms in days gone by.

The Publishing House today publishes books under its own imprint distinctly for Methodist use, as the *Discipline*, the Hymnal, the Ritual, church-school training texts, and so forth; and under the imprint of "Abingdon-Cokesbury Press" when books are intended for the general book trade and the religious book market. "The Abingdon Press" was the trade name of the Methodist Book Concern previous to union, and "Cokesbury Press" was that of the Publishing House of the Methodist Episcopal Church, South. At union the two presses were united as Abingdon-Cokesbury Press and have functioned with great success in the worldwide religious and interdenominational field of book publication.

THE CHRISTIAN ADVOCATE

The Methodist Protestant movement played a decided part in the beginning of Methodist journalism as such, though there was, of course, pamphleteering and magazine publishing from the earliest days. John Dickins issued the *Arminian Magazine* in Philadelphia in 1798; and the *Methodist Magazine* in 1797-98. In 1818 the *Methodist Magazine* was started again by the Methodist Book Concern and continued under various titles (*The Methodist Review* during

[52] *Discipline*, 1952, ¶ 1120 § 5.
[53] *Ibid.*, ¶ 1147.
[54] *Ibid.*

later years) until within quite recent times. But when the *Methodist Magazine* of 1818 refused to publish the writings of the Methodist Protestant reformers, William S. Stockton, a layman of Trenton, New Jersey, began in 1821 the publication of a biweekly periodical called the *"Wesleyan Repository"* devoted to the cause of laity rights. In 1824 this was renamed *Mutual Rights of Ministers and Members of the Methodist Episcopal Church*. This paper was published in Baltimore and powerfully edited. It had great weight with many persons and ably represented the side of the reformers.

Partly to answer *Mutual Rights*, as well as to provide an effective medium for the voice of the church, the *Christian Advocate and Journal* was started in 1826 with Nathan Bangs and John Emory, who were publishing agents, acting as editors. For a time *Zion's Herald*, an independent Methodist paper published in New England, was joined to the *Christian Advocate*, and on September 5, 1828, the paper was known as the *Christian Advocate and Journal and Zion's Herald*. After five years the publication of *Zion's Herald* as a separate periodical began again and has been continued to this day as an able independent organ in close connection with The Methodist Church.

In 1866 the *Christian Advocate and Journal* became the *Christian Advocate*. Meanwhile it had come to enjoy remarkable success and to be taken as the official organ of the church.[55] It dealt with all manner of matters other than those connected with the immediate controversy over laity rights. The General Conference itself

[55] Abel Stevens, *History of the Methodist Episcopal Church*, IV (1867), 460-61.

put the editorship of this powerful organ under its direct control by electing the editors at its quadrennial sessions and thus making the publication truly "the official voice of the Church." The *Christian Advocate*, published in New York, was for a while the only general organ of the Methodist Episcopal Church, though after a few years there were other *Advocates* published in Cincinnati and other places, whose editions were likewise taken as "general and official."

In the South the *Christian Advocate*, published in Nashville, Tennessee, likewise became the official organ for the Methodist Episcopal Church, South, and its editor was elected by the General Conference. The Southern Annual Conferences meanwhile developed, and to this day maintain, their own system of privately owned conference organs many of them holding to the traditional name of Advocate—the *Wesleyan Christian Advocate*, the *North Carolina Christian Advocate*, the *Virginia Methodist Advocate*, and so forth. These "conference organs" exert a very great influence in the immediate conference territory which they each serve.

The Methodist Protestant Church, long after the days of *Mutual Rights*, in time came to publish two papers, the *Methodist Recorder* and the *Methodist Protestant*. A few years before Methodist union these two journals were merged and became the *Methodist Protestant Recorder*, published in Baltimore. Its editor was elected by the General Conference.

The Methodist Church has had in its long history some conspicuously able editors, especially in charge of its respective general organs. Such men as Abel Stevens, Thomas E. Bond, and James M. Buckley, at New

York, and in the Southern church, O. P. Fitzgerald and Elijah Embree Hoss, and with the Methodist Protestants, Ancel H. Bassett, Frank Benson, Edward J. Drinkhouse, were able to give drive and direction to the mind of their entire connection in a remarkable way.

At Methodist union a real problem was presented in the merging of the extant official organs of the three churches. The issue was between the advantage of publishing one official organ for the whole church or of creating a number of regional organs or papers. At the Uniting Conference the debate within the Committee on Publishing Interests over the value of these respective proposals will not be forgotten by those who participated in it. The vote in the committee to create a single organ stood finally fifty-five to fifty-five with former Governor Alfred M. Landon, of Kansas, acting as chairman. A committee was thereupon appointed to work out this matter and did so after the General Conference adjourned, recommending a single organ. So the *Christian Advocate* was established and its publication arranged for at the Chicago headquarters of The Methodist Publishing House.

The editor of the *Christian Advocate* is elected quadrennially by the Board of Publication. The board is empowered also to elect such associate editors as may be necessary. Other editions of the *Christian Advocate* may be issued as the Board of Publication may determine. An edition of the *Central Christian Advocate* for the Central Jurisdiction was provided for by unanimous consent in 1939 and has been continued since.[56]

From time to time there is dis-

cussion as to the number and types of official *Advocates* or papers put out by the church. The General Conference of 1952 referred to the Board of Publication, with power to act, a recommendation of the Survey Commission suggesting a special periodical for pastors and one for the home and family.

CHURCH-SCHOOL PUBLICATIONS

The bulk of material produced by The Methodist Publishing House is in the field of church-school publications and supplies of all sorts. This material is produced under the direction of the editor of church-school publications and his staff, who work closely with the Curriculum Committee, and under its direction provide church and church schools with the needed materials.

The publication, distribution, and sale of such materials, however, is the responsibility of the Publishing House, which in turn collects all money accruing from the sale of these publications, and for its part pays the salaries of all persons employed in the editorial departments of church-school publications. There is thus a very close tie-in between the Board of Education and the Publishing House with reference to the production of church-school literature. It is uncritically assumed that since the imprint of The Methodist Publishing House is upon all church-school literature, adult training texts, and so forth, that these therefore are put out by the Publishing House on its own responsibility. But as has been indicated, the House acts here simply as the publisher for the editorial department of the Board of Education. To be sure, the editorial department

[56] *Discipline,* 1952, ¶ 1148 § 5.

249

of the Board of Education must be guided by the Curriculum Committee and on this committee the Publishing House is represented by the book editor and publishing agents. There are also other general church officers upon this committee, as has been shown. Nevertheless in accordance with the rule that to whom chief authority is delegated upon him devolves the greatest responsibility, the church looks to the Board of Education through its editorial department for the actual leadership in the production of church-school materials of all sorts.[57]

5. BOARD OF PENSIONS

The care of preachers, who, for one cause or another, are unable to continue in active service has been constantly in the mind of the church since Wesley's day. In early years the American conferences were made up predominantly of young men. But even some of these, because of ill health, became a care to their brethren, and soon age and death were presenting the church with superannuated preachers, and with widows and orphans. The formative years in the United States reflect the pressing necessity for action. The *Discipline* of 1797 asks:

Question: What further provision shall be made for the distressed Traveling Preachers, for the families of Traveling Preachers, and for the Superannuated and Worn-out Preachers, and the widows and orphans of Preachers?

Answer: There shall be a Chartered Fund, to be supported by the voluntary contributions of our friends, the principal stock of which shall be funded under the direction of the Trustees, and the interest applied under the direction of the General Conference according to the following regulations:

1. That no sum exceeding sixty-four dollars shall in any one year be applied to the use of an Itinerant, Superannuated, or Worn-out *single* Preacher.
2. That no sum exceeding one hundred and twenty-eight dollars in any one year shall be applied to the use of any Itinerant, Superannuated, or Worn-out *married* Preacher.
3. That no sum exceeding sixty-four dollars in any one year shall be applied for the use of each widow of any Itinerant, Superannuated, or Worn-out Preachers.
4. That no sum exceeding sixteen dollars shall be applied in any one year for the use of each child or orphan of Itinerant, Superannuated, or Worn-out Preachers.

Such was the origin of the Chartered Fund, which for years represented the resources and the provisions of the church as these were directed toward caring for its "Worn-out" preachers. Bishops Coke and Asbury waxed warm in urging support of this measure:

Our brethren who have laboured on the mountains, on the western waters, and in the poorer circuits in general, have suffered unspeakable hardships, merely for the want of some established fund, in which the competent members of our society might safely lodge what their benevolent hearts would rejoice to give, for the spread of the gospel. On the same account, many of our worn-out preachers, some of whom quickly consumed their strength by their great exertions for the salvation of souls, have been brought into deep distress; and the widows and orphans of our preachers have been sometimes reduced to extreme necessity, who might have lived in comfort,

[57] *Ibid.,* ¶¶ 1149-57.

if not in affluence, enjoying the sweets of domestic life, if the preachers who were the husbands on one hand, and the fathers on the other, had not loved their Redeemer better than wife or children, or life itself. And it is to be lamented, if possible, with tears of blood, that we have lost scores of our most able married ministers—men who, like good householders, could upon all occasions bring things new and old out of their treasury, but were obliged to retire from the general work, because they saw nothing before them for their wives and children, if they continued itinerants, but misery and ruin. But the present institution will, we trust, under the blessing of God, greatly relieve us in, if not entirely deliver us from, these mighty evils.[58]

The Chartered Fund was thus commenced. It has been added to through the years and is yet a trust in the keeping of the church. However, it was necessary for the Annual Conferences and sometimes for local churches to provide funds to care for the superannuates, and while there was some centralized administration, the chief care of retired ministers and of widows and orphans usually fell upon the local conference or those who were close to the claimants themselves.

Especially in the Methodist Episcopal Church, South, was this matter for many years left more or less to general collections and to local conference administration. The *Discipline* of 1858 of the Southern church called for "weekly class collections in all our churches." At the same time it was ordered that at every Annual and General Conference there should be collections for this cause, as well as to care for other ministerial assistance. In 1866 the Southern church put this whole matter upon a better basis by creating in each Annual Conference a powerful committee known as the Joint Board of Finance.[59] This powerful board became an institution in each of the Annual Conferences of the Methodist Episcopal Church, South, from that time on, and these conference committees, as they really were, exerted great power in collecting and distributing moneys for the Conference Claimants as well as for other needy causes. Each Annual Conference depended on its Board of Finance for all sorts of recommendations concerning assessments and finances, and continued to do so until 1918.

In the Methodist Episcopal Church, as has been said, the Chartered Fund was carried forward through the years. It was at first administered by a Board of Trustees of the church and in recent years by the Board of Pensions and Relief. But from an early day the Annual Conferences came to have chief responsibility for providing for their retired men. In 1908 the Methodist Episcopal Church created a Board of Conference Claimants,[60] and at the same time a "Connectional Fund" was created which was to be administered by this central agency.

In 1908 a plan of "Connectional Relief" was also established in the Methodist Episcopal Church. This plan took 5 per cent of the annual collections of the Annual Conferences and used it for the claimants. Then in 1916 the Board of Conference Claimants became the Board of Pensions and Relief of the Methodist Episcopal Church, and all the general funds were put under the control of this board. Thus it was enabled to correlate in a better way the whole

[58] *Discipline*, 1798. Notes by Bishops Coke and Asbury.

[59] *Discipline*, 1866, ¶¶ 249-53.
[60] *Discipline*, 1908, ¶ 423.

matter of caring for the superannuates.

In the Methodist Episcopal Church, South, it became increasingly apparent, as the twentieth century moved on, that a better-integrated overhead organization to care for all conference claimants was a definite necessity. Therefore in 1918 the General Conference of the Methodist Episcopal Church, South, created a Board of Finance and directed that this should be incorporated under the laws of Missouri. It was ordered that "the support of Conference Claimants formerly administered by the Trustees of the Methodist Episcopal Church, South, and the Joint Boards of Finance of the several Annual Conferences shall hereafter be conducted by the Board of Finance of the Methodist Episcopal Church, South." This board at once took over the administration of these general funds and the various bequests which had been added to it. The board a little later promoted a church-wide Superannuate Endowment Fund which added to its holdings appreciably. Through it the Southern church took much better care of this whole matter, and provided sound regulations and rules to unify and correlate the support of the Conference Claimants over the whole connection.

The Methodist Protestant Church cared for its retired ministers in the same way as the Methodist Episcopal Church, that is, chiefly through local conference collections and appropriations. But in time a General Superannuate Fund was created by the Methodist Protestant Church, and the Executive Committee of the Methodist Protestant Church was given control of this fund.[61] It was managed under the direction of the General Conference by creating and holding part of it as a "Permanent Fund," which was added to by an agreed upon percentage each year; and a "Distributive Fund," which was to be turned over and administered according to the immediate needs of the several claimants. This was the practice and process of the Methodist Protestant Church just previous to union.

In 1939, at the organization of The Methodist Church, the whole matter of supporting the conference claimants was put under a Board of Pensions. This board was created to succeed and take over all the work of "The Board of Pensions and Relief of the Methodist Episcopal Church" (incorporated under the laws of Illinois); the Board of Managers of "The General Fund for Superannuates of the Methodist Protestant Church" (incorporated under the laws of Maryland); and "The Board of Finance of the Methodist Episcopal Church, South" (incorporated under the laws of Missouri). These three corporations were continued and exist as legal entities today, but their corporate names have been changed to "The Board of Pensions of The Methodist Church, Incorporated in Illinois"; "The Board of Pensions of The Methodist Church, Incorporated in Maryland"; and "The Board of Pensions of The Methodist Church, Incorporated in Missouri," respectively.

There was thus created a single overhead control for these three corporations. It was further decided that the Illinois Corporation should be responsible for the administration of

[61] *Discipline,* 1936, p. 115.

funds for the support of conference claimants in the Northeastern, the North Central, the Western, and the Central Jurisdictions; while the Missouri Corporation was made responsible for the administration of funds for the support of conference claimants in the Southeastern and the South Central Jurisdictions. By doing this the Illinois Corporation and the Missouri Corporation continued to look after the bulk of the conference claimants which they had respectively cared for previous to union.

There was, and probably will be from time to time, some overlapping of responsibility in a huge delimiting operation of this sort. The Maryland Corporation, having charge of the claimants of the former conferences of the Methodist Protestant Church, had to see that these were properly allocated and cared for in the new church. To work out all problems connected with the creation of the new board, time and attention and great care were given to every move, and to every item of legislation providing for all such matters. At both the Uniting Conference and the General Conference of 1940 the utmost consideration was shown in dealing with the equities involved. While many difficulties presented themselves, this entire situation has been worked out as equitably as possible and to general satisfaction.

The Board of Pensions for The Methodist Church consists of one bishop who is elected by the Council of Bishops for a term of four years, and one minister and one layman from each jurisdiction for every one million members in the jurisdiction, or major fraction thereof. Each of these is to be elected for a term of eight years. Where a jurisdiction does not have a million members it shall nevertheless be entitled to one ministerial and one lay member. In order that the members of this board shall not all go out of office at the same time, it is provided that one half shall be elected at one meeting of the Jurisdictional Conference for a period of four years and the other half for eight years. In addition to the above lay members, there shall be two members at large elected by the other members of the board for a term of four years. The executive secretaries of the board shall be ex officio members of the board without vote.

The members of the Board of Pensions are the members and directors of the Illinois Corporation, of the Maryland Corporation, and of the Missouri Corporation. The annual meetings of the three corporations are held at the same time and place, and it is provided that the corporations shall meet consecutively in the order mentioned. The Board of Pensions thus functions through each corporation or through all three as it may decide. The board really acts as a holding corporation, just as does the Board of Publication with its four respective corporations.

The officers of the Board of Pensions consist of a president, a vice-president, and recording secretary. These are elected quadrennially. There must also be two executive secretaries who are to be members of the Board of Pensions by virtue of their office. One of these secretaries has charge of the affairs of the Illinois Corporation and of the Maryland Corporation, with his office in Chicago; while the other has charge of the affairs of the Missouri Corporation with an office in St. Louis.

253

The two executive secretaries work under the direction of the board in the respective jurisdictional areas assigned to each, and have co-ordinate powers and duties.

Under the control of this board are the permanent funds of the church, including the old Chartered Fund, which is administered by the Illinois Corporation; and the Endowment Fund for Superannuates, which is administered by the Missouri Corporation. Careful rules are provided for the handling of these separate funds and the regulations treating of this matter may be found in the appropriate place in the *Discipline*. A mass of technical regulations having to do with the proper administration of endowments and the like is also to be found in the *Discipline*, and those unusual situations which occurred at union when two or more Annual Conferences were merged in whole or in part were likewise treated. The General Conference, of course, has the authority to change any of the present regulations should this be deemed wise, and in fact from time to time minor alterations are to be expected as need seems to demand.

Annual Conferences are at present authorized to establish and maintain investment funds, and the general Board of Pensions recommends that each Annual Conference shall provide an incorporated board to administer its own permanent funds. To avoid confusion, however, it is suggested that such conference boards shall adopt some other corporate name than the one used by the Board of Pensions.

In each Annual Conference there must be organized a conference board which is auxiliary to the Board of Pensions. Such conference board is to be known as the Board of Conference Claimants. This board in each conference shall have charge of the interests and work of caring for the support of the claimants of that conference, except as otherwise provided for by the Board of Pensions.

The Board of Conference Claimants in the Annual Conference must be composed of twelve or more members, with effective ministers and laymen in equal number. Each conference board was elected at the first session of the Annual Conference following the General Conference of 1940, and it was so arranged that one third of each conference board was, or is, to be elected annually after that date.

The regulations by which each Annual Conference Board of Conference Claimants carries on its special work are carefully prescribed in the *Discipline*. Other rights and privileges of the conference boards are likewise listed.[62]

A great amount of care has gone into the making of the general pension regulations of The Methodist Church. There are special regulations effective in the territory of the Illinois Corporation, and special regulations effective in the territory of the Missouri Corporation. These supplant, and in some cases supersede, the general regulations for the whole church, but all has been done with a view to safeguarding the equities involved.

Under the Board of Pensions, the Minister's Reserve Pension Fund has been established, and this fund, under proper regulations, is to be administered by the Board of Pensions for the benefit of the ministers and future conference claimants of the church.

[62] *Discipline*, 1952, ¶ 1613.

6. BOARD OF EVANGELISM

Said the *Year Book* of the Commission on Evangelism—as it then was—in 1941:

Evangelism has always been Methodism's supreme task. Methodism needs today to return to her first love, her passion for souls, if she would recover the lost radiance of the warmed heart.

To win adults, young people, and children to a firm faith in Jesus Christ and a loving loyalty to Him; to persuade them to believe in Him as their personal Saviour and Guide; and to hold Him before the whole world as the redeemer of men from sin, greed, hate, and war—this commission still holds for the people called Methodists.

With this as its announced goal the General Commission on Evangelism of The Methodist Church became incorporated under the laws of Tennessee with and under the authority of the General Conference of The Methodist Church meeting in 1940. Thus was created for the church an agency which has matched its zeal with its vigor, and which has continued to emphasize through a well-integrated program the tremendous ideal to which it has given itself.

Before union there were from time to time in the participating Methodist churches various movements and organizations of an evangelistic nature. These served in their day and time to awaken a too sluggish church or generation upon this matter, or to emphasize in an unusual way the need to evangelize. But as the tacitly assumed program of every church and minister was the calling of sinners to repentance and the conversion of the world, there was not until within comparatively recent years a call for the creation of a special agency which might have in charge evangelism as such.

In the Methodist Episcopal Church there was created a Commission on Evangelism which appeared in the *Discipline* for the first time in 1932.[63] This organization accomplished in its way a work similar to that now entrusted to the general board. Likewise the Methodist Episcopal Church, South, had an organization within the framework of its Board of Missions. The Department of Home Missions, Evangelism and Hospitals was instructed to work "through a Committee on Evangelism" by the General Conference of 1934, while as early as 1914 the Southern church called for and created a General Committee on Evangelism under the work of Home Missions.[64]

At the time of union it was seen that the church must correlate and establish on a broad base all its work of this nature, and by the creation of a general agency, not only keep alive but promote with the utmost vigor the entire program of evangelism. Against the expressed fears of those who felt that localizing responsibility for evangelism in one board would thereby seem to relieve the local church and other church agencies of their part in this, it was stated that local churches and ministers everywhere needed encouragement and all the help that a board of evangelism might give them. The Uniting Conference therefore created a general Commission on Evangelism and the General Conference of 1940 further

[63] ¶ 557 (2).
[64] *Discipline*, 1934, ¶ 532, Art. XX; *Discipline*, 1914, ¶ 411, Art. XVII.

correlated this into the general organization of the church.[65]

Pursuant to directions, the bishops, boards, jurisdictions, and youth agencies elected their respective representives, and the general Commission on Evangelism, as it then was, met and organized in Chicago, July 27, 1940. At a later date in the same quadrennium the commission became incorporated with headquarters in Nashville, Tennessee. Subsequently the General Conference of 1944 changed its name from the general Commission on Evangelism to the General Board of Evangelism and provided that its headquarters should be "wherever fixed by the General Conference, or [as] the present Tennessee charter of the Commission on Evangelism may be amended."

The board is composed of seven bishops (six were called for in 1940) chosen by the Council of Bishops at the time of the General Conference. These bishops are elected, one each from the six jurisdictions, with one from the church at large, who is, by virtue of this selection, the chairman of the general board.[66] Also on the board are two ministers, one lay man, and one lay woman from each jurisdiction, elected by the Jurisdictional Conferences. There are also three youth members elected by the National Conference of Methodist Youth; and twelve members from the church at large, elected by the board. Previous to 1952 several of the executive secretaries of the boards of the church were members of the Board of Evangelism, but at the instance of the Survey Commission, these were not named members of the present board.

[65] *Discipline,* 1939, ¶¶ 1271-80.
[66] *Discipline,* 1952, ¶¶ 1468-69.

As has been stated, the chairman is the bishop elected by the bishops to represent the church at large upon the board. There are also elected by the board from among its members a vice-chairman and a recording secretary. The executive committee consists of seven members including the general chairman. The other six members are to come each from a separate jurisdiction.

The executive officers consist of an executive secretary elected by the board, such other secretaries and editors as the board may elect "on nomination by the executive committee," and a treasurer.

The board meets annually and at such other times as it may decide necessary. The board is supported by the general benevolence funds of the church and by the sale of its literature.

In carrying out its program, the Board of Evangelism is as aggressive as its task is important. The bishop who is chairman of the board must "make a report and present a program of work for the board to the Council of Bishops for their approval at each regular meeting of the council." The board has authority also to set up standards for conference evangelists. It co-operates with other agencies of the church in such matters as training ministers to serve the cause of evangelism, and in the preparation of literature designed to help this cause. It has furthered all sorts of meetings, conferences, training schools, and other agencies designed to awaken the church to the need of carrying the gospel aggressively to all people, and its literature has come to be widely known as helpful in the extreme in accomplishing this purpose.

The General Board of Evangelism

puts out its literature through two separate internal departments which it has organized for its own more efficient work. One of these produces the *Upper Room*, a bimonthly devotional booklet begun originally by Grover C. Emmons when he was secretary of the Department of Home Missions of the Methodist Episcopal Church, South. The other department produces promotional materials on evangelism, on the church, and the Christian life.

The *Upper Room* has increased in popularity until its present circulation is 2,300,000. At union the sponsors of the *Upper Room* made arrangements for the Commission on Evangelism, as it then was, to take over the publication of this booklet and this was subsequently done to the great benefit of all concerned.

The revenue from the *Upper Room* enables the General Board of Evangelism to produce and distribute many other helpful tracts, periodicals, and small books for the cultivation of the devotional life. However, the General Conference provides that no income from the *Upper Room* shall be used "for the support of other features of the board's work." That is, all the income from the publications put out by this department must be used "for the purpose of preparing and circulating such literature." It is, however, specified that this regulation does not forbid the Board of Evangelism from setting up a "reserve fund" out of its profits.[67]

Another department of the board —called by the board its *Tidings* department—produces all the promotional evangelistic literature of the Board of Evangelism. This includes numerous leaflets and small books on evangelism and the work of the church, visitation evangelism literature, literature on public evangelism, and a monthly journal of evangelism, which is sent to every active pastor and district superintendent, and to the evangelistic leadership of the church.

Though the *Tidings* department is not required by the regulations to be self-sustaining, as is the *Upper Room* department, the small portion of the world service dollar that the General Board of Evangelism receives makes it necessary that this department likewise be self-supporting. In order that the funds which the board receives from benevolences may be applied to a large and vigorous field work in evangelism, the board makes a nominal charge for the many evangelistic cards, leaflets, and booklets which it makes available to pastors and churches upon order from its *Tidings* department.

Boards of Evangelism for jurisdictions are permissive under present regulations, but compulsory for each Annual Conference. Every Annual Conference "shall provide for a Conference Board of Evangelism, which shall promote the program of evangelism as outlined by the General Board." Upon the Annual Conference Board, the district superintendents, one pastor and one lay member from each of the districts, and certain others as specified in the *Discipline*, are to serve. Upon nomination of the conference board the Annual Conference must elect annually a "conference secretary of evangelism, to be publicly assigned by the bishop." It is the duty of this official to promote the policies and program of the General, Jurisdictional, and Conference

---

[67] *Ibid.*, ¶ 1485.

Boards of Evangelism in the Annual Conference. The Conference Board of Evangelism also has the right to recommend to the conference for appointment by the bishop those who are to be "conference evangelists." The bishop, providing the conference by a two-thirds vote agrees, may make such appointments and often does.

District Committees on Evangelism are made mandatory by the *Discipline*, and each charge is instructed to provide a Commission on Membership and Evangelism.[68]

7. BOARD OF LAY ACTIVITIES

Laymen have always found a vital and important place of service in Methodism. Wesley's first preachers were laymen, even in his view as well as in the view of the Church of England of his day. Stewards and class leaders became keystones of the Methodist economy, while the class meeting of lay people in both Britain and America, formed in platoons in the British church, to use a military figure, enabled members the better to work, live, and serve God and others. In spite of the fact that American Methodism was controlled by preachers, against the Methodist Protestant fathers' insistence that it should not be, it carried on its vast work in days gone by, as it does now, largely through the life, character, and numbers of its devoted laity.

There was not, however, during the early years of American Methodism any thought of an organization specifically designed to develop or integrate lay work as such. That came in time, as with millions of adherents and with thousands of able and remarkable men in her ranks, it was felt that the church would be greatly benefited if laymen could be provided with opportunities to know each other, to work together, and to develop the latent resources inherent in the enormous number of lay people over the land.

The inception for the modern organization of laymen within the church seems to have come from the impetus given by the Laymen's Missionary Movement, which was organized, as an interdenominational agency, in New York in 1906. This movement tied in with the Student Volunteer Movement of that day and showed the determination of many men throughout the country to assist these volunteers and to support and call for others. In the South a number of prominent Methodist laymen became interested and organized the Laymen's Missionary Movement within their church. Among the leaders of this were John R. Pepper, C. H. Ireland, Judge E. D. Newman, and others. Organization meetings were held at Knoxville, Tennessee, in 1907, and in Chattanooga in 1908, when Ambassador James Bryce spoke, and while the movement as such was not legally authorized by the General Conference of the Southern church, its work was recognized as of high value, as the subsequent participation in the Centenary Movement and the Christian Education Movement made clear. Not the least of its valuable contributions was the discovering or the awakening of outstanding laymen who thus learned

[68] *Ibid.,* ¶¶ 219-22.

how to participate in a more active way in general church work.

The plan of financing the work of this organization through voluntary contributions proved unsuccessful and the General Board of Missions came to the rescue with small appropriations. This naturally brought the movement under the sponsorship of the Board of Missions. Then in 1922 the Episcopal Address recommended, "Anything which the General Conference can do to still further mobilize the laymen of our communion for doing fully the work which has been so fairly begun, is worthy of your most sincere and prayerful thought," [69] and the General Conference thereupon provided for the organization of a Board of Lay Activities. The board as organized had an executive committee and a general executive secretary in charge of its work. The General Conference made provision for its support in the regular benevolence budget, as with other boards. It had its headquarters in Nashville.

In the Methodist Episcopal Church there was a Commission on Men's Work which functioned for a number of years previous to church union. The commission had upon it some exceedingly able laymen, including Edgar T. Welch, Branch Rickey, Judge Snavely. It was provided with an executive secretary and the finances of the organization were received as an appropriation from the Board of Education. Also, for some years previous to union there was provision for Annual Conference and General Conference Laymen's Associations, designed to cultivate "the more effective participation of men in the total activities of the Church." [70]

The Methodist Protestant Church, stressing, as it did, lay activity and lay representation at every point, had no special organization emphasizing this matter at the time of union.

Previous to union a representative group of laymen of the three churches, among them Dr. George L. Morelock, general secretary of the Board of Lay Activities of the Methodist Episcopal Church, South, and Dr. J. Russell Throckmorton, secretary of men's work and adult work of the Board of Education of the Methodist Episcopal Church, met in St. Louis in 1938 to decide what sort of laymen's organization might profitably be recommended to the Uniting Conference. An autonomous organization similar to the one then in the Methodist Episcopal Church, South, was decided upon, and at the Uniting Conference, and in the first General Conference of The Methodist Church, the wishes and plans of the laymen were duly put into effect.[71] The Board of Lay Activities of The Methodist Church was thereupon organized, its headquarters established in Chicago, and it became incorporated under the laws of Illinois.

The board consists of three effective bishops, who are elected by the Council of Bishops; of six effective ministers, one from each jurisdiction; and of thirty-two lay members, distributed among the several jurisdictions on the basis of church membership. It is provided that no jurisdiction shall have fewer than two lay members. In electing the six ministers and the thirty-two lay members, the Jurisdictional Conferences do

[69] First Quadrennial Report, Board of Lay Activities, 1926, p. 9.

[70] Discipline, 1936, ¶ 263.
[71] Discipline, 1939, ¶¶ 1211-17.

this upon nomination from the Committee on Lay Activities of their respective Jurisdictional Conferences. The lay members to be elected are from the conference lay leaders of the several Annual Conferences in the jurisdiction; and if any man upon the Board of Lay Activities retires from the office of conference lay leader, he automatically vacates his membership on the board.

The board organizes by electing a president, a vice-president, a recording secretary, and a treasurer. It fixes a time for its own annual sessions and reports quadrennially to the General Conference and to the several Jurisdictional Conferences.[72]

An executive secretary is elected by the board, and this secretary has general supervision of the work under the direction of the board. Associate secretaries are elected by the board on nomination of the executive secretary. Any vacancies occurring in office shall be filled by the board itself.

The work of the Board of Lay Activities is affirmed by the *Discipline* to be a "benevolence interest of the church," and its support therefore devolves upon the Council on World Service and Finance.[73]

A wide and comprehensive program of lay activity is outlined for this board and its staff, under the provisions of the *Discipline*.[74] This includes Christian stewardship, Christian fellowship, personal evangelism, lay speaking or preaching, the circulation of church papers and other Christian literature, the benevolences, adequate support of the ministry, sound church finance in the local church, attendance upon worship services, men's work, the training of Official Boards, the Christianizing of personal and community life, co-operation with other general boards and agencies, and district and conference lay organizations to make more effective the program of lay activities.

It is provided that a Jurisdictional Board of Lay Activities may be organized and that a conference board must be. These Annual Conference boards nominate by ballot the conference lay leader for each Annual Conference, who in turn must be elected to that position by the conference. The conference lay leader is chairman of the Conference Board of Lay Activities by virtue of his office, and is entitled to a seat in the Annual Conference, if he is not a member of the same, but without vote.[75] Annual Conference Boards of Lay Activities have a specified membership and a definite assignment of work and program at each session of the Annual Conference.

District and Charge Boards of Lay Activities are also made mandatory by the *Discipline*.[76] The Official Board, in co-operation with the pastor, is made responsible for the program of lay activities within the station charge, as are official boards on circuit charges. A well-integrated program for all these undertakings, including the work of lay leaders in conferences, districts, and charges is laid out in the *Discipline*.

To crystallize the thought of the church upon the importance of the work of this board, one Sunday in each year is designated as "Laymen's Day" and the program put under the direction of the general board.

[72] *Discipline*, 1952, ¶ 1497.
[73] *Ibid.*, ¶ 1496.
[74] *Ibid.*, ¶ 1492.
[75] *Ibid.*, ¶ 1504.
[76] *Ibid.*, ¶ 1508.

The Methodist Church has an agency of great importance in the Council on World Service and Finance. It would be tedious and difficult to trace throughout the past history of the uniting churches the various steps which led at last to the creation of this central agency for the receiving, administrating, and disbursing the general budget of the entire Methodist Church. But that is what this powerful body does and must do, as well as make a careful estimate of needed budgetary expense ahead of time. The work of the church does require the support of our people, and participation therein through service and gifts is a Christian duty and a means of grace. But it is patent that in order to secure proper support for all needy causes, to select those which should have the right of way over others, and to see that all church interests receive their proper share of the funds raised upon a proportionate basis, there must be a central organization with authority to apportion as well as to administer all such funds. Up to 1952 the church knew this body as the General Commission on World Service and Finance. Under that name it was a corporation licensed under the laws of Illinois. But the General Conference of 1952, following the recommendations of the Survey Commission, directed that the name of the body should thereafter be the Council on World Service and Finance, and that its legal and corporate name should be changed in accordance with the enabling acts which the General Conference passed for that purpose.

The strengthening of the Council on World Service and Finance by the work of the Survey Commission was one marked feature of the reorganization of boards and agencies brought about in 1952. Two minor agencies of the church, the Statistical Office and the former Commission on Records, Forms, and Statistical Blanks, were both put under the reorganized Council on World Service and Finance. It was likewise given many important powers of review, as may be seen in studying the other agencies of the church.

The legislation of 1952 creates an incorporated body known as the Council on World Service and Finance, whose members are to be elected by the General Conference. No jurisdiction elects any of the members of this council, though the bishops of each jurisdiction may nominate to the General Conference the particular members who are to represent their own jurisdiction. These consist of: two bishops nominated by the Council of Bishops; two ministers and two lay persons from each jurisdiction; and seven members at large, at least three of whom shall be women, nominated by the Council of Bishops without regard to jurisdictions. No member, not even a bishop, shall be eligible for membership on, or employment by, any other general agency of the church except the Board of Trustees.

Officers of the council, beside a president, a vice-president, and a recording secretary, include an executive secretary, who also is the treasurer of the council. The executive secretary has the right to sit with the council and its executive committee at all sessions, and has the right to the floor without the privilege of vot-

261

ing. There are annual meetings called for, and one fifth of the members may empower the president to call a special meeting if this is deemed necessary. Sixteen members constitute a quorum.

The executive committee of the council consists of the officers of that body and six members who are elected annually by the council itself. This body is given great powers in acting between sessions of the council, but "it shall not take any action contrary to or in conflict with any action or policy of the council." [77]

DUTIES AND RESPONSIBILITIES

The duties and responsibilities of this agency can be listed as follows: (1) The preparation and presentation of the report concerning budgets and assessments to the General Conference. (2) The administration of the huge funds entrusted to its keeping.

The council must recommend to the General Conference, for its action and determination, the amount needed for the World Service budget and the percentage of the budget which is to be distributed annually to each World Service agency. The total amount thus designated, when approved by the General Conference, becomes the "annual world service budget" for the ensuing quadrennium. The world service agencies are: the Board of Missions, the Board of Education (including a special budget for in-service ministerial education), the theological schools, the Board of Temperance, the Board of Hospitals and Homes, the Board of Pensions, the Board of Lay Activities, the Board of Evangelism, the Board

of World Peace, the Board of Social and Economic Relations, the Radio and Film Commission, American University, Scarritt College, and the American Bible Society.

An equitable schedule of apportionment, by which the total World Service budgets shall be distributed to the several Annual Conferences, must also be worked out by the council and presented to the General Conference for "action and determination."

In addition to the general duties of the council, it must maintain and supervise the Statistical Office; must prepare and edit all official statistical blanks, records, and forms; and must maintain and supervise the Transportation Bureau of the Church. These last three duties were put upon the council by the General Conference at the recommendation of the Church Survey Commission.

Whenever there is any general board or agency which expects to make a church-wide financial appeal during any one quadrennium, such board or agency must come before the Council on World Service and Finance and present its reasons for making such a general appeal. The council has the right to make an appropriate recommendation to the ensuing General Conference as to what its attitude may be with reference to such special appeals.

Careful regulations are prescribed whereby no one board, agency, or "benevolence interest" is allowed to have a prior or preferred claim or an increased financial participation in World Service once the budget for that agency has been adopted by the General Conference. It is provided, however, that in order to meet an emergency, a three-quarters vote of

[77] *Ibid.*, ¶ 1119.

the council, with three quarters of the Council of Bishops concurring, may alter the above regulation so as to provide for special cases.

THE GENERAL FUNDS

The General Commission has under its care and administration the following important funds: (1) the World Service Fund; (2) the General Administration Fund; (3) the Episcopal Fund; and (4) miscellaneous funds.

Something has been said as to World Service, indicating that this represents the general budget of the church to be administered for the support of the executive agencies of the church. This fund, therefore, represents the larger portion of the church's budget in any one year or in any one quadrennium.

The General Administration Fund provides for the expenses of the sessions of the General Conference, for those of the Judicial Council, and for such committees and commissions as may be constituted by the General Conference (other than the World Service boards and agencies).

This fund is to be administered by the council. It is apportioned to the Annual Conferences, when the General Conference has adopted it, on the same ratio and percentage that each conference shares in the total World Service budget. No Annual Conference and no charge or local church is allowed to change or revise their apportionments for the General Administration budget.

THE EPISCOPAL FUND

The Episcopal Fund is raised separately from all other funds and is a part of the money raised for ministerial support. It provides for the salaries and expenses of effective bishops, for the support of retired bishops, and for that of the widows and minor children of deceased bishops. In case there is need, and the Council on World Service and Finance approves, the executive officer of that council has authority to borrow for the benefit of the Episcopal Fund such amounts as may be necessary.

In the Methodist Episcopal churches before union, for long years the Episcopal Fund was in the care of the Book Committee of the respective churches. These fixed the salaries of the bishops and appointed a treasurer—often one of the publishing agents—to act as custodian of the fund itself. The Committee on Episcopacy of the respective General Conferences in time came to review matters of salary, and to recommend retirement pensions and the allotment which should go to widows of bishops. This was the way the matter was handled at the time of union. The Methodist Protestant Church, of course, had no Episcopal Fund.

At present the Council on World Service and Finance recommends to each General Conference the amounts to be fixed as salaries for the effective bishops, and estimates regarding house, office, and travel expenses. It recommends the amount to be fixed as pensions for retired bishops, and the allowances for widows and minor children of deceased bishops. It also furnishes a "grant-in-aid" to each Central Conference to assist in the support of the Central Conference episcopal budget. Thus is obtained the "estimated episcopal budget."

The budget, when adopted, is apportioned to the several charges of the whole church in proportion to each pastor's current cash salary. This makes the Episcopal Fund depend upon each and every charge of the church. This is done upon a percentage basis (of the pastor's cash salary), as such basis has been determined by the General Conference. The support of the ministry, which includes bishops, thus rests directly upon each individual charge of The Methodist Church and not upon the Annual Conferences or District Conferences as entities.

STATISTICAL OFFICE

The Statistical Office has in charge the publication of the *General Minutes* of the church and the collecting and publication of statistical material. The *General Minutes* are the summation of the figures reported to the separate Annual Conferences on church membership, number of ministers and lay people, moneys raised for various purposes, and the like. Each Annual Conference publishes through its own journal the total statistics for its own activities during each year. The Statistical Office combines all these, so that the *General Minutes* represent the totals for the whole church.

At the time of union the Statistical Office was under the direction of the book editor and established through the publishing agents. The support for the office was paid out of the General Administrative Fund. But in 1952 the Statistical Office was put under the Council on World Service and Finance. Under the direction of that council the office is empowered to prepare the material for the *General Minutes* and such other related publications and year books as may be ordered by the council. The specialized services of this office are available to any official agency of the church for the conduct of special surveys, researches, and studies as these may be required in the work of such agencies. The General Administrative Fund continues to bear the expense of this particular office.

A further task of the council on World Service and Finance is "to prepare and edit all official statistical blanks, record forms, and record books required for use in The Methodist Church." [78] Before 1952 such records and forms were prepared by a special commission which was independent in its relationship to any particular board or agency of the church. This commission, however, was done away by the 1952 General Conference and its work given to the council on World Service and Finance. While records and forms impress one as being a minor part in the church's work, it is surprising to learn the number of such special forms and blanks. These run from a certificate of transfer of church membership or a small baptismal certificate to the long list of printed questions which the bishop or district superintendent must call at each conference. In the quadrennium which ended in 1952, 135 separate pieces of printed material, some in great quantity, were called for. The Council on World Service and Finance does its work in this field by appointing special individuals to act as a committee and prepare or revise the needed forms.

THE TRANSPORTATION BUREAU

A Transportation Bureau was created in the Methodist Episcopal Church, South, before union in 1939.

[78] *Ibid.,* ¶ 1120 § 6.

It fulfilled a felt need for some responsible person to have in charge the matter of constantly securing reservations for travel on the part of the officials of the church and those doing church business; of clearing matters of passport and advising with reference to needed travel and methods of travel. Mr. W. M. Cassetty, Jr., had in charge this matter for the Southern church at its headquarters at 810 Broadway, Nashville, Tennessee.

At the time of union the transportation office was moved into Chicago as a more convenient headquarters with Mr. Cassetty as its director. Its support for a time devolved upon several co-operating boards and agencies whose offices were expected to use its service. At the reorganization in 1952 the Transportation Bureau was recognized as a general administrative agency of the church, and put under the supervision of the Council on World Service and Finance.

This bureau is directed to represent the church in its relation with responsible persons or concerns operating the several modes of public transportation. At the time of large church gatherings, such as the General Conference, the Transportation Bureau is enabled to save the church enormously by discovering and advising the best methods of travel. A great amount of time is saved the officials of the church, and all those who travel on church business, when such persons have the benefit of consultation with the Transportation Bureau. It is an expense against the General Administration Fund of the church.

Beside these special duties the Council on World Service and Finance is ordered also to maintain an official file of pastors and church officials. Adequate records must be kept of the mail addresses of all bishops, ministers in the effective relation, supply pastors, retired ministers serving charges, conference lay leaders, and lists of general, jurisdictional, conference, and district boards, commissions, and committees as may be deemed necessary. The central treasury is to maintain cost of keeping such a file, and the executive secretary of the Council on World Service and Finance is authorized and directed to make equitable charges for its use by various bodies. It is stipulated, however, that these bodies must be authorized agencies or officers of The Methodist Church. The file cannot be made available to others.

A Personnel Registration Bureau is to be maintained by the Council on World Service and Finance, if in its judgment such a bureau is necessary. This acts as a clearing center for persons seeking positions with the general agencies of the church.

MISCELLANEOUS

The Council on World Service and Finance receives reports from all boards and agencies receiving financial support from the funds under its control. The council also has the right, as any incorporated body, to receive, sell, or hold in trust, property for the benefit of the funds under its control. Other regulations treating of this agency are found in the appropriate place in the *Discipline*.

ANNUAL CONFERENCE COMMISSIONS

Each Annual Conference has its own Conference Commission on World Service and Finance, which acts within the conference in support of the activities and duties of the

265

council, and of conference finances in particular. The conference commission has in charge the conference benevolence budget, which has to do with such Annual Conference agencies and work as may be sponsored or supported by the Annual Conference itself.

It is the duty of the Annual Conference commission to combine in one total sum the World Service and Annual Conference benevolences—that is, add the amount of the apportionment which has come from the general church and the apportionment which the conference itself votes for its own causes or work. The total World Service and Benevolence Fund budget thus established must be distributed equitably among the districts of the conference, or directly to the charges by whatever method and according to whatever ratio the conference itself approves. The conference has the right to decide whether it shall apportion its total budget to the separate districts or to separate individual charges. If it is apportioned to the districts, then the distribution to the charges of these districts must be made by the district stewards. If the apportionment is made directly to the charges, the conference may order the district superintendents to make the apportionment to the separate charges.

The Conference Commission on World Service and Finance, unless it be directed otherwise, has the right to estimate the total amount necessary for the support of the district superintendents and to determine the amount needed for their salaries. However, Annual Conferences which wish to do so, may provide support for the several district superintendents through the Board of District Stewards in each of the several districts.

9. COMMISSION ON PROMOTION AND CULTIVATION

Up until 1952 a Council of Secretaries of the church met from time to time to assist in promoting the various causes supported by the general funds of the church. These secretaries were the executive officers of the various boards and agencies, with the exception of The Methodist Publishing House. But in 1952 the work of promoting the causes of the church was put by the General Conference in the hands of a special Commission on Promotion and Cultivation. This commission, recommended by the Survey Commission, was created to the end that duplication, overlapping, and competition might be eliminated in the promotion of the general financial causes of the church. It also has as its goal the giving of information to the people of the church so that they may adequately support the several causes so dear to the heart of Methodism.

As ordered by the General Conference, this commission is composed of three bishops selected by the Council of Bishops; one member each from the Division of the Local Church and the Division of Educational Institutions of the Board of Education; one each from the Joint Section of Education and Cultivation and the Woman's Division of Christian Service of the Board of Missions; one each from the Board of Lay Activities, the Board of Evangelism, the Board of Temperance, the Board of World

Peace, the Board of Social and Economic Relations, the Board of Hospitals and Homes, the Board of Publication, the Commission on Chaplains, the Methodist Committee for Overseas Relief, the Commission on Public Relations and Methodist Information, the Radio and Film Commission, and the Advance Committee. The executive secretaries of the several agencies are ex officio members of the commission, but without vote.

This commission elects quadrennially the following officers: chairman, vice-chairman, and executive director. "The executive director shall be secretary of the commission, and the executive secretary of the Council on World Service and Finance shall be its treasurer." [79]

The *Discipline* gives minute directions for carrying out the work of this commission which has the right to co-ordinate and promote on a church-wide basis the program of world service, and other general financial causes. It must review at least annually the several and combined plans of the general boards and agencies for the production and distribution of all free literature and for promotional and resource periodicals (except the church-school literature). It does this in order that it may co-ordinate the content, distribution, and the timing of the release of such materials. If the timing and distribution of such materials do not impress the commission as being satisfactory, the commission must refer the matter at issue to the Co-ordinating Council.

This commission must also study the problems of co-ordinating and simplifying the methods and facilities for the distribution of materials. It is directed to co-operate with the Boards of Education and Lay Activities in certain of their moves. It has a right to commit to its central promotional office any cause or undertaking, financial or otherwise, not otherwise provided for, when this may demand church-wide promotion or publicity. However, such cause must be previously approved by the Council of Bishops and the Council on World Service and Finance, or by their executive committees, if it is to be so supported.

The world service funds support the expenses of the commission, except that constituent agencies that do not participate in world service funds may be called upon to help support the commission upon a pro rata basis.

Following up the work of this general commission, there may be constituted at each Annual Conference a Conference Commission on Promotion and Cultivation. This is empowered to promote the program of world service and other benevolence causes in the pastoral charges of the conference.

The creation of this commission for the general church does away with the unusual power which the Council of Secretaries exercised from 1940 until 1952 as promotional and planning agents. However, the executive secretaries are now members ex officio of the commission on Promotion and Cultivation, and by virtue of their leadership in their respective fields, and their own personal abilities, will be able to assist and direct in the work of promotion and cultivation in a very helpful way.

10. BOARD OF HOSPITALS AND HOMES

The Christian church has cared for the sick from its very beginning. Before Christian virtues flowered out in all the manifold activities which we see today, primitive charity centered itself largely upon hospitals. The hospice in the Middle Ages came to symbolize the charitable work of the church, and that in turn was followed by orphanages and asylums of various types. Methodism was in the true succession here and had no more than passed its formative years when it began movements of all sorts designed to look after the sick and the orphaned. In time the aged were also taken care of by established institutions, and with the coming of the social-gospel impetus all this was multiplied in an increasing way.

In the Methodist Episcopal Church there early sprang up small and, at first, scattered charitable institutions. Coupled with these there were also formal gifts and bequests given to the church for the founding or support of such institutions. Conferences and sometimes local philanthropic groups often sponsored such moves.

There was a home for the aged established in New York in 1850, and after a time there came homes for children, homes for working young men and women, and even sanitariums for the tubercular. These institutions grew up without relation to one another and there was an overlapping of service and finances, sometimes in the same city, until some organizations were in actual competition each with the other. Others were very poorly financed with scarcely any relation to Methodism, while at the same time they tried to secure the help of the church for the payment of debt, the erection of buildings, and the like.

During the later years of the nineteenth century there was a national Methodist Hospital and Home Association, which was a voluntary organization of superintendents, friends and workers in these hospitals. But it was clearly seen during the early years of the twentieth century that something more of overhead control was needed, and so the Board of Hospitals and Homes of the Methodist Episcopal Church was organized by the authority of the General Conference held at Des Moines, Iowa, in May, 1920. The General Conference itself elected a board of directors for this board and approved a plan for securing funds for the maintenance and operation of the board.

At the same time there had grown up in the Methodist Episcopal Church a kindred work under the General Deaconess Board. The work of the deaconesses was recognized by the General Conference of 1888, and for a time this was placed under the Board of Bishops. The Women's Home Missionary Society also trained deaconesses and had established hospitals and homes through them in various cities. At length the General Conference of 1912 decided to put all deaconess work under a General Deaconess Board, which was organized and chartered by the state of New York, and headquarters were established in Buffalo.

The overlapping interests and kindred problems of the General Deaconess Board and of the Board of Hospitals and Homes all pointed to the need for a merger of these boards. This merger took place by action of the General Conference of 1924, at Springfield, Massachusetts. In time the two boards were merged into one, and there was produced "an organization which had supervision of the best trained and largest personnel in the Protestant Church in America." [80]

In the Methodist Episcopal Church, South, a similar growth of interest in hospital and orphanage work had taken place through the midyears of the nineteenth century. There were certain Annual Conference organizations which took a prominent part in sponsoring orphanages and hospitals through the South, and some of these to this day are in existence and doing noble work. Sometimes there were local corporations doing good work without any relation to the general church.

The oldest hospital building connected with Methodist work in the United States is said to be the Warren A. Candler Hospital, Savannah, Georgia, whose organization date is given as 1830. In 1922 the General Board of Hospitals of the Methodist Episcopal Church, South, was organized under an order of the General Conference of that year, with Bishop Warren A. Candler as president. This board had the general oversight of the hospital work of the church and held an advisory sponsorship over local and conference institutions of healing. The Golden Cross, which will subsequently be discussed, was ably sponsored by this board over the South.

In 1938, when the Southern church reorganized certain of its boards and

departments, the General Board of Hospitals was placed under the Board of Home Missions and assigned to the supervision of the secretary of the Department of Home Missions, Grover C. Emmons. In 1939 and 1940, of course, the union of the Methodist churches called for a merging of all work under one board.

The Methodist Protestant Church carried on its philanthropic program under the general direction of the Executive Committee of that church. At the time of union it had three outstanding institutions, but there was great interest in the church itself upon the whole matter of hospitalization.

The Methodist Church at its reorganization in 1939 and 1940 created the present Board of Hospitals and Homes to take over all the work carried on by, and under, the official direction of the kindred boards in the uniting churches. The new board was ordered to secure articles of incorporation according to the laws of Illinois, and this it did, with headquarters in Chicago.

The board is to be managed by a Board of Managers consisting of eighteen persons. There are two bishops elected by the Council of Bishops, one minister and one lay member from each jurisdiction elected by the Jurisdictional Conference. At least one of these must be an active administrator of an institution under the general supervision of the board. Also there are to be four members at large elected by the board after it organizes. Everyone on the Board of Managers, it is provided, must be members of The Methodist Church. Should there be a vacancy among any of those elected by the jurisdictions, the College of Bishops

[80] A Report, by Newton E. Davis, detailing a history of the organization of the Board of Hospitals and Homes of the Methodist Episcopal Church, February 2, 1942, p. 15.

where such vacancy occurs, must elect the person who is to fill the unexpired term. All other vacancies, however, are to be filled by the electing body. In this respect the Board of Hospitals and Homes differs from other boards which are empowered to fill their own vacancies.

The officers of the board are to be a president, elected by the board from among the bishops who are members; four vice-presidents, each of whom shall represent one of the major interests of the board—namely hospitals, child welfare, homes for aged, and homes for youth. There is also to be a recording secretary and a treasurer. All these officers are elected for four years.

The executive of the board is known as the executive secretary. His salary is provided for by the board, and he has the right to obtain necessary help and to carry on his work subject to the authority and control of the board itself.

There is an executive committee of twelve members including, of course, the officers of the board and five additional members who are elected by the board. Each jurisdiction must be represented on the committee by an elected member and the executive secretary is a member ex officio without vote. Seven members of the executive committee constitute a quorum.

The financial support of the Board of Hospitals and Homes comes from two sources: from gifts, devises, wills, bequests, and the administration of trust funds as these have been given in whole or in part to the board; and from the general benevolences of the church, as the General Conference may determine.

The Board of Hospitals and Homes

has a well-wrought program in which it makes surveys, disseminates information, provides agencies for carrying out its own work, and renders assistance other than financial in the promotion and establishment of new institutions. Whenever requested to do so by conferences, groups, or officials of the church, the board may make appraisals and pass upon the wisdom of accepting or rejecting institutions such as hospitals and homes whenever these are suggested as beneficiaries or are to have in any way the approval or support of The Methodist Church. As an incorporated body, of course the board can act as trustee for the administration of bequests or endowments for institutions of the church.

Another very important function of the board under the authority of the General Conference is to establish a Personnel Bureau:

(1) To help institutions of philanthropic service in The Methodist Church to find adequately trained Christian personnel to conduct the various types of work represented by Methodist hospitals and homes.

(2) To encourage Methodist youth who are socially minded and who are desirous of investing their lives in some form of Christian institutional work.[81]

There is one important provision which the General Conference has determined shall be kept to the fore by this board:

The Board of Hospitals and Homes shall not be responsible, legally or morally, for the debts, contracts, or obligations, or for any other financial commitments of any character or description, created, undertaken, or assumed by any institution, agency, or interest of The Methodist Church, whether or not such institution, agency, or interest shall be approved, accepted, or

[81] *Discipline,* 1952, ¶ 1574.

recognized by the board, or shall be affiliated with the board, or whether or not the promotion or establishment of the same shall be approved, under any of the provisions of this constitution, or otherwise. No such institution, agency, or interest of The Methodist Church, and no officer or member of the Board of Managers of this board, shall have any authority whatsoever to take any action, directly or by implication, at variance with, or deviating from, the limitation contained in the preceding sentence hereof.[82]

This very positive direction acts as a blanket protection against financial involvement which might come by reason of a gift to the church of an institution not financially secure, or that might have great liabilities.

WHITE CROSS AND GOLDEN CROSS

To support the hospital program in both the Methodist Episcopal Church and the Methodist Episcopal Church, South, the White Cross Society and the Golden Cross Society were authorized and organized within the respective churches. The White Cross was organized in 1917 at Omaha by Bishop Homer Stuntz and L. O. Jones, who is credited as being the author of the plan. The Golden Cross in the Southern Church was organized in 1922. The guiding spirit behind the movement was Dr. C. C. Selecman, now bishop, who was then pastor of the First Methodist Church of Dallas, Texas.

These organizations were patterned after the plan of the American Red Cross and they were designed to enlist general support by enrolling members in their respective societies. Small contributions, or a definite fee, was charged for such enrollment. The income derived from these respective organizations was used to support the

philanthropic work of the church in its hospitals, and to a certain extent it was also used in administering to the indigent sick who might be beyond the reach of a regular church hospital. Both organizations did splendid work and both continued until church union. At that time plans were made to combine these two organizations.[83]

For a time the regulations regarding such combination were rather indefinite but at the General Conference of 1944 it was decided to carry on this whole work under the name of the Golden Cross Society. It was directed that this should include the "interests and activities formerly promoted by the White Cross Sociey of the Methodist Episcopal Church and the Golden Cross Society of the Methodist Episcopal Church, South, and which shall promote the hospitals and homes work under the direction of the Board of Hospitals and Homes."[84]

An annual enrollment for the Golden Cross Society was directed to be held in every congregation "in such manner and on such date as determined by the patronizing Annual Conference or Annual Conferences." The week following Golden Cross Enrollment Sunday is to be known as "Hospitals and Homes Week." Funds raised through the enrollment shall be used as directed by the Annual Conference in keeping with the policies of the society.

The Golden Cross has proved to be a popular philanthropic agency of the church, as were the White Cross and the former Golden Cross in their respective churches. Under certain provisions of the present Golden Cross

[82] *Ibid.*, ¶ 1568 (6).

[83] *Discipline*, 1940, ¶ 1259.
[84] *Discipline*, 1952, ¶1569 § 1.

program, funds are made available for hospitalization of needy persons in other than Methodist institutions.

Jurisdictional Boards of Hospitals and Homes may be organized as the respective Jurisdictional Conferences may determine. Annual Conference boards are practically mandatory since the *Discipline* directs that each Annual Conference "shall promote within its bounds a Conference Board of Hospitals and Homes." [85] The composition and organization of such conference boards are carefully outlined in the *Discipline*. The work of this board extends to the pastoral charge and women's auxiliaries. These last, when connected with the various philanthropic institutions of the church, may be organized under or be given approval upon compliance with established standard requirements and procedures.

A National Association of Methodist Hospitals and Homes must be organized by order of the General Conference. The method of organization and other procedures having to do with it are carefully outlined in the *Discipline*. It must work under the general direction of the Board of Hospitals and Homes.

11. BOARD OF TEMPERANCE

Methodism has always been unalterably opposed to the evils of strong drink. When Wesley first banded together his small groups, the General Rules of the United Society had a measure forbidding "drunkenness, the buying or selling of spirituous liquors, or the drinking of them except in cases of extreme necessity." One could not become a Methodist without abstaining from the use of intoxicating liquor, nor could he join that fellowship without standing for a high type of public morality. More evils, of course, were listed in the General Rules than the buying, selling, or drinking of spirituous liquor, but against all of whatever sort, public or private, Methodist people set themselves. Our Methodist Church may have been indeterminate in its attitude toward doctrinal differences or upon matters of church polity or liturgy, but toward liquor and public morality the whole world knows exactly where we stand.

As the various Christian denominations late in the last century began to emphasize the social gospel, and to give greater effect to the desire to purge the social order of evils of all sorts, the several branches of Methodism moved to implement their own feelings and teachings in this direction. Moral suasion and a direct plea to the individual conscience was, and is, the church's most enduring weapon; but there is a social sanitation which can and should be put into effect through education, teaching, and legislation, where this is required to protect human rights. Into the underlying philosophy of all this we need not go, but in all activist movements looking toward social betterment, The Methodist Church has always taken a leading part. Not least among these efforts has been the temperance movement, as the whole drive against alcoholic liquors of all sorts came to be called. It is therefore not surprising to find that both the great branches of Episcopal Methodism had

[85] *Ibid.*, ¶ 1571 § 1.

their well-organized commissions or Boards of Temperance for several years preceding church union.

In the Methodist Episcopal Church, there was created a Permanent Committee on Temperance and Prohibition at the General Conference of 1888, with Dr. J. G. Evans as chairman. In 1904 the General Conference changed the name of this committee to the Temperance Society, and named Bishop W. F. McDowell as president. In 1908 the constitution of the society was broadened and $25,000 apportioned to its support, although this income was not fully drawn upon as there was no full-time secretarial service.

In July, 1910, the Rev. Clarence True Wilson and the Rev. Alfred Smith were named field secretary and assistant field secretary respectively, and a period of unusual activity followed. Much campaigning was done and a great deal of literature circulated.

The 1912 General Conference moved the society from its headquarters in Chicago to Topeka, Kansas, increased its apportionment to $50,000 annually, and gave it a "column in the Minutes." During the next four years, the society participated in twenty-seven state prohibition campaigns, circulated millions of leaflets, and founded a research department, with Deets Pickett as secretary. This department established The Voice and The Clipsheet, both of which are still in effective use.

In 1916 the General Conference increased the society's income, authorized the change of name to the Board of Temperance, Prohibition, and Public Morals of the Methodist Episcopal Church, and moved it to Washington, D. C., where its first offices were in an old residence back of the Library of Congress. From this location offices were moved to 110 Maryland Avenue, N. E. Present headquarters are in the Methodist Building, 100 Maryland Avenue, N. E. This building was erected by the board and is one of the best-known buildings in the city. Upon the retirement of Dr. Clarence True Wilson in 1936, Dr. Ernest Hurst Cherrington became executive secretary.

In the Methodist Episcopal Church, South, the work of temperance was headed up for a time by the Commission on Temperance and Social Service, established in 1918.[86] In 1926 this became the Board of Temperance and consisted of seventeen members, one of whom was a bishop.[87] The organization was incorporated under the laws of Tennessee. Bishop James Cannon, Jr., came to be head of this powerful board, and his leadership of the temperance movement and the prohibition work of his church attracted national attention. The Board of Temperance was later made a department of the Board of Missions of the Methodist Episcopal Church, South, at the General Conference of 1938.

At union in 1939 it was decided to carry on the whole work of the church in this field by the creation of a Board of Temperance. Its avowed purpose was to make "more effectual the efforts of The Methodist Church in creating a Christian public sentiment, . . . and in crystallizing . . . opposition to all public violations of the moral law." [88] The board's

[86] Discipline, 1918, ¶ 416.
[87] Discipline, 1926, ¶ 505.
[88] Discipline, 1952, ¶ 1530.

avowed aim is to promote, by an intensive educational program, including publication and distribution of literature,

voluntary total abstinence from all intoxicants and narcotics; to promote observance and enforcement of constitutional provisions and statutory enactments which suppress the traffic in alcoholic liquors and in narcotic drugs; and to aid and promote such legislation in townships, counties, villages, cities, states, and throughout the nation and the world. It shall be the object and duty of this board also actively to seek the suppression of salacious and corrupting literature and degrading amusements, lotteries, and other forms of gambling, and in every wise way to promote the public morals.[89]

In practice the board does its work largely through field promotion, education for temperance within the church, dramatic presentations, visitation of schools and colleges, the compilation and classification of material and its publication as books, leaflets, pamphlets, periodical discussion, and publicity. It has an effective Department of Work Among Colored People.

The board as constituted and organized consists of: one bishop from each jurisdiction, elected by the bishops of the jurisdiction; one minister and one lay member from each jurisdiction elected by the Jurisdictional Conference; and five members at large, elected by the board itself. The board also was given the right to fill vacancies occurring between the meetings of the Jurisdictional Conferences, having due regard for jurisdictional representation.

The board organizes with a president, who must be a bishop; one or two vice-presidents, a recording secretary, a treasurer, and an assistant

treasurer. In addition, here are an executive secretary and such other officers as the board may determine.

The executive committee consists of the officers who are members of the board and of seven additional members selected by the board. This committee has the power *ad interim* to fill any vacancy and to transact such other business as is necessary between the annual meetings.

The executive secretary is ex officio a member of the board and sits with the executive committee, but without vote.

Annual meetings of the board are called for at a time and place fixed by the executive committee. The board has power to solicit and create special funds, to hold property, and so forth, as any other corporation, and in accordance with the provisions of the *Discipline*. It looks to the Council on World Service and Finance for its support and must furnish that commission with its "askings" quadrennially.

Jurisdictional boards auxiliary to the general board are suggested, and in case such are organized their membership is carefully provided for in the *Discipline*.

Annual Conference boards are made mandatory and must be elected on the nomination of the Cabinet— that is, of the district superintendents —or "otherwise as the conference may direct." Such conference boards must have not less than ten or more than eighteen members. Ministers and laymen on conference boards are to be in equal numbers. However, among the lay members of the conference board there must be two young persons of less than twenty-five years of age, "the remainder of the lay mem-

[89] *Ibid.,* ¶ 1531.

bership consisting of an equal number of men and women." [90] Conference boards carry on the work and program of the general board within their own area, and can elect their own officers and raise their own funds. But no funds collected for the general board may be allocated to the conference board without the consent of the general board.

12. BOARD OF WORLD PEACE

This board was created to implement the effort of The Methodist Church "to advance the interests of the Kingdom of our Lord" through international justice and good will. It endeavors "to create the will to peace, the conditions for peace, and the organization for peace." It is supported by church-wide benevolences and takes its share of the General Benevolence budget.

It was in 1924 that the General Conference of the Methodist Episcopal Church adopted a ringing declaration on world peace which was printed in the *Discipline* of that year. This declaration, the report of an important committee, called for the appointment of a commission of twenty-five members, five of whom were to be bishops, ten ministers, and ten laymen, all to be "authorized and instructed to invite the religious forces of the world to unite in a conference to consider the best plans and methods for making the impact of a world-wide religious sentiment against the evils we deplore." [91]

The commission was duly appointed, and subsequently at the Conference of 1928, the peace commission was continued. So it became a part of the organization of the Methodist Episcopal Church and was so at time of union.

The Uniting Conference created a peace commission for The Methodist Church. This took over the work of the former commission and crystallized for all Methodism the aims and hopes of the church for a warless world.

The Commission on World Peace was reorganized as a board by the General Conference of 1952. This board is now composed of three bishops, elected by the Council of Bishops; one minister and one layman from each jurisdiction, elected by the Jurisdictional Conference; three ministers and three laymen, elected at large by the Council of Bishops; and two youth members, who must be under twenty-one years of age at the time of their election. The youth members are elected by the board upon nomination by the National Conference of Methodist Youth. Certain boards and agencies of the church are represented on the board by the executive secretaries of these respective agencies.

The Board meets at such time during the quadrennium as it may be advisable. Its executive agent is known as the executive secretary, and to assist him the board elects such assistants as it may consider necessary.

Functions include the cultivation and education and action for peace throughout the church, consultation with the Department of State and

[90] *Ibid.*, ¶ 1541.
[91] *Discipline*, 1924, ¶ 572.

275

United Nations, and with various ecumenical bodies. Jurisdictional Committees on World Peace, auxiliary to the general board, may be elected by such Jurisdictional Conferences as may decide to create them; but each Annual Conference must elect a Conference Committee on World Peace. This committee, under proper regulations, is empowered to promote the work of world peace within the boundaries of the conference, and to support the general program of world peace as directed by the general board. Annual Conference committees must report each year to their creating conference.

Each local charge is likewise directed by the *Discipline* to "provide for the promotion of world peace" through a local Church Committee on World Peace. This must report to the Official Board concerning its activities.

13. CO-ORDINATING COUNCIL

This body, new in Methodist polity, was created by the General Conference of 1952. Its establishment was a prime object of the church Survey Commission. It was felt by the members of the commission that not only should the agencies of the church be immediately reconstructed according to plan, but that there should be a continuing body empowered to act as arbiter between the boards in the ongoing of their work. The commission therefore proposed that the church should create a powerful independent body which would have sweeping rights to supervise and control the other boards. The Co-ordinating Council, so recommended, was to be allowed to examine into the inner workings of any and all agencies of the church, and was given great power in blocking board actions of which it disapproved and in mandating actions which it considered wise. "Practically the General Conference in session," its opponents declared of it.

Against the formation of such a strong "oligarchy," as it was called, there was much opposition. Especially bitterly contested was the proviso giving it summary control over all board actions. The result was that the General Conference, after debate, finally adopted a plan creating a much weaker Co-ordinating Council than the one the Survey Report had called for. This body, however, does have rights and privileges which may be of great value if properly exerted.

As created and organized, the Co-ordinating Council consists of one bishop, one minister, one lay man, and one lay woman from each jurisdiction. In addition to these there are one minister and one lay person for each additional million members, or major fraction thereof, above the first million members in each jurisdiction. All of these are nominated by the Council of Bishops and must be elected by the General Conference. In addition there are two additional persons appointed by the Council of Bishops from among the members of the church overseas who are in the United States at the time of the meetings of the council. It is planned that the overseas members shall be replaced by others when they leave the United States. Staff members of

276

general agencies, of course, are not eligible for membership.

The Co-ordinating Council elects a president, a vice-president, and a recording secretary, and must file copies of its minutes with the secretary of the General Conference and with the Council on World Service and Finance. Annual meetings are called for, and one fifth of the members may direct the president to call a special meeting.

The council has the right to review questions involving the overlapping in activity or lack of co-operation among or within general agencies, when either a general board or other agency or an Annual Conference may ask that this be done. In case it does review such an overlapping, it must make recommendations to the boards or agencies involved, how they may resolve such issues. It cannot itself enforce the settling of any difficulty, but must report each one of its recommendations to the Council of Bishops, the Council on World Service and Finance, and to the secretary of the General Conference.

The council will act as a continuing Survey Commission in the power it has to study the general organizational structure of The Methodist Church, and to recommend to the General Conference such changes as it considers essential. It also has the right to formulate and present to the General Conference plans for a unified ongoing program of the church, including long-range objectives, but it can only do this after consultation with the Council of Bishops, the executive secretary of each general agency, and the president and treasurer of the Woman's Division of Christian Service. If any financial ob-

jectives are involved, the recommendations concerning these must wait upon the Council of World Service and Finance for transmitting these to the General Conference.

The council has the right to recommend to the General Conference, after certain consultations, the number and timing of all special days; the right to designate any agency which shall undertake any special study authorized by the General Conference, if such agency has not already been indicated; and it has a further right to consider the plans of any general agency proposing to acquire real estate or erect a building. It may determine whether the proposed acquisition or erection is in the best interest of the church. In case such a move is disapproved by the council, the project shall be delayed until it can be considered by the next General Conference.

The expenses of the Co-ordinating Council are borne by the General Administration Fund.

During the 1952-56 quadrennium, the Co-ordinating Council has been given a great grant of power in having the right to "consider and decide what, if any, action shall be taken in regard to those recommendations in the report of the Church Survey Commission which have not been specifically covered in legislation adopted by the General Conference of 1952." [92] Under this proviso the council seems to have the full power of the General Conference with regard to any recommendation of the Survey Report which was not specially taken up by the 1952 General Conference.

[92] *Discipline*, 1952, ¶ 1115 § 8.

14. BOARD OF SOCIAL AND ECONOMIC RELATIONS

Methodism has always been interested in social welfare. In the earlier days of the church's life this was thought to be brought about best by reconstituting the individual rather than by bringing pressure upon society or government for legislative enactments aimed at social reform. It is said that after John Wesley passed through the towns and villages of England, the grog shops closed up for some weeks, not because he had crusaded against them, but because he had taken away their trade. The drunkards and patrons of ale houses had been converted! The personal approach is the fundamental approach of Christianity, and the world will never be redeemed until there is a world of redeemed men.

But the Methodists are an aggressive people and especially in America have always thrown themselves wholeheartedly into all methods which made for moral advancement and for social sanitation. In every crusade for righteousness Methodists have been in the forefront of the battle. So when the era of social awakening broke upon the American scene late in the nineteenth century, Methodists in their conferences, their churches, and as individuals, threw themselves wholeheartedly into every cause that promised a moral advancement. The church began to utter resolutions calling for the rights of childhood, in behalf of the laboring man, and against the plays, pictures, and books which might debauch public morals. Wholeheartedly and enthusiastically Methodism drew its sword against the liquor traffic and began a war with it that will never cease until one or the other is obliterated from the face of the earth.

To implement and organize movements of this sort, various church bodies appointed social action committees. There were also voluntary groups which endeavored to build a public opposition toward certain types of evil, or to secure the passage of laws which might safeguard the morals of the people. Eventually in New York there was organized the Methodist Federation for Social Action to which leading ministers and prominent bishops of the church lent their names and influence. Within the years 1944 to 1952 this federation came into national consciousness by reason of certain actions of its leaders and its expressed attitude upon certain matters of public moment. In the church press and in the councils of the church there ensued considerable discussion of the federation, much of it adverse. Especially was there objection to the idea of using the name "Methodist" in the masthead of such a body, even though it declared itself to be "unofficial."

This situation helped the General Conference of 1952 to decide that the time had come to create an official Methodist body. The General Conference thereupon established a Board of Social and Economic Relations which, as was explained at the time of its origin, would "have under its own review and control all moves which might implement the actions of the General Conference and the Methodist Social Creed in matters of social and economic relations."

The board is distinctly empowered to encourage and stimulate interest and activity in the program of the church with regard to social and economic problems. It may also establish "service projects" where Methodist youth may render Christian service and express their Christian convictions in pioneering and in other endeavors at home and abroad, coordinating such work with other general agencies of the church.

The board, as directed by the General Conference of 1952, organized by electing a bishop as its president, with a vice-president, a recording secretary, a treasurer, and such other officers as were necessary. These officers, together with four other elected members of the board, constitute the executive committee. The executive secretary is elected by the board and serves ex officio on its executive committee. The board meets annually and at such other times as may be necessary. It is supported by the general benevolences of the church.

In connection with this board, each Jurisdictional Conference may establish a Jurisdictional Board of Social and Economic Relations, and each Annual Conference may also establish a Conference Board by the same name. In the local church each charge may have as part of its Quarterly Conference a Committee on Social and Economic Relations. Thus Methodism endeavors to implement its thinking, its zeal, and its activity for social righteousness.

15. COMMISSION ON CHAPLAINS

In order to oversee the work of the many chaplains who are appointed to positions under the military, naval, or air force establishments, as well as those in federal and state hospitals, penal institutions, and the like. The Methodist Church has created a Commission on Chaplains. This is empowered to represent the church in "the procurement, endorsement, and general oversight of all Methodist ministers serving as chaplains in the Armed Forces, Veterans Administration, and federal prisons.[93] Also Methodist chaplains who are in private or public institutions other than those owned by The Methodist Church (or even chaplains serving in the world of industry) are under the general supervision of this agency.

The commission is composed of six bishops, one from each jurisdiction, and five ministers and five laymen elected by the General Conference on the nomination of the Council of Bishops. It is provided that "a Bishop who is a member of the body" must serve as chairman. One advisory member may be elected from each department of the Armed Forces (Army, Navy, or Air Force) and one from the Veterans Administration and from other fields of service where Methodist chaplains are serving.

During the years it has been in existence, the Commission on Chaplains has earned an enviable reputation for efficiency as well as for brotherly oversight of the ministers who are under its care. All Methodist chaplains while affiliated with or members of an Annual Conference somewhere, are nevertheless away from their conference brethren by reason of their separate stations. They very keenly feel the need of

[93] *Discipline*, 1952, ¶ 1581.

comradeship and co-operation on the part of their church and nearby ministers. Methodist Annual Conferences have not always been as alert to the interests of their members in the chaplaincy as they should have been and yet these men have a vastly important task to perform.

The Commission on Chaplains is endeavoring to keep in touch with each one under its care; to supply printed materials and helpful literature which may be distributed to the men; to have schools and meetings and conferences at various times to encourage the morale of the chaplains and to bring them together for mutual support and help.

16. COMMISSION ON PUBLIC RELATIONS AND METHODIST INFORMATION

Today "Methodist Information" is a familiar trade-mark in hundreds of newspaper and radio offices throughout the nation as the source of news of the major activities of the denomination.

Credit for the creation of the Commission on Public Relations and Methodist Information—more generally known as "Methodist Information"—goes back to the bishops at the time of the reorganization of Methodism in 1939. They had observed that social service organizations were establishing strong publicity departments, and that there were successful public relations operations in other religious bodies. They had also approvingly appraised the results of the successful publicists on the boards and commission staffs in the uniting churches. Therefore in their Episcopal Address to the Uniting Conference, the bishops, under the heading "An Intelligent Church," declared:

Methodism in this great day finds itself with large numbers of communicants and adherents who have little knowledge of its activities, plans, purposes, happenings, and movements. They are not, except in the most meager way, Methodistically informed. The Church must keep them in touch with its thought, life, and activity. . . . The greatest modern agencies for taking the message of this Church to its own people and to all people must be called into full action. No feature of possible work offers a larger field of service than this of Church and Christian intelligence. . . . A department of Methodist intelligence . . . adequate in equipment, capable in management, and vigorous in action will have extraordinary possibilities for the United Church.

The recommendation on the part of the bishops resulted in the adoption by the 1940 General Conference of the committee's report, which called for the establishment of a Commission on Public Information. It was directed that this commission should consist of six persons, one of whom should be a bishop. An annual budget of $25,000 was set apart for the work of the commission, and the General Administration Fund was designated as the source of the commission's support. In 1944 the appropriation was increased to $26,-500, and the commission members increased to nine. The General Conference elects the members of the commission upon nomination of the Council of Bishops. The bishops also nominate the bishop appointed to the commission, who thus by disciplinary action becomes its chairman. The duties of the commission as defined by the *Discipline* are to "gather news of public interest concerning Methodist activities and opinion and disseminate it through the secular press, the religious press, radio, television, and other legitimate media of public information." [94]

The commission was duly organized on July 29, 1940, in Chicago, and at the organization meeting, after electing its own officers, it elected an executive director and established New York as its headquarters. There an office was opened in October, 1940. Now the headquarters of the commission, it has functioned steadily since that date.

At first it was not entirely clear what plan of news gathering and news dissemination would most effectively serve the church. Soon the commission decided to center its work in New York, Nashville, and Chicago, since, because of the locations of the principal boards, commissions, and publishing interests, most Methodist news on the General Conference level either originates in or gravitates to one or another of these cities. It has become increasingly apparent that this was a strategic move.

In 1944 a part-time representative to the Negro press was engaged and, later, part-time correspondents responsible to him were established in each of the episcopal areas of the Central Jurisdiction.

In conducting its work the commission divides its program into these general catagories: straight news coverage of events; service to boards, commissions, and other agencies; promotional campaigns; service to church publications; personal news stories; feature stories, cartoons, photographs; religious radio; education for church publicity; public information; and miscellaneous services.

The commission's proposed budget must be presented quadrennially to the Council on World Service and Finance, and that council provides for its support out of the general funds of the church.

The commission meets annually, at which time the executive director and the associate directors make their reports and such recommendations as they feel the commission should have. Audits of all the books of the commission are regularly made and become a part of its records, as is the case with other boards.

The 1948 General Conference increased the annual appropriations to the commission to $75,000. In addition to strengthening its staff, two projects were thereby made possible. One was the support of two-day press relations seminars for district superintendents and selected pastors; the other was the financial encouragement of public relations officers on the episcopal area level. By 1952 there were eight such offices, in the main supported locally, given initial assistance followed by a reduced subsidy.

The 1952 General Conference enlarged the commission's scope by changing its name to the Commission on Public Relations and Methodist Information. It also designated the commission as "the sole general news gathering and distributing agency for The Methodist Church and its general agencies."

[94] *Ibid.*, ¶ 1593.

INDEX

INDEX

Board—cont'd

Hospitals and Homes, 268-72; of Lay Activities, 258-60; of Ministerial Training, Annual Conference, 234; of Missions, 222-28; Official (local church), 159; of Pensions, 250-54; of Pensions and Relief, 251; of Publication, 239-50; of Social and Economic Relations, 278-79; of Stewards, 159; of Temperance, 272-75; of Trustees, 158; of World Peace, 275-76

Bond, Thomas E., 248

Book agents, 241, 242

Book Committee, 240

Book Concern, 240

Book editor, 245-47

Book publications, 245-47

Boundaries: Annual Conference, 177-78, 185; episcopal areas, 37, 63, 71-72; jurisdictional, how changed, 178

Buckley, James M., 45, 248

Budget: conference benevolence, 263, 266; episcopal, 263; general administration, 263; unified, 262-63; World Service, 262; World Service, local church, 263

Cabinet: bishop's, 31, 85; pastor's, 151

Candler, Warren A., quoted, 22

Censure, as penalty, 192

Central Conference: areas, 183; assignment of bishops in, 184; authorization, 107, 184; bishops, 107, 184-85; boundaries, 138; election of bishops by, 51, 107; episcopal administration of, 107, 184; history of, 183; powers and duties, 184

Central Jurisdiction, 174-75, 180-81

Chaplains, Commission on, 279-80

Character, passage of, 139

Charge lay leaders, 260

Chartered Fund, 250

Christian Advocate, 247-49

Christian Advocate, Central Edition, 248

Christian Advocate, Nashville, 248

Christian Advocate and Journal, 248

Christmas Conference, 16, 97

Church Conference, 152, 161-62

Church Extension, Section of, 225

Church schools, 234-35

Church-school publications, 236, 237

Church-school superintendent, 153

Cincinnati and Book Concern, 241

Civil courts and church trials, 192-94

Clair, Matthew W., Jr., cited, 180

Clerical members and rights, 129

Coke, Thomas, 15, 26, 50

College of Bishops, 47, 132

Colleges, standards regarding, 238

Commission: on chaplains, 279-80; on Deaconess Work, 227; distinction from "board," 218; on In-Service Training,

Commission—cont'd

234; on Laymen's Work, Methodist Episcopal, 259; on Public Relations and Methodist Information, 280-81; on Promotion and Cultivation, 266-67; on Theological Education, 234

Committee: administrative, 124; co-ordinating, 221; on Admissions, 129; on Appeals, 177, 185, 197-98; on Conference Relations, 129; on Episcopacy, 64-65, 126-27; of investigation, 192; legislative, 124; on Ministerial Qualifications, 129; on Ministerial Qualifications (District), 146; on Nominations, 153; on Pastoral Relations, 129, 155; of Quarterly Conference, 155

Concurrence, on memorials, 125

Conference benevolence budget, 262, 263

Conference Claimants, Board of, 254

Conference Commission on World Service, 265-66

Conference organs, 248

Conference president, 81, 139

Conference Relations, Committee on, 129

Confirmation, question regarding, 25

Connectional enterprises and General Conference, 217

Connectional Fund, 239

Constitution: amendments to, 110-15, 134; conditions of, 114; of Methodist Episcopal Church, 114; of Methodist Episcopal Church, South, 114; of Methodist Protestant Church, 115; Plan of Union, 115, 171; relation to General Conference, 112-13; First Restrictive Rule, 100; Second Restrictive Rule, 102; of Woman's Division of Christian Service, 226

Constitutionality: and the Southern bishops, 47, 49; and Judicial Council, 207

Contrary doctrines, questions regarding, 101

Co-ordinating Committee, 221

Co-ordinating Council, 276-77

"Council, The," of Asbury, 99

Council of Bishops, 61, 74, 132

Council of Secretaries, 266, 267

Council on World Service and Finance, 261-66

Courses of study for ministers, 232-34

Curriculum Committee, 236-37

Daily Advocate, 125

Deaconess Work, Commission on, 227

Deaconesses, members of Quarterly Conference, 149

Deacons, 87, 130

Debates: over eligibility of women, 121; over episcopacy (in 1844), 39-41; over lay representation, 117, 121

288